GREAT SHIPWRECKS
and CASTAWAYS

GREAT SHIPWRECKS
and CASTAWAYS

Authentic Accounts of Disasters at Sea

Edited, with an Introduction, by

C H A R L E S   N E I D E R

DORSET PRESS
New York

To TESS and SAM

This edition published by Dorset Press
a division of Marboro Books Corporation,
by arrangement with Charles Neider
1990 Dorset Press

ISBN 0–88029–464–7

Printed in the United States of America

M 9 8 7 6 5 4

Contents

Stranger Than Fiction

MANY YEARS AGO, while I was vacationing in Northeast Harbor, Maine at the home of John Adams (the most wry-humored barber that yachting village has probably ever boasted), I went deep-sea fishing off Bar Harbor in Frenchman's Bay with a guy named Davis, who owned an old gray tub. We started out after lunch. Bar Harbor rolled behind us and disappeared around a point, and we saw the Porcupine Islands in the bay. The sun, glancing off the water, seemed to shower our faces with glass splinters.

I asked Davis if we were going to veer southeast toward Schooner Head. He said he didn't know the fish over there whereas he knew them pretty well over here and we'd slow down and try for a spot. He anchored the tub and got out a keg of clams, which he and I shucked while the others readied their drop lines—heavy cord with large double hooks and huge lead sinkers. The clams stank. Davis cursed the man who had sold them to him. Davis was about thirty, with a lean figure in his basque shirt and dungarees, and his face and neck had been seamed by the sun.

It was lovely in that stinking old tub. Cormorants flew by close to us, and as I paused in my work to watch them I was aware of the intensely blue water and the spines of the green and lavender mountains on Mt. Desert Island. We dropped our lines. Soon cod and haddock started to take our bait, big fat pink and gray fish, oily and cold, which I gaffed onto the deck. They flopped noisily in the stern, the gulls watching them, first one eye and then the other. We tossed the small fish high into the air, and the large Arctic gulls (which Davis called attic gulls) swooped and tore them out of the beaks of the screaming herring gulls. A fog set in and soon we had trouble seeing the water. We stopped fishing, and it was then that someone in the party of six got on the subject of shipwrecks.

"Now, if you want to hear about a shipwreck, Charley can tell you one," said Davis. "Tell him, Charley."

Charley Empson, a widower of seventy-one who worked as a caretaker on the Atwater Kent estate, had a belly like a blowfish's and a baked face red as a boiled lobster. While Davis sounded his fog horn and the buoy bells clanged softly in the distance, Empson told us the story of Jeb Cannon.

It was the afternoon of July 22, 1904, and the small herring fleet that operated out of Southwest Harbor stood about two miles off Otter Cliffs when a storm struck, scattering the boats. The boat Cannon was on split wide open and quickly foundered. Jeb Cannon of Southwest Harbor, Jim Thomas of Damariscotta and Clem Mallory of Elsworth, having managed to reach a small lifeboat, were the only survivors of a crew of ten. They had neither food nor water, but it rained a great deal and they caught the rain in their shirts and wrung it out into the bailing can. The search for them was widespread but futile.

About a month later Cannon was picked up by a herring boat out of Gloucester. There were large chunks of meat in his boat—the remains of Jim Thomas. Cannon had been eating him. You could see were he'd been working over him with his knife. The head was gone but there was the name tattooed on the left arm. Cannon was blackened and blistered by the sun. His hair was now gray; it had been brown. His lips were black. His nose looked like a bit of black bone. His hands were as green as a crab. When he became hysterical aboard the herring boat, the men soothed him with rum. The story he told them was that first Clem Mallory and then Jim Thomas had died of exposure, and he had been forced to eat them to stay alive.

He continued to live alone in Southwest Harbor near where the sardine factory later stood. He kept mostly to himself. As he put it, he wasn't one for much jawing. Fourteen years after his shipwreck he caught a fever and, sensing he was dying, called in his neighbors and gave them the following account.

He and Clem Mallory and Jim Thomas had drifted day after day, growing so weak they lay in the bottom of the boat, barely stirring, waiting to die. One night about two weeks after the storm, Cannon had shot Clem Mallory in the head with a pistol he had managed to salvage from the wreck and had hidden.

"Cut him up, we're going to eat," he had said to Jim Thomas.

Jim Thomas had glared at him, muttering something that Jeb Cannon couldn't make out.

"I'll kill you too," Cannon said, and, crawling close to Thomas, pointed the gun at his head.

Jim Thomas spat weakly and continued to mutter and glare.

"No," Cannon said. "I need fresh meat."

He had cut up Mallory and eaten him for several days. But Mallory went bad, and Cannon had to toss him piecemeal overboard. He slept with his gun in his fist. Three days before being picked up, he had shot Jim Thomas.

Charley Empson, finishing his tale, said, "His neighbors, they went out and left him to die alone. And after he died they wouldn't let him be buried in Southwest. They hauled him out in a dinghy and dropped him over the side."

I have set down only the outlines of Charley Empson's story. The story as he gave it to us was incomparably richer and more interesting. It cast a spell over us. The fog didn't lift that afternoon. Davis made his way to the dock by chart, compass and buoy bells.

As I drove toward Northeast Harbor over the mountain road I kept thinking of Jeb Cannon and his experience. I thought: the naked truth here is just as fascinating as the great fictional shipwrecks, such as those of Sinbad, Odysseus, Crusoe and Gulliver. And I decided to gather the greatest true stories of shipwreck and castaways. So it is Charley Empson whom I must thank for the idea of the present collection.

In the old days every third mariner had a tale of woes and marvels to tell. Sinbad and Odysseus weren't just awesome legends, they were fellow sea sufferers who had suffered the sea change. This wasn't remarkable, considering the hazards of attempting the sea in the old sailing ships. One such vessel was lost each day during a period of English history. The least articulate, least literate and least reverent sailor somehow had access to a parson and a printer, and with their help fashioned the story of his glory days. The incentive was no doubt largely profit, but there was also fame to think of, and the tradition of honorable behavior. Death was less to be feared than dishonor when the conditions of society made anonymous dishonorable behavior difficult to achieve.

In the days of many of the present accounts, disaster on the sea wore a visible face, men *saw* it, and because they saw it or thought they did, great dreams were possible to them. In such modern shipwrecks as the *General Slocum,* the *Titanic* and the *Lusitania,* fate came faceless to the party. Things "just happened" and, as on the *Titanic,* many were long unaware of the forfeit of their lives, strolling and conversing while their ship foundered.

A shipwreck in which all are saved stirs gladness in us but it doesn't necessarily make either for high drama or fine literature. Whenever I felt I had to make a choice between a famous wreck poorly related and an unknown one that produced a fascinating narrative I unhesitatingly favored the latter. Man's ingenuity, his will to survive, his behavior in primitive and terrible situations, his passion on the cross of his environment: these are the motifs I found entrancing and significant.

I have preferred accounts by eyewitnesses and participants, and in most cases have preferred the narratives of nonliterary correspondents over those by professionals. I have also featured such narrative forms as diaries, journals and letters, which offer some warrant of authenticity. I strove for variety of setting, time, subject and style. Since it was my intention to make a readable and interesting book, I have not hesitated to modernize spelling, capitalization and punctuation where necessary. For the convenience of readers who may wish to consult the original accounts, I have appended a detailed list of sources.

In general, the older accounts were written in a finer style than those of the nineteenth and twentieth centuries. Narratives of the past century abound in cliches, sermonizing, bowdlerizing and romantic verbiage. It's by no accident that I have allowed tales of the sixteenth and seventeenth centuries to dominate the present collection. The style of the sixteenth is perhaps the finest of all, but reports from that time are not plentiful. I have slighted the nineteenth century, having chosen only two items from it; one of these, *Murder Without Malice*, is an account of an occurrence of 1841, which I have accepted because its subject matter is extraordinary. As for Robert Falcon Scott's *The Last March*, I owe the reader an explanation.

Scott and his comrades in tragedy were not, strictly speaking, shipwrecked, nor were they cast away. They were brought to the barrier ice (now known as the Ross Ice Shelf) and left there with supplies, the ship returning to civilization. It was while the ship was away that the tragedy occurred. But if the Scott party were not actually cast away, in a sense they were voluntary castaways. The most famous of all castaways, Alexander Selkirk, was such a one. Having disagreed with the captain of the vessel he was on, he asked to be put ashore on the island of Juan Fernandez off Chile. More than four years elapsed before he was rescued. I have decided to label the Scott group voluntary castaways in order to include his account, believing that the advantages of such a decision justify the risk of being accused of sophistry. Scott's superb account of his tragic journey, in which the entire polar party was lost, does honor to a great explorer and to the great tradition of log-keeping. Its kinship with the account by Thomas Candish is readily evident. The basic elements are there: courage, indomitability, style and the urge to record.

CHARLES NEIDER

New York
October, 1989

GREAT SHIPWRECKS
and CASTAWAYS

1540 The Adventures of Peter Serrano,

who lived seven years on a sandy island off the coast of Peru.

PETER SERRANO escaped from shipwreck by swimming to that desert island which from him received its name, being, as he reported, about two leagues in compass. It was Peter Serrano's misfortune to be lost upon these places and to save his life on this disconsolate island, where was neither water, wood, grass or anything for support of human life, at least not for maintenance of him so long a time as until some ship passing by might redeem him from perishing by hunger and thirst; which languishing manner of death is much more miserable than by a speedy suffocation in the waters. With the sad thoughts hereof he passed the first night, lamenting his affliction with as many melancholy reflections as we may imagine capable to enter into the mind of a wretch in like extremities.

So soon as it grew day he began to traverse his island and found on the shore some cockles, shrimps and other creatures of like nature which the sea had thrown up and which he was forced to eat raw because he wanted fire to roast them.

With this small entertainment he passed his time, till observing some turtles not far from the shore, he watched until they came within his reach, and then, throwing them on their backs (which is the manner of taking that sort of fish), he cut the throat, drinking the blood instead of water. And, slicing out the flesh with a knife which was fastened to his girdle, he laid the pieces to be dried and roasted by the sun. The shell he made use of to rake up the rainwater,

1

which lay in little puddles, for that is a country often subject to great and sudden rains.

In this manner he passed the first of his days, by killing all the turtles that he was able, some of which were so large that their shells were as big as targets or bucklers. Others were so great that he was not able to turn them or stop them in their way to the sea; so that in a short time experience taught him which sort he was able to deal with and which were too unwieldly for his force. With his lesser shells he poured water into the greater, some of which contained twelve gallons; so that having made sufficient provisions both of meat and drink, he began to contrive some way to strike fire, that he might not only dress his meat with it but also make a smoke to give a sign to any ship which was passing.

Considering of this invention (for seamen are much more ingenious in all times of extremity than men bred at land), he searched everywhere to find out a couple of hard pebbles instead of flints, his knife serving in the place of a steel. But the island being all covered over with a dead sand and no stone appearing, he swam into the sea and, diving often to the bottom, he at length found a couple of stones fit for his purpose, which he rubbed together until he got them to an edge, with which, being able to strike fire, he drew some thread out of his shirt, which he worked so small that it was like cotton and served for tinder. So that, having contrived a means to kindle fire, he gathered a great quantity of seaweeds thrown up by the waves, which, with the shells of fish, and the planks of ships which had been wrecked on those shoals, afforded nourishment for his fuel. And lest sudden showers should extinguish his fire he made a little covering like a small hut with the shells of the largest turtles or tortoises that he had killed, taking great care that his fire should not go out.

In the space of two months and sooner he was as unprovided of all things as he was at first, for with the great rains, heat and moisture of that climate his provisions were corrupted. And the great heat of the sun was so violent on him, having neither clothes to cover him nor shadow for a shelter, that when he was, as it were, broiled in the sun, he had no remedy but to run into the sea.

In this misery and care he passed three years, during which time he saw several ships at sea and as often made his smoke; but none turned out of their way to see what it meant, for fear of those shelves and sands which wary pilots avoid with all imaginable circumspection. So that the poor wretch, despairing of all manner of relief, esteemed it a mercy for him to die.

Being exposed in this manner to all weathers, the hair of his body grew in such manner that he was covered all over with bristles, the hair of his head and beard reaching to his waist, so that he appeared like some wild and savage creature.

At the end of three years Serrano was strangely surprised with the appearance of a man in his island, whose ship had, the night before, been cast away upon those sands, and who had saved himself on a plank of the vessel. So soon as it was day he espied the smoke and, imagining whence it was, he made towards it.

As soon as they saw each other it is hard to say which was the most amazed. Serrano imagined that it was the Devil who came in the shape of a man to tempt him to despair. The newcomer believed Serrano to be the Devil in his own proper shape and figure, being covered over with hair and beard. In fine they were both afraid, flying one from the other. Peter Serrano cried out, as he ran, "Jesus, Jesus, deliver me from the Devil." The other, hearing this, took courage; and, returning again to him, called out, "Brother, Brother, don't fly from me, for I am a Christian, as thou art." And because he saw that Serrano still ran from him he repeated the Credo or Apostles' Creed in words aloud. Which, when Serrano heard, he knew it was no Devil that would recite those words, and thereupon gave a stop to his flight. And returning with great kindness, they embraced each other with sighs and tears, lamenting their sad estate, without any hopes of deliverance. Serrano, supposing that his guest wanted refreshments, entertained him with such provisions as his miserable life afforded. And, having a little comforted each other, they began to recount the manner and occasion of their sad disasters.

For the better government of their way of living they designed their hours of day and night to certain services. Such a time was appointed to kill fish for eating; such hours for gathering weeds, fish bones and other matters which the sea threw up, to maintain their constant fire; and especial care had they to observe their watches and relieve each other at certain hours, that so they might be sure their fire went not out.

In this manner they lived amicably together for certain days. But many did not pass before a quarrel arose between them, so high that they were ready to fight. The occasion proceeded from some words that one gave the other that he took not that care and labor as the extremity of their condition required. This difference so increased (for to such misery do our passions often betray us) that at length they separated and lived apart one from the other. However, in a short time, having experienced the want of that comfort which mutual society procures, their choler was appeased. And so they returned to enjoy converse and the assistance which friendship and company afforded, in which condition they passed four years, during all which time they saw many ships sail near them. Yet none would be so charitable or curious as to be invited by their smoke and flame. So that, being now almost desperate, they expected no other remedy besides death to put an end to their miseries.

However, at length a ship, venturing to pass nearer than ordinary, espied the smoke; and, rightly judging that it must be made by some shipwrecked persons escaped to those sands, hoisted out their boat to take them in. Serrano and his companion readily ran to the place where they saw the boat coming. But as soon as the mariners approached so near as to distinguish the strange figure and looks of these two men they were so affrighted that they began to row back. But the poor men cried out and, that they might believe them not to be Devils or evil spirits, they rehearsed the Creed and called aloud on the name of Jesus. With which words the mariners returned, took them into the boat and carried them to the ship, to the great wonder of all present, who with admiration beheld their hairy shapes, not like men but beasts, and with singular pleasure heard them relate the story of their past misfortunes.

The companion died in his voyage to Spain but Serrano lived to come thither; from whence he traveled into Germany, where the Emperor then resided. All which time he nourished his hair and beard to serve as an evidence and proof of his past life. Wheresoever he came the people pressed as to a sight, to see him for money. Persons of quality, having the same curiosity, gave him sufficient to defray his charges. And his Imperial Majesty, having seen him and heard his discourses, bestowed a rent upon him of four thousand pieces of eight a year, which make 4800 ducats in Peru. And, going to the possession of this income, he died at Panama without further enjoyment.

1578 The True Relation of Peter Carder,

of Saint Verian in Cornwall, within seven miles of
Falmouth, which went with Sir Francis in his voyage
about the world, begun 1577; who with seven others
in an open pinnace or shallop of five tons, with eight
oars, was separated from his General by foul weather
in the South Sea, in October, Anno 1578; who, returning by the Straits of Magellan toward Brazil,
were all cast away, save this one only aforenamed,
who came into England nine years after miraculously,
having escaped many strange dangers, as well among
divers savages as Christians.

AFTER Sir Francis Drake had passed the Straits
of Magellan, the sixth of September, 1578, and was driven down to
the southwards in the South Sea, unto the latitude of fifty-five degrees and a third, with such accidents as are mentioned in his voyage,
and returning back toward the Straits again, the eighth of October
we lost sight of the Elizabeth, one of our consorts. Shortly after his
separation from our company, our General commanded eight men
to furnish our small pinnace or shallop with eight men, whose names
were these: myself, Peter Carder aforesaid, Richard Burnish of London, John Cottle and another, both servants to Master John Haw-
kins, Artyur, a Dutch trumpeter, Richard Joyner, servant to Vincent
Scoble of Plymouth, Pasche Gidie of Salt Ashe, and William Pitcher
of London.

This company was commanded to wait upon the ship for all necessary uses, but having not passed one day's victuals in us, nor any
chart nor compass, saving only the benefit of eight oars, in the night

time by foul weather suddenly arising, we lost the sight of our ship, and though our ship sought us and we them for a fortnight together, yet could we never meet together again. Howbeit, within two days after we lost them, we recovered the shore and relieved ourselves with mussels, oysters, crabs and some sorts of roots in the woods, and within a fortnight after the loss of our consorts we returned back into the Straits of Magellan, and in two places came on land on the main of America, to relieve ourselves in certain bays, where we found oysters, mussels and crabs as before, and filled our barricos with fresh water, and in one of these places we found savages, but they fled from us.

Afterward we came to Penguin Island in the Straits, and there we salted and dried many of the penguins for our sustenance. Thence we shaped our course for Port Saint Indian, where Sir Francis Drake not many months before had beheaded Captain Doughty. In this port we stayed a day or two and took fish like breams and mackerels with hooks and lines. Then coasting the land for some fortnight, some hundred leagues beyond the River Plata, we found a small island three leagues from the main full of seals, whereof we killed good store to our sustenance; the young ones we found best and ate them roasted. Then passing over the River Plata to the north side, we put into a small river, and went up into the woods six of us: other two remaining on the shore to look to the boat.

While we were thus seeking food in the woods the people of the country, called Tapines, some sixty or seventy armed with bows and arrows shot fiercely at us and wounded us all very grievously, and four of us were taken by them and never recovered: the rest of us they pursued to our pinnace and wounded us all, but in the end we put them to flight. Thence we went to an island some three leagues off in the sea, not above a league in compass, where we cured ourselves as well as we might, yet so that two of us died of our late wounds, and that which was worse for want of help. Through foul weather our pinnace was dashed against the rocky shore and broken, and there remained alive of us eight no more, but myself, Peter Carder and William Pitcher.

Here we remained the space of two months, in all which time for our victuals we had a fruit somewhat like unto oranges, growing upon a high tree, the leaf whereof was somewhat like the aspen leaf, and small; white crabs creeping upon the sand, and little eels which we found under the sands, but in all this island we could not find any fresh water in the world, insomuch that we were driven to drink our own urine, which we saved in some shards of certain jars which we had out of our pinnace, and set our urine all night to cool therein, to drink it the next morning; which thus being drunk often and often voided, became in a while exceeding red.

In all this time we had no rain, not any good means to save it, if it had fallen; whereupon, seeing ourselves in so great extremity, we devised how we might get unto the main, and by good fortune found a plank of some ten foot in length, which of likelihood had driven from the River Plata, whereunto with withes we bound some other wood, and furnishing ourselves with the foresaid fruit, eels and crabs, we committed ourselves to God; hoping with the setting in of the tide and with the help of two poles which we used instead of oars to attain unto the main, which was some three leagues off, but we made it in three days and two nights before we could come to the main.

At our coming first on land, we found a little river of very sweet and pleasant water, where William Pitcher, my only comfort and companion (although I dissuaded him to the contrary) overdrank himself, being pinched before with extreme thirst, and to my unspeakable grief and discomfort within half an hour after died in my presence, whom I buried as well as I could in the sand.

The next day following, as I traveled along the shore towards Brazil, having mine arming sword and target* with me, I met with some thirty of the savages of the country, called Tuppan Basse, which being armed with bows and arrows and having two or three great rattles with stones in them, and a kind of tabrets that they used instead of drums, they went dancing before me about a musket shot off, and then they stayed and hanged up a piece of a white net

* a small shield or buckler

of cotton-wool, upon a stick's end of four foot high, and went from it about a musket shot off: then I coming unto it, took it in my hand, viewed it and hung it up again, which (as afterward I understood, by living long among them) was as much as "Come hither." Then I came to them, and they friendly led me along some half a mile, all the way dancing, as well men as women, whereof there were some eight in the company, until we came to another riverside, where they hanged up their beds, tying them fast to a couple of trees, being a kind of white cotton netting, which hanged two feet from the ground, and kindled fire of two sticks, which they made on both sides of their beds for warmth and for driving away of wild beasts, and having fed me with such as they had, we took our rest for that night.

The next day early in the morning they took down and trussed up their beds, crying *tiasso, tiasso*, which is to say, *away, away*, and marched that day towards Brazil some twenty miles, and came to their town where their chief governor was. This town was built four-square, with four houses only, every house containing about two bowshot in length, and the houses made with small trees like an arbor, being thatched over down to the ground with palm tree leaves. They have no windows, but some thirty or forty doors on every side of this squadron, by which each family passes in and out. Their chief lord, whose name was Caiou, being a man of some forty years old, had nine wives; but the rest have only one wife, except such as are counted more valiant than the rest, which are permitted two wives, one to look to their children at home and the other to go to the wars with them. This town contained very near 4,000 persons of all sorts.

The next day the governor sent divers of his people abroad to bring in all sorts of victual which the country yielded and offered them onto me to see which of them I liked best, among which there was great store of fish, as well sea fish as fresh-water fishes, many sorts of fowls, many sorts of roots and divers land beasts, as armadillos, which afterward I found to be very good meat. Of all these at the first I only took one fowl and a couple of fishes and bestowed the

rest among their children, which procured me no small good will
among them.

Here I stayed among them (being well entertained) for certain
months, until I had learned most part of their language, in which
mean space I noted their manners, which were as follows. They went
out to the wars armed as at my first coming, only with bows and
arrows, some three or four hundred at a time, and when they had the
victory of their enemies, they tied one of their captives to one of their
company with cotton cords fast arm to arm, and bringing them
home, within two or three days after they would tie them to a post,
and with a massy club of red wood one of the strongest of the company (after they have drunk a certain strong drink with dancing
round about him) at one blow slits his head asunder: this drink is
made by their women of a certain root called I.P. which first they
seethe and afterward chew in their mouths and then spit it out again
into a long trough and mingle it with water, and there let it work
two or three days and gather yeast upon it, like to our ale. Which
done, they take the liquor and put it into broad-mouth jars of earth,
and of this both their men and women do drink at their feasts, till
they be as drunk as apes.

I could observe no religion amongst them, but only that they rev-
erence and worship the moon, especially the new moon; whereat
they do rejoice in leaping, dancing and clapping their hands. The
merchantable commodities of this country are Brazil wood, tobacco,
red pepper and cotton wool. They have also great stores of apes,
monkeys, armadillos, hogs without tails as big as ours; their birds are
parrots, parraketos, black fowls as big as doves, and ostriches as high
as a man.

After I had lived about half a year amongst them, and learned their
language, the king requested me to go to the wars with him against
his enemies the Tapwees, which I granted; but before we set out, I
showed them a way for making of certain targets, of the bark of a
tree, some three-quarters of a yard long for defense against arrows,
whereof we made some hundred; and withal I wished them to make
some two hundred of clubs. Which being done we marched forward

some 700 in number, which by mine advice were all marked with a red kind of balsam from the knee downward upon one leg, to be known from our enemies (by the way it is to be noted that there are three sorts of balsamum in that country, to wit, white, red and black, very odoriferous and excellent good for a green wound, and the white I esteem to be best). In three days' march we came to another town built foursquare, as before I have declared, but much lesser; we set upon the town about four of the clock in the morning. The enemy standing upon defense of their arrows were much deceived by reason of our targets, which being seconded by our clubs, we immediately knocked down to the number of two hundred. The rest, except some twenty prisoners, escaped into the woods. Here the king stayed one day and caused many of their carcasses to be broiled upon the coals and eaten.

The chiefest riches which we found here was their drink which they used to make themselves drunk withal; their cotton beds and their tobacco. As for gold and silver they neither seek nor make any account thereof. This is to be noted, that how many men these savages do kill, so many holes they will have in their visage, beginning first in their nether lip, then in their cheeks, thirdly in both their eyebrows and lastly in their ears. Those twenty prisoners which we brought home were afterward killed, roasted and eaten.

While I remained here amongst these people, certain Portuguese accompanied with certain Negroes and Brazilians came within some ten leagues of our town to see whether they could surprise any of our savages and to harken what was become of me, for that they had heard by this time that some of Sir Francis Drake's company were cast ashore amongst the savage people; but their coming was not so secret but that two of the Portuguese and certain Negroes were taken and, after their confession of the intent of their coming thither, they were brained with clubs, broiled and eaten. These things thus passing, I became suitor to the king to give me leave to depart his country and to go to some river of Brazil not planted by the Portuguese, to see if I could spy out any English or French ship to pass me into my country, which he in the end favorably granted; and sent four of his people with me to furnish me with victuals, which they did very plentifully of birds, fish and roots for the space of nine or ten weeks, all which time they did accompany me; and I desiring to go toward the Line, they brought me into the town of Bahia de Todos os Santos.

But about four or five miles before we came to the town, I yielded myself to a Portuguese called Michael Jonas, declaring unto him that I was an Englishman, and inquired whether there were any Englishmen dwelling in the town. He told me that there was one Antonio de Pava in the town which could speak good English and was a lover of our nation, and brought me directly unto his house.

This Antonio de Pava, pitying my case and advising me not to be known, that I understood the Portuguese tongue, brought me to the governor, whose name was Diego Vas. This governor told me by Antonio de Pava, which became my interpreter, that seeing I was found in the inland of their country westward, being a stranger, contrary to their laws, he could do no less than commit me to prison and send me into Portugal to be committed to the galleys for term of life. To this I answered by the advice of my good friend Antonio de Pava that I came not willingly into those dominions, but being by casualty once come there, I was not taken prisoner but sought them out and came and yielded myself into their hands, laying down my weapons at one of his nationals' feet.

Nevertheless he sent me to prison where by the means of Antonio de Pava and other of his friends I was sufficiently relieved and within one fortnight after brought again publicly to the bar in the town house to mine answer. There I answered the second time by Antonio de Pava, my interpreter, that I thought it sufficient, that when I might have kept out, yet of mine own free will I had made a long journey with great hazard of my life through the countries of savages, being man-eaters, which favored me to seek the Portuguese Christians out and peaceably to put myself into their hands. Hereupon the governor and his assistants consulted and concluded together that I should be committed to the house of Antonio de Pava and there remain until they might write into Portugal to know the King's pleasure concerning me. Within one year they received answer from

Lisbon concerning me, that I should be forthcoming and that hereafter the King would send further order for my transporting into
Portugal.

But about two years passed before this order came: in which mean
space, first I spent part of my time in going into the fields as overseer
of my friends, Negroes and savages, in their planting and dressing
of their sugar canes and in planting of gingers, which grow there exceeding well, but is a forbidden trade to be transported out for
hindering of other places, and in cutting down of Brazil wood, and
in bringing it down by rivers upon rafts unto the port where the ships
do lade it, and in seeing them gather their cotton wool and picking
the seeds out of it, and packing the same, and in gathering of the
long pepper both white and red.

After I had spent some year and a half in this business, my friend
Antonio de Pava having a small bark of his own, which he employed
in carrying of wares from port to port and for bringing of sugars to
places where ships should lade, used me, knowing I had been brought
up to the sea, in these his businesses. Our first voyage was to Ilhéus,
where we left some wares, and stayed there some month: then we
went to Pôrto Seguro, and there took in some sugars for linen cloth,
bays, wine and oil. Then returning home, shortly after we were set
forth again in the same bark to Espírito Santo, and Saint Vincent,
and the River Jenero, where discharging our wares to certain factors
and receiving sugars and cotton wool aboard, we returned safely
home. In my first voyage one Master David Leake, an English surgeon, lost there out of an English ship in the country, being much
sought for because of his skill, had passage with us from Bahia to
Espírito Santo. Upon my return of my second voyage, my good friend
Antonio de Pava advertised me that a ship was shortly to arrive there
to carry me into Portugal prisoner, telling me that he should not be
able any longer to help me and therefore wished me to look to myself;
but kindly offered me his help to convey me away.

Whereupon I took his boat and four of his Negroes, pretending to
go on fishing to the sea; and so of purpose going much to leeward
of the place, I put in to Pernambuco: where the Negroes, being ex-

amined whence we came and for what cause, being utterly ignorant of mine intent, answered that they were drawn thither by force of weather, and for their master's sake were well treated and returned home with the next wind, myself remaining secretly behind them.

Within certain months there came thither a hulk with eight Englishmen and fourteen Portuguese, who after some three months had laden the same with English and Portuguese goods to come for England. The English goods belonged to M. Cordal, M. Beecher and M. Sadler, worshipful merchants of the city of London; which had been left in the country before by the Merchant Royal. Thus passing homeward in our course as far as the Isles of the Azores, within sight of the Isle of Pike, being five Portuguese ships in consort, we met with Captain Raymond and Captain George Drake of Exeter, with English ships of war, who, because the peace between England and Spain was broken the year before, commanded us to yield ourselves to them as their lawful prizes, which we did all five accordingly without any resistance. But by contrary weather we were driven into Baltimore in Ireland, and within a while after we arrived in the narrow seas in the haven of Chichester, in the end of November, 1586, nine years and fourteen days after my departure out of England with Sir Francis Drake in his voyage about the world.

My strange adventures and long living among cruel savages being known to the right honorable the Lord Charles Howard, Lord High Admiral of England, he certified the Queen's Majesty thereof with speed and brought me to her presence at Whitehall, where it pleased her to talk with me a long hour's space of my travails and wonderful escape, and among other things of the manner of M. Doughty's execution; and afterward bestowed 22 angels* on me, willing my Lord to have consideration of me: with many gracious words I was dismissed, humbly thanking the Almighty for my miraculous preservation and safe return into my native country.

* English gold coins, issued 1470-1634

1583 *By Richard Clarke of Weymouth,*

master of the ship called the Admiral, going for the
discovery of Norumbega with Sir Humfrey Gilbert,
1583. Written in excuse of that fault of casting away
the ship and men imputed to his oversight.

DEPARTING out of Saint Johns, Yarborough,
in the Newfoundland the twentieth of August unto Cape Raz, from
thence we directed our course unto the Isle of Sablon (or the Isle of
Sand), which the general Sir Humfrey Gilbert would willingly have
seen.

But when we came within twenty leagues of the Isle of Sablon,
we fell to controversy of our course. The General came up in his
frigate and demanded of me, Richard Clarke, master of the Admiral,
what course was best to keep. I said that west southwest was best,
because the wind was at south and night at hand and unknown sands
lay off a great way from the land. The General commanded me to
go west northwest. I told him again that the Isle of Sablon was west
northwest and but fifteen leagues off, and that he should be upon
the island before day if he went that course.

The General said my reckoning was untrue and charged me in her
Majesty's name, and as I would show myself in her country to follow
his commandment; and about seven of the clock in the morning the
ship struck on ground, where she was cast away. Then the General
went off to sea, the course that I would have had them go before,
and saw the ship cast away men and all, and was not able to save
a man, for there was not water upon the sand for either of them
much less for the Admiral that drew fourteen foot.

15

Now as God would, the day before it was very calm, and a soldier of the ship had killed some fowl with his piece, and some of the company desired me that they might hoist out the boat to recover the fowl, which I granted them: and when they came aboard they did not hoist it in again that night. And when the ship was cast away the boat was after being in burden one ton and a half: there was left in the boat one oar and nothing else. Some of the company could swim and recovered the boat and did haul in out of the water as many men as they could; among the rest they had a care to watch for the captain, or the master. They happened on myself being the master, but could never see the captain; then they hauled into the boat as many men as they could, in number sixteen.

And when the sixteen were in the boat, some had small remembrance and some had none; for they did not make account to live but to prolong their lives as long as it pleased God, and looked every moment of an hour when the sea would eat them up, the boat being so little and so many men in her, and so foul weather that it was not possible for a ship to brook half a course of sail. Thus while we remained two days and nights and that we saw it pleased God our boat lived in the sea (although we had nothing to help us withal but one oar, which we kept up the boat withal upon the sea, and so went even as the sea would drive us), there was in our company one Master Hedely that put forth this question to me the master: I do see that it doth please God that our boat liveth in the sea, and it may please God that some of us may come to the land if our boat were not over laden. Let us make sixteen lots, and those four that have the four shortest lots we will cast overboard, preserving the master among us all.

I replied unto him saying, No, we will live and die together. Master Hedely asked me if my remembrance were good. I answered I gave God praise it was good, and knew how far I was off the land and was in hope to come to the land within two or three days, and said they were but threescore leagues from the land (when they were seventy), all to put them in comfort.

Thus we continued the third and fourth day without any sustenance, save only the weeds that swam in the sea, and salt water to drink. The fifth day Hedely died and another moreover. Then we desired all to die, for in all these five days and five nights we saw the sun but once and the stars but one night, it was so foul weather. Thus we did remain the sixth day: then we were very weak and wished all to die saving only myself which did comfort them and promised they should soon to land by the help of God. But the company were very importunate and were in doubt they should never come to land, but that I promised them the seventh day they should come to shore or else they should cast me overboard; which did happen true the seventh day, for at eleven of the clock we had sight of the land, and at three of the clock at afternoon we came on land.

All these days and seven nights the wind kept continually south. If the wind had in the meantime shifted upon any other point, we had never come to land: we were no sooner come to the land, but the wind came clean contrary at north within half an hour after our arrival. But we were so weak that one could scarcely help another of us out of the boat, yet with much ado being come all on shore we kneeled down upon our knees and gave God praise that he had dealt so mercifully with us.

Afterwards those which were strongest helped their fellows unto a fresh brook, where we gratified ourselves with water and berries very well. There were of all sorts of berries plenty, and as good as ever I saw. We found a very fair plain champaign ground that a man might see very far every way. By the sea side was here and there a little wood with goodly trees as good as any I saw ever in Norway, able to mast any ship, of pine trees, spruce trees, fir and very great birch trees.

Where we came on land we made a little house with boughs, where we rested all that night. In the morning I divided the company three and three to go every way to see what food they could find to sustain themselves, and appointed them to meet there all again at noon with such food as they could get.

As we went aboard we found great store of pease as good as any we have in England: a man would think they had been sowed there. We rested there three days and three nights and lived very well with pease and berries. We named the place Saint Laurence, because it was a very goodly river like the river of St. Laurence in Canada, and we found it very full of salmons.

When we had well rested ourselves we rowed our boat along the shore, thinking to have gone to the Grande Bay to have come home with some Spaniards which are yearly there to kill the whale; and when we were hungry or athirst we put our boat on land and gathered pease and berries. Thus we rowed our boat along the shore five days: about which time we came to a very goodly river that ran far up into the country and saw very goodly grown trees of all sorts.

There we happened upon a ship of St. John de Luz, which ship brought us into Biscay to an harbor called the Passage. The master of the ship was our great friend or else we had been put to death if he had not kept our counsel. For when the visitors came aboard, as it is the order in Spain, they demanding what we were, he said we were poor fishermen that had cast away our ship in Newfoundland, and so the visitors inquired no more of the matter at that time.

As soon as night was come he put us on land and had us shift for ourselves. Then had we but ten or twelve miles into France, which we went that night, and then cared not for the Spaniard. And so shortly after we came into England toward the end of the year 1583.

1592   *Master Thomas Candish His Discourse.*

Of his fatal and disastrous voyage towards the South
Sea, with his many disadventures in the Magellan
Straits and other places; written with his own hand to
Sir Tristram Gorges, his executor.

M o s t loving friend, there is nothing in this
world that makes a truer trial of friendship than at death to show
mindfulness of love and friendship, which now you shall make a
perfect experience of: desiring you to hold my love as dear dying poor,
as if I had been most infinitely rich. The success of this most unfortunate action, the bitter torments thereof lie so heavy upon me, as
with much pain am I able to write these few lines, much less to make
discovery unto you of all the adverse haps that have befallen me in
this voyage, the least whereof is my death: but because you shall not
be ignorant of them, I have appointed some of the most sensiblest
men that I left behind me to make discourse unto you of all these
accidents. I have made a simple will, wherein I have made you sole
and only disposer of all such little as is left. . . .

We were beaten out of the Straits with a most monstrous storm at
west-southwest, from which place we continued together till we came
in the latitude of forty-seven, in which place Davis in the Desire,
and my pinnace, lost me in the night, after which time I never heard
of them but (as I since understood), Davis' intention was ever to run
away. This is God's will, that I should put him in trust that should
be the end of my life and the decay of the whole action. For had not
these two small ships parted from us, we would not have miscarried
on the coast of Brazil; for the only decay of us was that we could

not get into their barred harbors. What became of these small ships I am not able to judge, but sure, it is most like they went back again without danger, and being so few men they might relieve themselves with seals and birds and so take a good time of the year and pass the Straits. The men in these small ships were all lusty and in health, wherefore the likelier to hold out. The short of all is this: Davis' only intent was utterly to overthrow me, which he hath well performed.

These ships being parted from us, we, little suspecting any treachery, the Roebuck and myself held our course for Brazil and kept together till we came in the latitude of thirty-six, where we encountered the most grievous storm that ever any Christians endured upon the seas to live, in which storm we lost company. We with most extreme labor and great danger got the coast of Brazil, where we were fifteen days and never heard of the Roebuck. We came to an anchor in the Bay of Saint Vincent, and being at anchor there, the gentlemen desired me to give them leave to go ashore to some of the Portuguese farmhouses to get some fresh victuals, which I granted, willing them to make present return, knowing very well the whole country was not able to prejudice them if they willingly would not endanger themselves. They went to a sugar mill hard by me where I rode (for that was my special charge, that they should never go a mile from the ship), where they got some victual and came aboard again very well.

The next day in the morning betimes an Indian came unto me with Captain Barker; which Indian ran away from his master at my last being there; this savage knew all the country. He came unto me and said that beyond a point, not a culvering-shot off, there was a very rich farmhouse and desired ten or twelve men to go thither. Captain Barker, being one whom I most trusted in the conduct of men and who ever was the most careful in such matters of service, I appointed to go and to take some twenty or thirty men with him; and willed him (as he had any respect or regard of my commandment) not to stay but to come presently away, finding anything or nothing. He forthwith took five-and-twenty men of the most principal men in the ship, and then your cousin Stafford would by no means be left behind. They departed by four of the clock in the morning, so as

I did not see their company. But what should I write more than this unto you? They were all such as neither respected me nor anything that I commanded. Away they went, and by one of the clock they sent my boat again with Ginny wheat and six hens and a small hog. I seeing no return again of the company (for they had sent away the boat only with men to row her aboard) was very much grieved and presently returned the boat again with message: That I much marveled they would tarry at a place so long with so few men; and further, that it was not a hog and six hens could relieve us. And seeing there was no other relief to be had, I charged them straightly to come aboard presently. Thus having dispatched away my boat for them, I still expected their present coming aboard. All that night I heard nothing of them. The next morning I shot ordnance, yet I saw no boat come. Then I weighed anchor and made aboard into the bay, yet for all this I heard nothing of them. Then I doubted with myself very greatly, knowing there were no means left to make any manifester signs to them to hasten away. All that day I heard nothing of them, in the morning I set sail again and ran into the shore. All that night I heard no news of them.

The next morning I saw an Indian come down to the seaside and wave unto the ship. We being desirous to hear some news, caused a raft to be made, for boat we had none, and sent it ashore and set the Indian aboard. When we saw him we found him to be our own Indian, which had escaped away, being sore hurt in three places; who told us that all the rest of our men were slain by three hundred Indians and eighty Portuguese which in the evening set upon them suddenly. Then I demanded why they came not aboard. The Indian answered me that some were unwilling to come and the rest did nothing but eat hens and hogs, which they had there in abundance and that they minded nothing to come aboard. I leave you to judge in what grief I was to see five-and-twenty of my principal men thus basely and willfully cast away; but I leave you to inquire of others the practices of these men, lest in writing unto you it should be thought I did it of malice, which (I protest) is far from me, they being now dead and myself looking imminently to follow them.

Thus I was left destitute of my principal men and a boat; and had I not (by great hap the day before) taken an old boat from the Portuguese I had been utterly undone. This boat I sent to an island fifteen leagues off, to see if they could hear any news of the rest of my ships; she returned within eight days, all which time I remained without a boat. Thus I was six days before I heard news of any of my consorts. The seventeenth day, came in the Roebuck, having spent all her masts but their mizzen, their sails blown clean away and in the most miserable case that ever ship was in. All which mishaps falling upon me, and then missing my small ships wherein (upon that coast) consisted all my strength, having no pinnaces nor great boats left to land my men in, for they were all cast away going to the Straits, I (notwithstanding the want of boats and pinnaces) determined rather than not to be revenged of so base dogs to venture the ships to go down the river afore their town and to have beaten it to the ground. Which forthwith I put in execution. And having gotten down half the way, we found the river so narrow by reason of a shoal, as all the company affirmed plainly it was both desperate and most dangerous. For the river is all ooze, and if a ship come aground it is impossible ever to get off, for there riseth not above a foot water and no anchor will hold to hale off any of my ships in so narrow a place, as we were almost aground in wending. Seeing this apparent danger, I forthwith bare up out of the river, where we escaped no small danger to get well out, for we had not little more water then we drew; and if she had come aground it had been impossible ever to have gotten her off. . . .

There was a Portuguese aboard me who took upon him to be a pilot, who came unto me and told me upon his life that he would take upon him to carry both my ships over the bar at Espírito Santo, a place indeed of great relief and the only place in Brazil for victual and all other wants that we were in. I knew very well that if I could bring my ships within shot of the town I should land my men and further, it could not be in them to make resistance. The whole company desired this course, affirming that there was no way left to relieve all our wants but this; and that there they were in hope to find some ships to repair the Roebuck again. I finding their willingness and charging the Portuguese upon his life to tell me truly whether the ships might pass over the bar without danger, he willed me to take his life if ever the ships came in less water than five fathoms, with such constant affirmations as he desired not to live if he should not perform this. I, considering the greatness of our wants and knowing right well the place to be the only wished town on all the coast to relieve us, forthwith gave my consent, and thither we went, leaving all other intentions. We anchored before the bar and sent my boat to sound the bar and found the deepest water to be but fifteen and seventeen foot (the Portuguese himself going with them, all over the bar), the most water to be but three fathoms. They coming aboard, brought me word of the truth. I called for the Portuguese and demanded of him why he had so lied unto me, who affirmed that he never sounded the bar before and that he had brought in ships of one hundred tons, and that he made account there had not been less water than five fathoms.

This mishap was no small amazement to me and all the company, considering our distress for water and other necessaries, and that the road was so ill as we were scant able to ride there, so as we could neither take in water nor do any other business. In this meantime while we were scanning of these matters, the Roebuck's boat, rowing further into the bay, saw where three ships were at an anchor not far from the town, and came aboard and brought me word thereof; at which news the company seemed much to rejoice, and all affirmed that they would go with our boats and bring them out of the harbor. I showed them how much the taking of them imported us and told them that although the day was spent yet I thought the night not to be altogether inconvenient if they would put on minds to perform it. Resolutely my reasons were these: first they were not so sufficiently provided to defend themselves at that instant as they would be in the morning; and further I told them that if they were not able to defend them, they would take the principal and best things out of them, being so near the shore; and that if they had wherewith to defend themselves it would be less offensive to us in the night than in the day, and we in greatest security, and more offensive to the enemy, especially this exploit being to be done on the water, not landing.

These persuasions seemed a little to move them, for they all desired to stay all morning; yet some of them prepared themselves. Coming amongst them, I found them all, or for the most part, utterly unwilling to go that night; upon which occasion (I confess) I was much moved and gave them some bitter words and showed them our case was not to make detractions but to take that opportunity which was offered us and not to fear a night more than a day, and told them plainly that in refusing of this I could stay there no longer, for over the bar we could not go, and the road so dangerous as never ships rode in a worse. And further, we saw all the country to be fired round about, and that to land we could not without utter spoil to us all, for our boats were naught; and further, we could by no means be succored by our ships; so as I intended to depart. The next morning there was almost an uproar amongst them, the most of them swearing that if I would not give them leave they would take the boats and bring away those ships of themselves. I coming among them, began to reprehend them for their rashness, and told them that now all opportunity was past and that they must be contented, for go they should not. They very much importuned me and some of the chiefest of them desired me with tears in their eyes that they might go, affirming that there was no danger to be feared at all, for if they were able to take them they would return again, and that to depart without attempting to do this was a thing that most greatly grieved them.

I knew right well that if they landed not they could receive no prejudice, for if their ships had been able to withstand them it was in their power to go from them, being stark calm. And further I knew that no ships use Brazil that be able to defend themselves from a cockboat; much less that they should be of force to offend those boats wherein there were so many musketeers as could sit one by another. I, seeing their great importunity, was contented to give them leave to go. And this was my charge to Captain Morgan (to whom at that present I left my directions): that first, upon pain of his life, he should not land at all, whatever opportunity was offered; and that if he saw any danger in coming to these ships he should attempt no further, but return aboard again; but contrariwise if he saw that the place was such as we might land without too much disadvantage and if we might land on plain ground, free from woods or bushes, hard before the town, that then he would presently repair unto me again, and I, and so many as these bad boats would carry, would presently land upon them.

Thus my boats departed from me, having some eighty men, as well furnished with weapons as it is possible to sort such a number withal. Now you shall understand that in the night the Portuguese had hailed the ships hard afore the town. The river where the town stood was not above a bird-bolt-shot over, and half a mile from the town. Where the ships rode, the night we came in, they had cast up two small trenches, on each side the river one, where they had planted some two small bases apiece upon a hill. Right over them were thick woods and great rocks, so that if any were possessed of them they might but tumble stones down and beat away a thousand men. The trench on the western side of the river shot at our boats once or twice; upon that they began to think with themselves what to do, Captain Morgan affirming the place to be very narrow and that they could not well pass it without danger, considering the many men in their boats and also the charge which I had given was such if they saw any danger they should presently repair aboard and certify me and not to pass any further till they had understood my further determination. This Master Morgan made known amongst them, whereupon some of the harebrain sailors began to swear that they never thought other but that he was a coward and now he will show it that durst not land upon a bable ditch, as they termed it. Upon this the gentleman was very much moved and answered them that they should find him to be none such as they accounted him and that, come what could happen to him, he would land.

Upon this, they put the boats between the two sconces (that on the eastern side they had not seen) and the boats being hard upon it were shot at, and in the biggest boat they hurt two and killed one with that shot. Upon this they determined that the smallest boat with their company should land on the western side and the other to land on the eastern side. The small boat landed first, and that place having but few in it, they being not able to defend themselves, ran away, so that our men entered peaceably without hurt of any. The other boat, drawing much water, was aground before they came near the shore, so as they that landed were fain to wade above knee high in water. Now the place, or sconce, was in height some ten foot, made of stone. Captain Morgan more resolutely than discreetly scaled the wall, and ten more with him, which went out of the boat together. Then the Indians and Portuguese showed themselves, and with great stones from over the trench killed Morgan and five more, and the rest of them being sore hurt, retired to the boat, which by this time was so filled with Indian arrows as of forty-five men being in the boat there escaped not eight of them unhurt, some having three arrows sticking in them, some two and there was none which escaped without wound. The fury of those arrows coming so thick and so many of them being spoiled, they put the boat from the shore, leaving the rest on land, a spoil for the Indians.

By this time there came two boats full of lusty Portuguese and some Spaniards who, knowing the sconce on the western side to be weakly manned, came with their boats to the fort's side. One of them ran ashore which was fullest of men, then our men let fly their muskets at them and spoiled and killed all that were in that boat. The others, seeing their fellows speed so ill, rowed back again with all their force and got the town again. In this meantime the great boat being gotten off, they called to them in the sconce and willed them to forsake the fort and to come and help them; for they told them that all their men were spoiled and slain. Upon this they straight came out of the sconce again and retired to their boat; who rushing in all together into the boat she came on ground, so that they could not get her, but some must go out of her again. Ten of the lustiest men went out, and by that time the Indians were come down into the fort again and shot at our men. They which were a land (perceiving the arrows fly among them) ran again to the fort's side and shot in at the lower hold with their muskets. By this the boat was got off, and one that was the master of the Roebuck (a most cowardly villain that ever was born of a woman) caused them in the boat to row away and so left those brave men a spoil for the Portuguese. Yet they waded up to the necks in the water to them, but those merciless villains in the boat would have no pity on them. Their excuse was that the boat was so full of water that had they come in she would have sunk with all them in her; thus vilely were those poor men lost.

By this time they which were landed on the other side (the great boat not being able to row near the shore to relieve them) were killed with stones by the Indians, being thus willfully and indiscreetly spoiled, which you may well perceive if you look into their landing, especially in such a place, as they could not escape killing with stones. They returned aboard again, having lost five-and-twenty men, whereof ten of them were left ashore in such sort as I have showed you. When the boats came to the ship's side there were not eight men in the biggest boat which were not most grievously wounded. I demanded of them the cause of their mishaps and how they durst land, considering my straight commandment to the contrary; they answered me that there was no fault in Captain Morgan but the greatest occasion of all this spoil to them happened upon a controversy between the captain and those soldiers that landed with him and were killed at the fort, for their ill speeches and urging of Captain Morgan was the cause that he landed contrary to my commandment and upon such a place as they all confessed forty men were sufficient to spoil five hundred. . . .

The next morning looking for the Roebuck, she could nowhere be seen. I leave to you to judge in what plight my company was, being now destitute of surgeons, victuals and all other relief; which in truth was so great a discomfort to them as they held themselves dead men, as well whole as hurt. The scantness of water made us that could seek after them but were forced to seek to this island with all possible speed, having to beat back again thither two hundred leagues; which place God suffered us to get with our last cask of water, the poor men being most extremely pinched for want thereof. Where (after we had a little refreshed ourselves) we presently mended our boat in such sort as with great labor and danger we brought forty tons of water aboard. And in the meantime searching our stores of ropes, tackle and sails, we found ourselves utterly unfurnished both of ropes and sails; which accident pleased the company not a little, for by these wants they assuredly accounted to go home. Then making a survey of the victual, we found to be remaining in the ship (according to the rate we then lived at) fourteen weeks victuals large.

Having rigged our ships in such sort as our small store would furnish us, which was most meanly, for we had but four sails (our spritsail and foretop being wanting) which two the ship most principally loveth, and those which we had (except her mainsail) were more than half worn. In this poor case being furnished and our water taken in, my company knowing my determination (which was to hail my boat aground and build her anew) they forthwith openly began to murmur and mutiny, affirming plainly that I need not mend the boat, for they would go home and then there should be no use of her. I, hearing their speeches, thought it was now time to look amongst them. Calling them together, I told them that although we had many mishaps fallen upon us, yet I hoped that their minds would not in such sort be overcome with any of these misfortunes, that they would go about to undertake any base or disordered course; but that they would cheerfully go forward to attempt either to make themselves famous in resolutely dying, or in living to perform that which would be to their perpetual reputation. And the more we attempted, being in so weak a case, the more (if we performed) would be to our honors. But contrariwise, if we died in attempting, we did but that which we came for, which was either to perform or die.

And then I showed them my determination to go again for the Straits of Magellan; which words were no sooner uttered but forthwith they all with one consent affirmed plainly they would never go that way again; and that they would rather stay ashore in that desert island than in such case to go for the Straits. I sought by peaceable means to persuade them, showing them that in going that way we should relieve our victuals, by salting of seals and birds, which they did well know we might do in greater quantity than our ship could carry. And further, if we got through the Straits (which we might now easily perform, considering we had the chiefest part of summer before us) we could not but make a most rich voyage and also meet again with the two small ships where were gone from us; and that it was but six hundred leagues thither; and to go into England they had two thousand. And further that they should be most infamous to the world, that being within six hundred leagues of the place which we so much desired, to return home again so far, being most infamous and beggarly. These persuasions took no place with them, but most boldly they all affirmed that they had sworn they would never go again to the Straits; neither by no means would they.

And one of the chiefest of their faction most proudly and stubbornly uttered these words to my face, in presence of all the rest; which, I seeing and finding my own faction to be so weak (for there were not any that favored my part but my poor cousin Locke and the master of the ship), I took this bold companion by the bosom and with mine own hands put a rope about his neck, meaning resolutely to strangle him, for weapon about me I had none. His companions seeing one of their chief champions in this case and perceiving me to go roundly to work with him, they all came to the master and desired him to speak, affirming they would be ready to take any course that I should think good of. I, hearing this, stayed myself and let the fellow go; after which time I found them something conformable, at least in speeches, though among themselves they still murmured at my intentions. Thus having something pacified them and persuaded them that by no means I would take no other course then to go for the Straits, I took ashore with me thirty soldiers and my carpenters, carrying fourteen days' victual with me for them. Thus going ashore, I hailed up my boat to new build her in such sort as she might be able to abide the seas, leaving aboard all my sailors and the rest to rig the ship and mend sails and to do other business.

And now to let you know in what case I lay ashore among these bad men, you shall understand that of these thirty there were very few of them which had not rather have gone to the Portuguese than to have remained with me; for there were some which, at my being ashore, were making rafts to go over to the main, which was not a mile over, where the Portuguese had continual watch of us, looking but for a fit opportunity to set upon us. Being in this case, always expecting the coming of the Portuguese against whom I could have made no resistance and, further, the treachery of some of my company which desired nothing more than to steal over so to betray me, I protest I lived hourly as he that still expecteth death. In this case I made all the speed I could to make an end of my boat, that we might be able to row her aboard, which in twelve days we mainly finished; which being done, I came aboard and found all my business in good forwardness. So I determined with all possible speed to dispatch and be gone for the Straits of Magellan.

But ere ever we could get in all our water and timber wood and other necessaries, an Irishman (a noble villain) having made a raft, got over the main and told the Portuguese which were there (watching nothing but an opportunity) that if they would go over in the night they should find most of our men ashore without weapons and that they might do with them what they would. Upon this, the next night they came over and having taken some of our men, they brought them where the rest lay, which they most cruelly killed, being sick men not able to stir to help themselves. Those which were ashore, more than the sick men, had stolen out of the ship, for it was all my care to keep them aboard, knowing well that the Portuguese sought to spoil us, the place being so fit for them, all overgrown with woods and bushes, as their Indians might go and spoil us with their arrows at their pleasures, and we not be able to hurt one of them. In the morning, perceiving their coming, I sent my boat ashore and rescued all my healthful men but five, which they found out in the night without weapons to defend them; whereof (besides the loss of our men) we having but four sails, left one ashore, which was no small mishap among the rest.

The Portuguese went presently again over to the main, but left their Indians to keep in the bushes. About the watering place, our men going ashore, were shot at and hurt and could by no means come to hurt them again, by reason of the wood and bushes. Wherefore finding my men hurt and that by no means I could do anything there without more loss of men (whereof I had no need) for I had not above ninety men left, or little over, notwithstanding my wants of wood and water, and my boat, not being sufficiently mended, was in no possibility to do me pleasure—in this case was I forced to depart, fortune never ceasing to lay her greatest adversities upon me.

But now I am grown so weak and faint as I am scarce able to hold the pen in my hand: wherefore I must leave you to inquire of the rest of our most unhappy proceedings, but know this, that for the Straits I could by no means get my company to give their consents to go. For after this misfortune and the want of our sails (which was a chief matter they alleged), and to tell you truth all the men left in the ship were no more than able to weigh our anchors. But in truth I desired nothing more than to attempt that course, rather desiring to die in going forward than basely in returning back again. But God would not suffer me to die so happy a man, although I sought all the ways I could still to attempt to perform somewhat. For after that by no means I saw they could be brought to go for the Straits, having so many reasonable reasons to allege against me as they had: first, having but three sails, and the place subject to such furious storms, and the loss of one of these was death; and further, our boat was not sufficiently repaired to abide the seas; and last of all, the fewness and feebleness of our company (wherein we had not left thirty sailors). These causes being alleged against me, I could not well answer them but resolved them plainly that to England I would never give my consent to go, and that if they would not take such courses as I intended I was then determined that ship and all should sink in the seas together. Upon this they began to be more tractable, and then I showed them that I would beat for Saint Helena and there to make ourselves happy by mending or ending. This course in truth pleased none of them; and yet, seeing my determination and supposing it would be more dangerous to resist me than in seeming to be willing, they were at quiet, until I had beaten from twenty-nine degrees to the southward of the Equator to twenty. At which time, finding that I was too far northerly to have good wind, I called them to tack about the ship to the southward again. They all plainly made answer they would not, and that they had rather die there than be starved in seeking an island which they thought that way we should never get.

What means I used to stand again to the southward I leave you to inquire of themselves; but from the latitude of twenty I beat back again into twenty-eight with such contrary winds as (I suppose) never man was troubled with the like so long a time together. Being in this latitude, I found the wind favorable and then I stood again to the northward, willing the master and his company to sail east-northeast, and they in the night (I being asleep) steered northeast, and mere northerly. Notwithstanding all this most vile usage, we got within two leagues of the island, and had the wind favored us so as that we might have stemmed from eighteen degrees to sixteen east-northeast, we had found the island. But it was not God's will so great a blessing should befall me. Being now in the latitude of the island, almost eighteen leagues to the westward of it, the wind being continually at east-southeast (the most contrary wind that could blow), I presently made a survey of my victual and found that according to that proportion which we then lived at there was not left in the ship eight weeks' victual; which, being so far from relief, was (as I suppose) as small a portion as ever men were at in the seas.

Being so uncertain of relief, I demanded of them whether they would venture (like good-minded men) to beat to the southward again to get this island, where we should not only relieve ourselves, but also to be in full assurance either to sink or take a carrack; and that by this means we would have a sufficient revenge of the Portuguese for all their villainies done unto us; or that they would pinch and bate half the allowance they had before and so to go for England. They all answered me they would pinch to death rather than to the southward again. I knew their dispositions, having lived among them in such continual torment and disquietness. And now to tell you of my greatest grief, which was the sickness of my dear kinsman John Locke, who by this time was grown in great weakness, by reason whereof he desired rather quietness and contentedness in our course than such continual disquietness which never ceased me. And now by this, what with grief for him and the continual trouble among such hellhounds, my spirits were clean spent; wishing myself upon any desert place in the world, there to die, rather than thus basely to return home again; which course I had put in execution had I found an island which the charts make to be in eight degrees to the southward of the Line. I swear to you, I sought it with all diligence, meaning (if I had found it) to have there ended my unfortunate life. But God suffered not such happiness to light upon me, for I could by no means find it. I was forced to go towards England; and having gotten eight degrees by north the Line, I lost my most dearest cousin.

And now consider whether a heart made of flesh be able to endure so many misfortunes, all falling upon me without intermission. I thank my God that in ending of me he hath pleased to rid me of all further trouble and mishaps. And now to return to our private matters, I have made my will, wherein I have given special charge that all goods whatsoever belong unto me be delivered into your hands. For God's sake refuse not to do this last request for me. I owe little that I know of and therefore it will be the less trouble; but if there be any debt that of truth is owing by me, for God's sake see it paid. I have left a space in the will for another name, and (if you think it good) I pray take in my cousin Henry Sackford, he will ease you much in many businesses. There is a bill of adventure to my cousin Richard Locke. If it happen the other ship return home with anything, as it is not impossible, I pray remember him, for he hath nothing to show for it. And likewise Master Heton, the customer of Hampton, which is fifty pounds, and one Eliot of Ratcliffe by London, which is fifty pounds more, the rest have all bills of adventure but the ruin in the victual, only two excepted, which I have written unto you. I have given Sir George Carey the Desire, if ever she return, for I always promised him her if she returned, and a little part of her getting. If any such thing happen, I pray you see it performed.

To use compliments of love (now at my last breath) were frivolous, but know that I left none in England whom I loved half so well as yourself; which you in such sort deserved at my hands as I can by no means requite. I have left all (that little remaining) unto you, not to be accountable for anything. That which you will (if you find any overplus, yourself specially being satisfied to your own desire) give unto my sister Anne Candish. I have written to no man living but yourself, leaving all friends and kinsmen, only reputing you as dearest. Commend me to both your brethren, being glad that your brother Edward escaped so unfortunate a voyage. I pray give this copy of my unhappy proceedings in this action to none but only to Sir George Carey, and tell him that if I had thought the letter of a dead man would have been acceptable I would have written unto him. I have taken order with the master of my ship to see his pieces of ordnance delivered unto him, for he knoweth them. And if the Roebuck be not returned, then I have appointed him to deliver two brass pieces out of this ship, which I pray see performed. I have now no more to say but take this last farewell: that you have lost the lovingest friend that was lost by any. Commend me to your wife. No more, but as you love God do not refuse to undertake this last request of mine. I pray forget not Master Cary of Cockington, gratify him with something; for he used me kindly at my departure. Bear with this scribbling; for I protest, I am scant able to hold a pen in my hand.

1615 *A Poor Englishman Cast Away*

In 1614 Sir William Monson was sent to scour the Scotch and Irish Seas, which were much infested with pirates. Nevertheless the next year, 1615, the ordinary passage boat, sailing from England to Dublin, was taken by a French pirate. But a tempest arising immediately after, they were obliged to let it go again. There happened to be three persons then in it, who were thus left to the mercy of the wind and waves, which carried them between Ireland and Scotland, into the main sea, expecting to be cast away every minute. They had neither victuals or drink, except some sugar which happened to be in the boat. Upon this they lived, and drank their own urine till their bodies were so dried up that they could make no more.

In this doleful condition one of the company, being quite spent with fatigue and misery, died and was heaved overboard by the remaining two. After a while the second grew so feeble that he laid himself along in the boat, ready to yield up the ghost. In this plight the third providentially descried a small island towards the extremities of Scotland. It was a great way off but he encouraged the dying man to rouse himself with hopes of life; and accordingly upon this good news he raised himself up and by and by the boat was cast upon a rock and split, the two men escaping up into the island.

They found nothing at all growing there, neither grass, tree or anything else by which a man could procure subsistence, nor any shelter from the weather except about the middle of the island, where there were two long stones pitched in the ground and a third laid

35

upon them, like a table, which they judged to have been so placed by some fishermen to dry their fish upon; and under these they slept at night.

They now judged themselves to be in a more wretched condition than if, being swallowed up by the sea, they had been delivered from the extremities they were in for want of meat and drink. Yet God in his good Providence was pleased to make some provision for them; for they took some sea mews, which they dried in the wind and sun, and then ate raw. They also caught some sea dogs and found some eggs in the crevices of the rocks by the seaside. Thus, through God's good Providence, they had wherewithal to subsist so as to keep them from starving. But what they thought most insupportable was thirst, because the place afforded no fresh water except what fell from the clouds and was left in certain cavities which time had made in the rock. Neither could they have this at all seasons, because the island, or rather rock, being small and lying low, in stormy weather the waves dashed over it and filled the pits with salt water.

Before they had been here long they built a kind of hut with boards from the ruins of the boat, which served them for a more comfortable shelter than the stones against the rain and injuries of the wind and weather.

In this condition they lived together for about the space of six weeks, comforting one another and finding some ease in their common calamity, till at last the poor Englishman being left alone, the burden became almost insupportable. For one day, awakening in the morning, he missed his comrade and, getting up, went calling and seeking all about the island for him. Not being able by any means to find him, he fell into such despair that he frequently resolved to cast himself down headlong into the sea and so put a final period to that affliction of which he had endured but one half, while he had a friend to divide it with him.

What became of his companion he could not guess—whether despair forced him to that extremity or whether, getting up in the night, not fully awake, he had fallen into the sea. But he rather thought that, through want of proper care, he fell from the rock as he was looking for birds' eggs, for it was very steep on that side. He had discerned no distraction in him, neither could he imagine that he should, on a sudden, fall into that despair against which he had so fortified himself by frequent and fervent prayer.

His loss so affected the poor disconsolate survivor that he oft thought to have leaped from the rocks into the sea; yet still his conscience stopped him, suggesting to him that if he did it he would be utterly damned for his self-murder.

Being now entirely alone, another affliction befell him, which was this. His only knife, with which he used to cut up the sea dogs and sea mews, having a bloody cloth wrapped round it, was carried away, as he supposed, by some bird of prey. Being now not able to kill any more, he was reduced to the following extremity. With much difficulty he got a great nail out of one of the boards of his hut, which he made shift so to sharpen upon the stones that it served him instead of a knife.

By degrees his clothes wore out, and when winter came on and everything wore a more doleful aspect than before he endured the greatest misery imaginable. For many times the rock and his hut were so covered with snow that it was not possible for him to go abroad to provide his food, which extremity put him upon this invention. He thrust out a little stick at the crevice of his hut and, baiting it with a little sea dogs' fat, by that means caught some sea mews, which he took with his hand from under the snow and thus kept himself from starving.

In this sad and solitary condition he lived for about eleven months, expecting to end his days there, when the gracious Providence of God sent a ship thither, which delivered him out of as great misery as perhaps any man was ever in.

In the year 1616, a Fleming named Pickman, coming from Drontheim in Norway in a vessel laden with boards, was overtaken by a calm, during which the current carried him upon the rock of island where the poor Englishman dragged on his miserable existence.

This Pickman was well known in England and Holland for his art and dexterity in getting out of the sea the great guns of the Spanish

Armada, which was driven upon the coasts of Scotland and Ireland in 1588.

He was now in some danger of being cast away and, to avoid being wrecked, ordered some of his men to get into the shallop and to tow off the ship. They, having done so, would needs climb up into a certain rock to look for birds' eggs. As soon as they were got up they at some distance perceived the figure of a man, whence they imagined there were others lurking thereabout or that this man had made his escape thither to avoid some pirates who, if not prevented, might surprise their ship. On this, without stopping to relieve him, they returned with all the haste they could to their shallop and so got on board.

The calm continuing and the current of the sea still driving them upon the island, they were forced to get into the longboat and to tow the vessel off again. The man whom they had seen before was in the meantime come to the brink of the island and made signs with his hands lifted up, entreating them to come nearer; sometimes falling on his knees and joining his hands together, begging and crying to them for relief.

At first they made difficulty about going to him; but at length, being overcome by his lamentable signs, they went nearer the island, where they saw something that was more like a ghost than a living person: a body stark naked, black and hairy, a meagre and deformed countenance with hollow and distorted eyes, which raised such compassion in them that they endeavored to take him into the boat. But the rock was so steep thereabout that it was impossible for them to land. Whereupon they went about the island and came at last to a flat shore, where they took him on board at the same rock where he had been cast on shore. They saw neither grass nor tree on the island, or any shelter except the hut which the poor man and companion had built.

The sun was set ere they got to the ship, when the wind immediately rose and drove them off from the island. Observing this Providence so singularly displayed, they imagined that what they had brought with them was not a man, since he had not the figure of one;

whereupon they were the more inquisitive to know who he was and by what means he came to that uninhabitable place. Upon which he gave them his history as already related.

The master of the ship, commiserating his deplorable condition, treated him so well that within a few days he was quite another creature. He afterwards set him ashore at Londonderry and sometime after saw him again at Dublin; where such as had heard of his singular affliction gave him money to enable him to return to England, his native country.

1619   A Most Dangerous Voyage by Captain John Monck

CHRISTIAN IV, King of Denmark, being desirous to find out a passage betwixt Greenland and America to facilitate the voyage to the East Indies, did order one Captain Monck, a person of great bravery, to sail with two stout ships to the Straits which were not many years before discovered by one Mr. Hudson, an Englishman.

This Mr. Hudson, having been several times before on the northern coasts, was at last prevailed upon by some English merchants to try his fortune whether he could find out a passage betwixt Greenland and America to the East Indies. Accordingly, he set sail from England with one ship only in the year 1610 and, passing along the coast of Greenland, was, what with the fogs and what with storms, forced into a strait passage, which at last brought him into an open sea; which made him begin to conceive certain hopes that he had been so fortunate as to be the discoverer of the said passage.

But after he had for a considerable time cruised up and down this sea without being able to discover the desired passage, he resolved (contrary to the opinion of the rest) to pass the winter thereabouts, though he was not sufficiently stored with provisions for so long a time. And they must infallibly have perished for want of food if they had not met with several sorts of birds and among the rest with white partridges, of whom they catched about a hundred dozen. And these leaving that part of the country towards the Spring, they were in their stead supplied with swans, ducks, geese and other such like water fowl, which were easily catched. Besides, they met with a certain tree there of a most miraculous nature, its leaves being green inclining to yellow, had a strong taste of spice and, being boiled, afforded a balsamic oil, the decoction itself being a present remedy against the scurvy, the sciatica and other distempers occasioned by cold and vicious humors.

The approaching spring furnished them with such store of fish as would be sufficient to freight their whole ship if Mr. Hudson had not been more intent upon his intended discovery than anything else. Which, however, being not able to effect, he saw himself under a necessity of bending his course back to England. In the meanwhile there happened a mutiny against the captain, carried on by one Green, his clerk, who did force his cabin, from whence they took him and his son and, putting them with seven more in a shallop, committed them to the mercy of the sea.

But we must return to Captain Monck, who set sail from the Sound with two ships, one manned with forty-eight men, the other with sixteen, on the 16th day of May in the year 1619. He arrived on the 20th of June near Cape Farewell, being very rocky, covered with ice and snow, and situated under 62½ degrees. From thence steering his course to the northwest towards Hudson's Straits, he was much incommoded by the ice, which however did him no considerable damage, he having sea-room enough. Among other accidents that befell him, it froze so violently on the 18th of June at night, and the winds blew so hard and cold, that his sails were rendered useless by reason of the ice that adhered to them; yet the next following day proved so excessive hot in the afternoon that they were forced to lay by their clothes and to go in their shirts only.

He did not arrive at Hudson's Straits till the 17th of July, which he called, after the King of Denmark, Christian's Straits. His first landing was in an island directly opposite to Greenland; and, having sent some of his people to take a view of the country, they found no men, but by their footsteps were convinced there were some in this island. The next following day they saw some of the savages, who, seeming to be surprised at the sight of the Danes, hid their arms behind a great stone heap and then advanced toward them in a friendly posture, but kept continually a watchful eye upon their arms for fear the Danes should come too near them. Notwithstanding which, they found means to get betwixt them and their arms, which they seized. The savages seemed to be exceedingly troubled at this loss and in an humble posture begged the Danes to have them restored, without which they were not able to subsist, hunting being their only livelihood. They offered to exchange their clothes for them, which moved the Danes at last to compassion; so that they not only gave them back their arms but also presented them with several toys, which they received very thankfully, and in lieu of them brought the Danes several sorts of fowl and fish.

One among them having got a small looking-glass, and seeing himself in it, was so overjoyed that he put it into his bosom and did run away as fast as his legs could carry him. The Danes laughed heartily at his simplicity; but what diverted them more than all the rest was that they perceived some of these savages to make their courtship, after their way, to one of the ship's crew, who having long black hair and being of a swarthy complexion, with a flattish nose, they took him for one of their countrymen who perhaps had been carried away from Greenland some time before; which often furnished them afterwards with matter of laughter, so that the poor fellow was always jeered as long as the voyage lasted.

On the 19th of the same month Captain Monck ordered the sails to be hoisted up in order to leave this island, but was forced to return into the same harbor by reason of the ice, which obstructed his passage. In the meanwhile they left no stone unturned to find out some of the inhabitants, but in vain. They found some nets spread near the seashore, on which they hung knives, looking-glasses and other such-like toys, in hopes to allure them to the seaside. But nobody appeared, whether out of fear of the Danes or because they were commanded to the contrary by their superiors is uncertain.

Captain Monck, being disappointed in his hopes of meeting with the inhabitants, ordered a wild reindeer to be shot, of which there were great numbers there; wherefore he gave the name of Reensund to the island, and to the harbor that of the Monckepes, being situated under 64 degrees and 20 minutes. And after he had planted the Danish arms there he once more left the said island on the 22nd of July but met with such bad weather and so many vast ice shoals at sea that on the 28th of the same month he was forced to seek for shelter betwixt two islands, near one of which he came to an anchor. But, finding it unsafe to continue thus, he brought his ships as near the shore as possible he could, so that at low water they lay upon the sand; and the high tide carried such a prodigious quantity of ice to the shore that they were in no small danger if by their industry they had not prevented it. There was a great ice shoal, near fifty foot thick, which, being loosened by the violence of the sea, carried all before it, and among the rest their shallops, which narrowly escaped sinking.

Ashore they saw several footsteps of men, a sign that the place was not destitute of inhabitants; but whatever care they took, they could not get sight of any. They also found there some mineral stones and a very good talc, of which they carried off several ton-weight. There were several other small islands thereabouts but the sea did run so high near the shore that the Danes durst not venture to land. These islands are situated under 62 degrees, 20 minutes, about fifty leagues within Hudson's, or as Monck calls it, Christian's, Straits. The bay where he came to an anchor he called Hareford, from the great number of hares they met with there. He again set up the arms of Denmark and the initial letter of his royal master, viz. C. IV, signifying Christian IV.

On the 9th of August he set sail again from this place with a northwest wind, steering his course west-southwest, and on the 10th came to the south of the straits of America and cast his anchor near a large island, unto which he gave the name of Snow Island because it was all covered with snow.

On the 20th of August he directed his course to the northwest, being then (as his own diary testifies) exactly under the elevation of 62 degrees, 20 minutes; but there fell so much snow, and the wind did blow so violently, that they could see no land, though the straits were not above sixteen leagues over thereabouts, which shows that they are broader in some other places. After having past these straits, he got into Hudson's sea, which he furnished with another name, or rather gave it two names instead of one. For that part of it which washes the American shore he called Mare Novum, or the New Sea. To the other part, which extends to Greenland (if it be really Greenland), he gave the name of Mare Christianum, or Christian's Sea. He continued his course west-northwest till he came to 63 degrees, 20 minutes, when, finding himself surrounded on all sides by the ice, he resolved to pass the winter there. The harbor he called Monck's Winter Harbor and the country New Denmark. In his relation he makes mention only of two islands in the Christian Sea, which he styles "the two sisters"; and in the New Sea, but one, called Dichles Oeland. He advises those who undertake the voyage through these straits to keep as much as possibly they can in the middle to avoid being carried away by the stormy tides and the great ice shoals which are of such a thickness there that if a ship happen to get betwixt them it seldom escapes. He says that it flows exactly five hours in the Christian Sea, the tide being regulated by the moon.

On the 7th of September Captain Monck cast anchor there, and after his people had refreshed themselves for some days he ordered them to bring the ships into a little creek, where they were sheltered against the violence of the winds and ice. The next thing they had to do was to provide themselves good huts against the approaching winter season. This harbor lay near the entrance of a river, which was not frozen up in October, though the sea was full of ice all round about.

On the 7th day of the same month Captain Monck had a mind to go up the river in a boat, but could not go further than about a league and a half by reason of the cataracts or rocky waterfalls that opposed his passage. He then marched with some of his men about four leagues deep into the country to see whether he could meet with any of the inhabitants; but, nobody appearing, he resolved to return another way. Here he met with a certain stone raised above the ground, upon which was painted an image resembling the Devil with claws and horns. Near this stone was a place of about eight foot square, enclosed with lesser stones. On one side of this enclosure there lay a heap of small flat stones intermixt with moss of trees. On the opposite side was a large flat stone laid upon two others in the shape of an altar, upon which they found three coals laid across. They saw several more of those altars as they were walking about, and some footsteps of men near each of them, though they did not come in sight at that time. It is very likely that the inhabitants used to sacrifice upon those altars, either with fire, or perhaps offer their sacrifices to the fire itself, for round about them they saw abundance of bones, which probably were the bones of the sacrificed beasts, whose flesh the savages had devoured raw, according to their custom. They met also with many trees, cut down to the roots with iron instruments; and with dogs that were muzzled. But what most confirmed them in their opinion that this isle was not destitute of inhabitants was that in many places they could discover the holes where they had fixed the poles belonging to their tents, and found many pieces of skins of bears, wolves, dogs and sea calves wherewith they used to cover them; which seemed to intimate that the inhabitants here did lead a vagabond life like the Tartars and Lapponians.

After the Danes had planted their huts they cut good store of wood to be laid up for the winter and killed abundance of wild fowl. Captain Monck killed a white bear with his own hands, which they ate, and he says expressly that it agreed very well with them. They catched abundance of hares, partridges and other fowl, besides four black foxes and some sables.

On the 27th of November there appeared three suns to them and on the next following 24th of January two. On the 10th of December (old style) there happened an eclipse of the moon, which they saw about eight o'clock at night; after which they saw the same night the moon surrounded with a very bright circle, through the middle of which was a cross which divided the moon in two. This seemed to be the forerunner of those evils which these poor wretches were to suffer hereafter, as will appear out of the following account.

The cold began to increase with the winter season to such a degree that they saw ice of three hundred, nay three hundred and sixty, foot thick. No beer, no wine or brandy was strong enough to be proof against it but froze to the bottom and the vessels split in pieces, so that they cut the frozen liquor with hatchets and melted it before the fire before they could drink it. If they happened to leave any quantity of water in their copper or tin vessels they found them all in pieces the next morning. Neither were the poor Danes able to resist so excessive a frost which mastered the metals, for they all fell sick and their sickness increased with the cold; they were generally seized with a griping looseness which did not leave them till it put an end to their days. Thus they dropped away one after another, so that about the beginning of March the Captain was fain to do duty as a sentry for want of others. The worst was that the Spring did augment their distemper, for their teeth were ready to fall out and their gums swelled to that degree that they could not take any other nourishment but bread soaked in water. The poor remnants of these unfortunate wretches were in the next following May seized with another looseness, with such violent pricking pains in their limbs as made them look like mere shadows, their arms and legs being quite lame and full of blue spots, as if they had been beaten, being a distemper not unknown to seamen, by whom it is commonly called the scurvy. So many of them died that there were not enough left to bury them, the rest being likewise sick and very weak. And to complete their misery they began to want bread, instead of which they made use of raspberries which they digged out from under the snow, which supplied the defect of bread. But they were fain to eat them as soon as they were taken from under the snow, where they kept fresh, but soon grew useless afterwards.

On the 12th day of April it rained the fifth time after seven months; and towards the end of May there appeared again all sorts of fowl, such as wild geese and ducks, swans, swallows, partridges, ravens, snipes, falcons and eagles; but they were too weak to catch them.

On the 4th of June Captain Monck himself fell down so dangerously ill that he did take no food for four days together; and expecting nothing else but present death, he made his last will, in which he desired those that might by chance come to this place to bury his corpse and to send the diary of his voyage to the King of Denmark. After four days were past he began however to recover a little and with much ado got out of his hut to see whether there were any of his ship's crew left alive, of whom he found no more than two of sixty-four persons he brought along with him. These two being overjoyed to see their captain in a condition to stir abroad, took him in their arms and carried him to a fire to refresh his spirits. They now began to encourage one another, promising to stand by one another to the last gasp. They digged everywhere among the snow till at last they met with a certain root, which being both restorative and food to them, they were restored in a few days. The ice began now to melt apace, so that on the 18th of June they catched some salmon and other fish, which with what exercise they used in hunting, so strengthened them in a little time that they resolved to return to Denmark.

The summer season approaching, they were extremely pestered with gnats, which made them hasten their departure. So that on the 16th of July they went aboard their lesser ship (leaving the biggest behind) and steered their course toward Monck's harbor. They were much incommoded by the ice and lost their boat and rudder. Whilst they were busy in making a new one they fastened their ship to an ice-rock, which being loosened by the tide, their ship was carried away with it. But the ice being melted soon after, they got clear again and met with their boat, which they had lost ten days before. It was not long before they got fast within the ice once more. But the weather changing almost every day, they were soon released again. Having at last repassed the Straits, they sailed by Cape Farewell into the ocean but were on the 8th of September overtaken by a most terrible tempest, which threatened no less than their total destruction, they being quite tired out, and not able to manage the ship. So that, leaving themselves to the mercy of the winds, they lost their mast, and the sails blew overboard, which however they made shift to save.

In this condition they were forced upon the coast of Norway, where they cast a piece of an anchor (the only one they had left) in a small creek, where they hoped to shelter themselves against the storm; but found themselves deceived in their hopes, for they were in most imminent danger of being dashed to pieces against the rocks, if by good fortune they had not got betwixt them and the shore; where after they had refreshed themselves for some days they pursued their voyage and arrived at last in Denmark.

Captain Monck had no sooner set foot ashore but he went to Copenhagen to give the king an account of his unfortunate voyage; who, not imagining him to be still among the living, received him with all imaginable marks of his favor. Thus we have seen the brave Captain Monck return to the Danish shore, which, as might reasonably be supposed, would put an end to all his sufferings. But it seems his ill destiny had preserved him for more, which was to put an unhappy period to the life of this brave man.

For whilst he was in Denmark he used often to ruminate upon his past adventures; and, being by degrees convinced of what had been the chief cause of his miscarriage in his voyage through the Straits, he took a resolution to try his fortune once more, in which he hoped to supply the defects of the former, arising from the want of knowledge of those seas and some other circumstances. Accordingly he proposed his design to some persons of quality, who, approving of it, equipped two ships which he was to command in chief.

Having provided himself with all necessaries for such a voyage, he was ready to set sail, when (as his ill fortune would have it) the king sent for him and, happening, among other things, to speak of his former unfortunate voyage, told him that he had lost two ships by his want of conduct. Which the captain answering somewhat briskly, the king took his cane and pushed it in anger against his breast. The captain took this affront so heinously that he immediately went home to bed and would not be persuaded to take the least nourishment. So that in ten days after he died for melancholy and want of food.

1654 An Account of the Shipwrecked Crew of a Dutch Vessel

WE SAILED out of the Texel on the 10th of
January, 1653-4 in the evening with a very fair gale, and after many
storms and much foul weather came to an anchor on the 1st of June
in the road of Batavia. As soon as we had refreshed ourselves there
for a few days the governor general of the India company commanded
us away to Tapowan, and accordingly we set sail the 14th of the
same month in our ship called the Sparrowhawk. We carried aboard
us Min Heer Cornelius Lessen, to take possession of the government
of Tapowan and Formosa with their dependencies in the place of
Min Heer Nicholas Verburge, who had resided there three years
according to custom. We had the good fortune to come to an anchor
at Tapowan on the 16th of July. Min Heer Lessen immediately
landed and caused our ship to be unloaded. Then, having advised
with the council, he ordered us to Japan; in pursuance whereof,
having our loading and discharge, we put to sea again on the 30th of
the same month. The next day held fair till towards the evening,
when, as we were getting out of the channel of Formosa, there arose
a storm which increased all night.

On the 1st of August early in the morning we perceived a small
island very near us. We used our utmost endeavors to get under
shelter of it and find some place to cast anchor, for in most parts of
that sea there is no bottom to be found. However, we compassed our
design, though with much difficulty because we were afraid to come
near a floating timber that burnt close by us. Our pilot, fortunately

49

looking out, had discovered that island, otherwise we had been lost, for we were not above a musketshot from it. The fog clearing up and the day growing bright, we found ourselves so near the coast of China that we could easily discern armed men scattered along the shore, expecting to make their advantage of our wreck. But, God be praised, they missed of their aim though the storm increased rather than diminished. There we continued all that day at an anchor in sight of them, as also the night following.

The next day the wind falling, we observed that the number of the Chinese was much increased, which made us stand upon our guard, resolving to remove further from them as soon as possible, but were hindered by a calm which lasted all day and next night.

The third day we perceived the storm had drove us twenty leagues from our course, so that we were again in sight of the island Formosa. We plied betwixt that island and the continent, the weather somewhat cold; and what troubled us most was that the uncertain winds and calms kept us in that channel till the 11th of that month, when a southwest wind grew up into a storm, with a heavy rain, and forced us to run northeast, and northeast by east. The three following days the weather continued still more tempestuous and the wind shifted so often that we were continually hoisting and lowering our sails. By this time the frequent beating of the sea had much weakened our vessel and the continual rain obstructed our making any observation, for which reason we were forced to take in all our sails, strike the yards and commit ourselves to the mercy of the waves.

On the 15th the wind blew so boisterously that we could not hear one another speak, nor durst we let fly an inch of sail. And, to add to our misfortunes, the ship took in so much water that there was no mastering of it. Besides, the waves every moment broke in upon us in such manner that we expected to perish every minute. That night our boat and the greatest part of our gallery were carried away, which shook our boltsprit and made us fear we should lose our prow. All possible means were used to repair the damage sustained and prevent the ill consequences it might produce. But in vain, for the gusts of wind were too violent and came too close one upon another, besides the breaking of the waves which were ready to sink us every moment. At length finding there was no way to save ourselves but by abandoning the vessel and the company's goods, we resolved to loose a foretopsail the better to avoid the greater surges. Whilst we were thus employed, a wave coming over our stern had like to have washed away all the seamen that were upon the deck. It filled the ship so full of water that the master cried out, "My mates, cut down the mast by the board immediately and recommend yourselves to the mercy of God! For if one or two such waves return we are all lost and all our skill and labor will not save us!"

This was our condition, when the second glass of the second watch being just running out, he that looked out ahead cried, "Land, land," adding that we were not above a musketshot from it, the darkness of the night and the rain having obstructed our discovering it sooner. We endeavored to anchor but in vain because we found no bottom, and the roughness of the sea and force of the wind obstructed. Thus the anchors having no hold, three successive waves sprung such a leak in the vessel that those who were in the hold were drowned before they could get out. Some of those that were on the deck leaped overboard and the rest were carried away by the sea. Fifteen of us got ashore in the same place, for the most part naked and much hurt, and thought at first none had escaped but ourselves; but, climbing the rocks, we heard the voices of some men complaining, yet could see nothing nor help anybody because of the darkness of the night.

On the 16th all of us that were in a condition to walk went calling and seeking about the strand to see if we could find any more that had got to land. Some were found scattered about, so that we made up thirty-six, most of us dangerously hurt. Then, searching the wreck, we discovered a man betwixt two planks, which had so pressed his body that he lived but three hours. It is needless to relate how sensibly we were touched at the loss of our ship and to see that of sixty-four men only thirty-six were left in a quarter of an hour. However, we went along the shore to pay the last duty to those bodies the sea had cast up. We found none but our Captain Egbertz of Amsterdam, stretched out on the sand, ten or twelve fathom from the water, with his arm under his head, whom we buried.

Having scarce taken any sustenance for two or three days past, because there had been no possibility of dressing anything, we searched along the sands to see whether the sea had not cast any of our provisions ashore, but could get only one sack of meal, a cask with some salt meat, a little bacon and, what was best for the wounded men, a hogshead of claret. Our greatest trouble was to contrive how to make a fire; for, having neither heard nor seen any living creature, we concluded we were on a desert island. Towards evening the wind and rain somewhat abating, we gathered enough of the wreck to contrive some shelter for us, making use to that purpose of the remainder of our sails.

On the 17th, as we were lamenting our deplorable condition, sometimes complaining that we saw nobody and sometimes flattering ourselves with the hopes of being near Japan, where we might find somebody that would put us in the way to get to the Dutch factory, our ship being in no condition to be refitted, we spied a man about a cannonshot from us. We called and made signs to him; but as soon as ever he saw us he fled. Soon after noon we spied three more, one of them with a musket and his companions with bows and arrows. Being come within gunshot of us, they halted; and perceiving we made towards them, ran way, though we endeavored by signs to show them we desired nothing but fire of them. At last one of us resolved to attack them; but they delivered up their arms without making any opposition, wherewith we lighted the fire we wanted. These men were clad after the Chinese fashion, excepting only their hats, which were made of horsehair, and we were much afraid lest they should be wild Chinese or pirates. Towards evening there came a hundred armed men clad like the other, who, after counting of us, kept us enclosed all night.

On the 18th we spent all the morning in enlarging our tent; and about noon there came down about two thousand men, horse and foot, who drew up in order of battle before our hut. Our secretary, the chief pilot and his mate, with a boy, went out to meet them.

When they came before the commander he ordered a great iron chain to be put about the neck of each of them, with a little bell, such as the bellwether wears in Holland. In that condition they forced them to fall down and prostrate themselves before that commander, all his men at the same time raising such a shout that we who were in our hut cried out, "We are lost and must prepare to be used after the same manner!" Which was immediately put in execution. When we had laid some time flat on our faces, they made signs to us to kneel. Being in this posture, they put some questions to us which we did not understand, and we on our side did all we could to let them know that we intended to have gone to Nagasaki in Japan. They were as far from understanding us as if they had never known Japan; for they call that country Jeenare, or Jirpon. The commander, perceiving he could make nothing of all we said, caused a cup of Arac to be filled to everyone of us and sent us back to our tent. They that conducted us to see what provisions we had, found only a little bacon and salt meat, which they showed to their chief. An hour later they brought us rice boiled in water and, believing we were almost starved, would not give us much for fear it should hurt us. After dinner they came with ropes in their hands, which very much surprised us, imagining they intended to strangle us; but our fear vanished when we saw them run altogether towards the wreck to draw ashore what might be of use to them. At night they gave us more rice to eat; and our master having made an observation, found we were in the island of Quelpaert, which is in 33 degrees, 32 minutes of latitude.

These people were employed all the 19th in getting ashore the sad remains of our wreck, drying the cloths and burning the wood to get the iron, being very fond of that metal. Beginning now to grow somewhat familiar, we went up to the commander of the forces and the admiral of the island, who was also come down, and presented each of them with a prospective glass and a pot of red wine, with our captain's silver cup, which we found among the rocks. They liked the liquor so well that they drank till they were very merry. They returned us the silver cup with many tokens of friendship and we retired to our tent.

On the 20th they made an end of burning all the wood of the ship and saving the iron; during which time a pleasant accident happened. The fire they made coming to two pieces of cannon which were loaded with ball, they gave so great a report that they all fled and durst not return a long while or go near the vessel till we had assured them by signs they need not to fear the like would happen any more. This day they brought us twice to eat.

On the 21st in the morning the commander gave us to understand by signs that we must bring before him all that we had saved in our tent, that it be sealed; which was done in our presence. Whilst this was doing some persons were brought before him who had converted to their own use some iron, hides and other things saved out of our wreck, which they had still in their possession. They were immediately punished before our faces to show us their design was not to wrong us of any of our goods. Each of those thieves had thirty or forty strokes given him on the soles of his feet, with a cudgel as thick as a man's arm and as tall as a man. This punishment is so severe that some of their toes dropped off. About noon they made signs to give us to understand we must depart. Those that were well had horses provided for them and the sick were carried in hammocks. Thus we set forward, attended by a numerous guard of horse and foot; and travelling four leagues, came at night to a little town called Tadiane, where, after a slender repast, they carried us into a warehouse much like a stable.

The 22nd in the morning, at break of day, we set out in the same order and travelled to a little fort, near which there were two galiots. Here we halted to dine, and at night came to the town of Moggan or Mocxo, where the governor of the island resides. We were all conducted to the square before the town-house, where about three thousand men were at their arms, some of whom, coming forwards, gave us water to drink in dishes; but they being armed after a dreadful manner, we thought they designed to rid themselves of us.

Our secretary, attended by the same persons with whom he appeared the first time before the commander of the troops, was carried to the governor. When they had lain a while prostrate on the ground a sign was made to us to do the same, after we had been brought near a sort of balcony which was before the house, where he sat like a king. The first thing he caused to be asked of us by signs was whence we came and whither we were bound. We answered as before that we were Hollanders and bound for Nagasaki in Japan; whereupon he gave us to understand, by bowing his head a little, that he understood something of what we said. Then he ordered us to pass before him by four and four at a time; and having put the same question to us all and received the same answer, he ordered us to be carried to the same house where the king's uncle, who had attempted to usurp the throne, had been confined and died.

As soon as we were in, the house was beset with armed men. We had a daily allowance of twelve ounces of rice a man and the same quantity of wheaten meal; but very little besides, and so ill dressed that we could not eat it. Thus our common meals were for the most part only rice, meal and salt, and we had nothing to drink but water. The governor seemed to us to be a very understanding man and we often found afterwards that we had not been deceived in our opinion. He was then threescore and ten years of age, had been born in the capital city of the kingdom and was in good esteem at court. When he dismissed us he made signs that he would write to the king to know what he was to do with us. It would be a considerable time before his answer could come because the distance was fourscore leagues, whereof all but ten leagues by land, and therefore we begged of him to order we should have flesh sometimes and something else to eat. We also obtained leave of him for six of us to go abroad every day by turns to take the air and wash our linen; which was granted, to our great satisfaction, for 'twas very heavy to be shut up and live on bread and water. He also did us the honor to send for us often and to make us write something before him, both in his tongue and in our own. There we first began to understand some words of that language; and he discoursing with us sometimes, and being pleased to divert us with some little amusements, we began to conceive some hopes of getting over one day to Japan. He also took such care of our sick that we may affirm we were better treated by that idolater than we should have been among Christians.

On the 29th of October our secretary, the master and surgeon's mate were carried before the governor, where they found a man sitting who had a great red beard. The governor asked us who we took that man to be; and having told him we supposed him to be a Dutchman, he fell a laughing and said we were mistaken, for he was a Koresian. After some discourse had passed between us, that man, who till then had been silent, asked us in Dutch who we were and of what country, to which we answered that we were Dutchmen come from Amsterdam in the service of the company and being bound by their command for Japan and a storm had thrown us upon that island. That our vessel being staved, we begged earnestly of God that we might be sent on our way. Then we took the boldness to ask his name and what countryman he was; to which he replied that his name was John Wettevree, born at Riip in Holland, whence he came as a volunteer in the year 1626 aboard the ship called the Hollandia; and that going to Japan in the year 1627, aboard the frigate called the Ouderkeres, the wind drove them on the coast of Korea. That, wanting water, and being one of those that were commanded ashore to get provisions, he and two more had been taken by the inhabitants. That his companions had been killed seventeen or eighteen years since in the wars, when the Tartars invaded Korea.

Asking him further, where he lived then and what accident had brought him into that island, he told us that his abode was in the capital city of Korea, whence the king had sent him to know what we were and what had brought us into his dominions. He added that during his long residence in Korea he had often asked leave of the king to go over to Japan, without ever obtaining any other answer than that he must never expect it, unless he had wings and could fly thither; that the custom of the country was to detain all strangers that came thither, but that they wanted for nothing, being provided with diet and clothes as long as they lived.

Thus all the comfort he could give us was that we should be treated as he had been if we were carried to the king. The joy of finding so good an interpreter dispelled our melancholy and made us forget all our misfortunes. 'Twas very surprising and even wonderful that a man of fifty-eight years of age, as he then was, should so forget his mother-tongue that we had much to do at first to understand him; but it must be observed he recovered it again in a month. The governor having caused all our depositions to be taken in form, sent 'em to court and bade us be of good cheer, for we should have an answer in a short time. In the meanwhile he daily bestowed new favors on us, insomuch that he gave leave to Wettevree and the officers that came with him to see us at all times and acquaint him with our wants.

About the beginning of December a new governor came, our benefactor's three years being expired. We were much concerned at it, as not doubting but that change might be prejudicial to us. 'Twould be a hard talk to express how much kindness and affection he showed us at his departure, insomuch that, seeing us ill-provided against winter, he caused two pair of shoes, a coat well lined and a pair of stockings of skins to be made for every one of us. Besides, he treated us nobly and assured us he was sorry it had not been in his power to send us over to Japan or to carry us over with him to the continent. He further added that we ought not to be troubled at his going away because, being at court, he would use all his endeavors to obtain our liberty or to have us carried thither. He restored us the books we had saved, with some other parcels of goods, giving us at the same time a bottle of precious oil which might be of use to us for the time to come. The first thing the new governor did was to reduce our allowance to rice, salt and water. We complained to the old governor, who was detained in the island by contrary winds, but he sent us this answer: That his time being expired, 'twas not lawful for him any longer to hear our complaints but that he would write to his successor. And as long as he was in the island, though sparingly, we were allowed as much as might stop our complaints.

After that good lord's departure, which was in the beginning of January, 1654, we were much worse used than we had been before, for they gave us barley instead of rice, and barley meal instead of wheat. Thus if we had a mind to eat any other food we must sell our barley and live upon the twelve ounces of meal. This hard usage forced us to think of making better use of our liberty of going abroad by six and six at a time than we had done before. We were invited by the approaching spring to make our escape, and the more because the king's orders did not come and we were in danger of ending our days on that island in captivity.

Therefore, after long consulting together how we might seize upon a boat in a dark night, at length six of us resolved to execute this design about the end of April. But one of the gang being got atop of the wall to discover the vessel we were to seize, he was unfortunately discovered by some dogs, whose barking made the guards more watchful, and us lose an excellent opportunity of making our escape.

About the beginning of May our master going abroad with five others, as he was walking observed that at a little hamlet near the city there was a barque well appointed, without anybody to guard it. He presently sent one of his company to get a little boat and some short planks. Then, making every one of his men drink a draught of water, he went aboard without taking care for any more. Whilst they were laboring to draw the barque over a little shoal that was by it, some of the inhabitants discovered their design and one of 'em, running out with a musket, went into the water to oblige them to return. Yet that did not hinder their getting out, except one, who not being able to get up to the others, was forced to go back to land. The other five going to hoist sail, both the mast and sail fell into the water. They soon got 'em up and, setting everything right with much labor, as they endeavored a second time to hoist sail the end of the mast broke off short and could not possibly be mended. All these delays gave the natives time to get into another barque and soon overtook them, our men having nothing to help 'em away. As soon as they came together our men nimbly boarded them, hoping to make themselves masters of the vessel, notwithstanding their enemies' weapons; but finding this barque was full of water and unfit for service, they all submitted.

Being brought ashore, they were carried before the governor, who caused their hands to be made fast to a great log with a strong chain, and having laid them flat on the ground and brought all us before them well bound and manacled, they were asked whether they had done that action without our knowledge or whether we had been made privy to it. They all positively asserted we knew nothing of it. Wettevree was set to examine what their design was, and they answering 'twas no other but to go to Japan. "How durst you," said the governor, "attempt that passage without bread and water?" They answered they had chose rather to expose themselves once for all to the danger of death than to die every moment. We were immediately unbound, but the six unfortunate wretches had every one twenty-five strokes on the bare buttocks with a cudgel a fathom long, four fingers broad and an inch thick, being flat on the side that strikes and round on the other. These strokes were so unmercifully laid on that they who received 'em were forced to keep their beds a month, and we were all of us deprived of our liberty and strictly guarded day and night.

About the latter end of May orders came to carry us to court, at which we knew not whether we ought to rejoice or be troubled. Six or seven days after, they put us into four boats, with fetters on our feet and one hand made fast to a block to prevent our leaping into the water, which otherwise we might easily have done, all the soldiers being seasick. After two days struggling with contrary winds we were put back and our irons taken off. We returned to our former prison at Quelpaert. This island, which the natives call Sehesure, lies twelve or thirteen leagues south of the coast of Korea and is about fourteen or fifteen leagues in compass. On the north side of it is a bay where several barques lie and whence they sail for the continent, which is of very dangerous access to those that are unacquainted with it, because of several hidden rocks, and that there is but one place where ships can anchor and tide under shelter, for in all other places they are often drove over to the coast of Japan. The island is all encompassed with rocks but abounds in horses and cattle, which pay great duties to the king; so that, notwithstanding their breeds of horses and herds of cattle, the islanders are very poor and despised by the inhabitants of the continent. In this island there's a mountain of a vast height, all covered with woods, and several small hills which are naked and enclose many vales abounding in rice.

Four or five days after, the wind came about and we were shipped again betimes in the morning, with the same precaution as before. Towards night we drew very near the continent and, having lain all night in the road, landed the next morning, where our chains were taken off but our guards doubled.

In the morning we had horses brought to carry us to the city Heynam; and having been separated at sea and landed in several places, we were very glad to meet all together again at that town. The next morning, having taken a very slender repast, we came to the town of Jeham, where Paul John Cools, our gunner, died, having never enjoyed his health since our shipwreck. Next day the governor of the town caused him to be buried, and we, mounting a horseback, came at night to the city Nadioo. The day following we lay at Sansiang, thence to Tongap after crossing a high mountain, on the top whereof is the fort Ilpam-Sansiang, which is very spacious. Thence we went to the city Teyn and the next day we baited at the little town of Kunige and at night came to the great town of Chintio, where the king formerly kept his court and where now the governor of the province of Thilado resides. 'Tis a city of great trade and very famous in that country, though a day's journey from the sea. Going thence, we lay at Jesan, the last town of the province of Thilado; then at the little town of Gunun, next at Jensan, and lastly at Confio, the residence of the governor of the province of Tiongsiando. Next day we crossed a great river and entered upon the province of Sengado, in which Sior, the capital of the kingdom, is seated. After lying many days in several places we crossed a river, a league from whence is the city of Sior, where the king keeps his court. We reckoned seventy-five leagues we had travelled from our landing to this city, all the way northward, only a little inclining to the west.

Being come to this town, they put us all together into a house, where they left us two or three days, after which time they put us into little huts, three and three, or four and four, with Chinese that are settled there. Then they carried us all in a body before the king, who examined us to all points by the help of Wettevree. Having answered him the best we could, we humbly beseeched his majesty that since we had lost our ship in the storm he would be pleased to send us over to Japan, that with the assistance of the Dutch there we might one day return to our country to enjoy the company of our wives, children and friends. The king told us 'twas not the custom of Korea to suffer strangers to depart the kingdom; that we must resolve to end our days in his dominions and he would provide us with all necessaries. Then he ordered us to do such things before him as we were best skilled in, as singing, dancing and leaping after our manner. Next he caused us to have meat given us, which was well enough after their manner, and gave each of us two pieces of cloth, to clothe us after their fashion.

The next day we were all sent before the general of the forces, who ordered Wettevree to tell us that the king had put us into his lifeguards and that, as such, he would allow us seventy catties of rice a month. Every one of us had a paper given him, in which was set down his name, his age, his country, what profession he had followed before and what he now was, all in their character, sealed with the king's great seal and the general's, the latter nothing but the print of a hot iron. Together with this commission they delivered to each a musket, powder and ball, with orders to give a volley before the general every first and fourth day of the month; to be always ready to march into the field with him, whither the king went, or upon any other account. In spring and autumn that general reviews his troops three times a month; and besides, the soldiers exercise as often in private.

A Chinese and Wettevree were appointed to command us, the former as sergeant, and t'other to have an eye over us and to teach us the customs and manner of behavior of the Koresians. Most of the great men, being fond of novelty, invited us to dine at their houses to see us exercise after our manner and to make us shoot and dance. But, above all, their wives and children were eager to see us because the meaner sort of the island of Quelpaert had spread abroad a report that we were monstrous and that when we drank we were forced for to tuck up our nose behind our ear. These absurd tales were the cause that the better sort of people at Sior were amazed to see us better shaped than the people of their own country. Above all they admired the fairness of our complexion and did so throng to see us that at first we had much ado to break through the crowd in the streets; and we could not be quiet at home, their curiosity was so great. At length the general put a stop to this, forbidding all persons whatsoever to come near us without his leave, and the more because the very slaves of great men took the boldness to come and fetch us out of our chambers to make a jest at and divert themselves with us.

In August the Tartar came to demand the usual tribute, whereupon the king was forced to send us to a great fort, to be kept there as long as the ambassador was in the country. This fort is about six or seven leagues from Sior, on a mountain they call Numma Sansiang. 'Tis three hours work to get up to it, and is so strong that the king retires to it in time of war, and most of the great men of the kingdom live there. 'Tis always provided for three years and for a great number of people. There we continued till the beginning of September, when the Tartar went away.

About the end of November the cold was so vehement that the river, which is a league from the capital city, was froze, and three hundred horses loaded passed over it. The general, taking compassion to see the cold we endured, gave the king an account of it, who ordered some hides we had saved from our shipwreck to be distributed among us, which were most of 'em rotten, allowing us to sell 'em and buy something to clothe us warm. Two or three resolved, with the money they got by these hides, to purchase to themselves a little hut, choosing rather to endure cold than to be eternally tormented by their landlords, who were continually sending of us to the mountains, two or three leagues distant, to fetch wood. This labor was intolerable, both by reason of the cold and because the ways are bad and uneasy. The little hovel they bought cost 'em nine or ten crowns; and the rest having clothed themselves the best they could, were forced to pass the remainder of the winter as they had done before.

The Tartar returning in March, 1655, we were forbid as before under severe penalties going out of our houses. The day he set forward to return home, Henry Jans of Amsterdam, our master, and Henry John Bos of Harlem, a gunner, resolved to go meet this ambassador on the way, upon pretense of going for wood. When they saw him appear at the head of several bodies of horse and foot that attended him, they laid hold of his horse's reins with one hand and with the other, turning aside their Koresian habit, showed him they were clad after the Dutch manner underneath. This at first caused a great confusion among the multitude, and the Tartar asked them earnestly who they were, but they could never make him understand them. However, the ambassador ordered 'em to follow and be where he was to lie that night. Being come thither, he made much inquiry whether there was anybody that could understand what they said to him; and having been told of Wettevree, he sent for him to come to him with all speed. That interpreter having advertised the king, a council was held, where 'twas resolved to make the ambassador a present, to the end he should so stifle the matter that it might not come to the chan's ear. Our two poor wretches were brought back to Sior and put into a prison, where they soon after died, but we could never know whether a violent or a natural death, none of us having been ever allowed to see them. As soon as this business was noised abroad we were carried before the council of war, where 'twas asked whether we had any intimation of our companions' design. And though we could truly assert we had not, yet that would not save us from being adjudged to have every one fifty strokes on the buttocks for not having given notice of our companions' going out. We had certainly received that correction had not the king remitted it, saying we were poor wretches cast into his country by storms rather than any design of plundering. All the penalty he laid on us was sending us home again with an injunction not to stir abroad without his orders.

The Tartar coming in August, we were commanded under pain of severe punishment not to stir out of our quarters till three days after he was gone. The day before he came we received letters from our companions, by an express, in which they gave us an account that they were confined on the southernmost borders of the kingdom, where they were strictly guarded to the end that if the great chan had received any intelligence concerning the two unhappy fellows that were dead and should demand the rest they might tell him they were all three cast away going to the island Quelpaert. The Tartar came again about the latter end of the year and we were by the king's order strictly confined to our houses, as we had been before.

Though the Tartar had sent twice into Korea since the attempt unfortunately made by our two companions without making any mention of it, yet most of the great men used all their endeavors with the king to destroy us. The council sat three days upon this affair, but the king, his brother, the general and some others were not altogether of that opinion. The general was for making each of us fight two Koresians, all with the same weapons, pretending that so the king would be rid of us and none would have it to say that the king had murdered poor strangers. Some more charitable persons, who knew we were kept shut up and ignorant of what was doing, gave us this intelligence privately. Hereupon Wettevree told us that if we lived three days we should in all likelihood live long enough after.

Now the king's brother, who was president of the council, passing by our quarters as he was going to it, and very near to us, we had the opportunity to cast ourselves at his feet and implore his favor, lying with our faces prostrate on the ground. This sight moved so much compassion in him that for the future he solicited our affair so earnestly that we owe our lives only to the king and him. This giving offense to many persons who might attempt other methods to destroy us, for the preventing their wicked designs, and to avoid our appearing before the Tartars, it was thought fit to banish us into the province of Thilado, where we were to be allowed fifty pounds of rice a month at the king's cost.

Accordingly, we departed from Sior in March, on horses provided for us, our acquaintance bearing us company as far as the river, which is a league from the city. There we took our last leave of Wettevree, for from that day to this we have never seen nor heard talk of him. We passed through all the same towns we had seen in our way to the court and, coming to lie at Jeam, we set out the next morning and about noon arrived at a great town called Diusiong, or Thillapening, commanded by a large citadel opposite to it. The Penigse, who is chief in the absence of the governor, resides there and has the title of colonel of the province. To him the sergeant that had the charge of us delivered us with the king's letters. He was immediately sent away to go fetch our three companions that had been sent away the year before, who were twelve leagues off, where the vice-admiral commanded. We were all lodged together in a public house, and three days after, those that were absent being brought to us, we were again together thirty-three of us, the miserable remains of our shipwreck.

In April they brought us some hides that had been left behind at Quelpaert, from which place we were but eighteen leagues, they not being worth sending to Sior. We fitted ourselves the best we could and laid up some small provisions in our new habitation. The only business we were charged with was to pull up the grass that grew in the square before the castle twice a month, and to keep it clean.

This year, 1657, our governor being accused of some misdemeanors, was forced to go to court to clear himself, where it is reported he was in danger of his life. But being well beloved by the people and favored by the great ones on account of his family, which was one of the noblest in the kingdom, he came off so well that his honors were increased. He was very good to us as well as to the natives. In February came a governor very unlike the other for, besides that he found us more work, he would oblige us to go three leagues off to the mountain to fetch wood, which his predecessor had caused to be brought home to us gratis. But, God be praised, an apoplexy delivered us from him in September following, which nobody was sorry for, so little was he liked.

In November came a new governor, who took so little care of us that when we asked him for clothes or anything else, he answered: the king had given him no orders as to that point, that he was only obliged to furnish our allowance of rice, and for other wants it was our business to provide as we thought fit. Our clothes being now worn out with carrying of wood, and the cold beginning to pinch us, we resolved to cast off shame among those people and to beg, making our advantage of their curiosity, which led them to ask us a thousand questions. Accordingly, that we might get something to clothe us and not be forced to run half a league for a handful of salt, we presented a petition to the governor for his leave to beg, representing that we could not possibly get our living any longer by carrying wood, because we were naked, and our labor would yield us nothing but a little salt and rice; therefore we humbly prayed he would permit us to go abroad in our turns. He granted it; and we made such good use of this favor that in a short time we were provided against the cold.

At the beginning of the year 1658 the governor was called away and his successor afflicted us with new crosses. He forbid us going abroad and told us that if we would work for him he would give each of us three pieces of cotton cloth. After having long considered upon his offers, which would not set us above other wants, especially in a scarce year as that was, and knowing we should wear out more clothes in his service than he would give us, we with all imaginable respect represented to him that he ought not to require that of us; after which an accident happened which obliged him to consent to our demands. Those people are so much afraid of a fever that only the thought of it terrifies them, and some of us being then under that disease, he consented that we should beg in companies, provided we were not absent above a fortnight or three weeks, and that we neither went towards the court nor Japan. The other half of us that remained at home he ordered should look to the sick and take care to pull up the grass in the square.

In April this year the king died, and his son succeeded him with the consent of the great chan. However, we went on in our trade, and particularly among their religious men, who are very charitable and grateful, for the pleasure we did them in giving an account of our adventures and showing them the customs of other countries. They were so much pleased to hear us that they could have spent days and nights in our company.

The next governor that came in the year 1660 was so kind to us that he often declared if it were in his power he would send us back into our country or at least to some place where there were country-men of ours. He granted us a confirmation of the liberty of going abroad without any restraint. This year happened such a drought that all sorts of provisions were very scarce. The following year, 1661, was yet more miserable, abundance of people were famished to death, and the roads were full of robbers. The king vigorously pursued them and by that means prevented many robberies and murders. He also ordered the dead bodies found in the fields to be buried.

Acorns, pineapples and other wild fruit were all the support of the people, and the famine was so great that villages were plundered and some of the king's stores broke open and none punished for it because those disorders were committed by the slaves of great men; and this calamity lasted all the year 1662. The next year, 1663, felt some share of it; for either the poor had not sowed or else they had no crop; however, that was remedied by the plentiful harvest in other places that were watered by rivers or lay near bogs, otherwise the country had been utterly destroyed. The place where we were being no longer able to furnish us, the governor writ about it to the intendant of the province, who answered that the king having appointed our subsistence to be furnished them, he could not remove us to another place without an order from his majesty.

About the end of February the governor, pursuant to the orders he had received from court, dispersed us into three towns. Twelve he sent to Saysiano, five to Siunschien and as many to Namman, for we were but twenty-two at this time. This parting was very grievous to us, it being a great satisfaction to be all together in a place where we were at our ease and had good provisions; whereas it was to be feared they might send us to some place that still labored under the hardships of famine. This our sorrow was turned into joy, for this alteration was the occasion of our getting away, as will appear in the sequel.

About the beginning of March, after taking leave of our governor and returning him abundance of thanks for his favors, we set out from thence afoot, carrying the sick and what baggage we had on the horses allowed us. Those that were going to Saysiano and to Siunschien went the same road with us and we lay all in the same town that first and second night. The third day we came to Siunschien, where we left five of our companions. The next night we lay in a country house, and setting out early in the morning came about nine to Saysiano, where those that conducted us delivered us to the governor, or admiral, of the province of Thilado, who resides there. He presently ordered us lodging and such furniture as was necessary, and the same allowance we had enjoyed till then. This seemed to us to be a very good worthy lord.

Two days after our coming he went away to court and three days after his departure came another to succeed him, who proved our scourge; for he would not suffer us to be far from him and left us exposed to all hardships of the summer and winter. The greatest favor he granted us was leave to go cut wood fit to make arrows for his men, whose only employment is continually shooting with the bow, the great men striving who shall keep the ablest archers. He put many more hardships upon us but God gave us our revenge. Winter drawing on, and the town we were in not having furnished us with necessaries against the cold, we represented to the governor in what a good condition our companions were in the other towns and humbly prayed he would vouchsafe to permit us to go seek out for something to defend us against the cold. He gave us leave to be absent three days, upon condition the one half of us should remain with him whilst the other half was abroad. This liberty was very beneficial to us, because the great men, who had compassion on us, favored our sallies, and we were sometimes allowed to be a month abroad. Whatsoever we got was brought and put in common with those that remained in the city.

This continued till the governor's departure, who was sent for by the king to come to court. At his arrival there he declared him general of his army, an employment always possessed by the second man in the kingdom. His successor eased us of all our burdens that had been imposed on us and ordered we should be as well treated as our companions were in the other towns. Thus we were only obliged to pass muster twice a month, to keep our house in our turns, and to ask when we would go abroad, or at least to give the secretary notice, that, if occasion were, they might know where to find us. We gave God thanks for having delivered us from such a wicked man and sending such a good one.

This man, besides the favors already mentioned, often treated us, and civilly condoling our misfortune, asked why, being so near the sea as we were, we did not attempt to pass over that small sea which parted us from Japan? We answered, we durst not venture upon such a thing contrary to the king's will; and besides, we knew not the way and had no vessel. To this he replied there were barques enough along the seacoast. We rejoined they did not belong to us and that if we missed our aim we should be punished as thieves and deserters. The governor laughed at our scruple, not imagining we talked after that manner only to prevent their being jealous of us and that all our thoughts day and night were employed in contriving how to seize a barque, and that our enemies had obstructed our buying one till that time.

Now we received the news that our late governor had not enjoyed his new honor above six months before he was summoned to answer before the king for his misdemeanors. He was accused of having put to death several persons, as well nobles as commoners, on very slight occasions. He was condemned to receive fourscore and ten strokes of a cudgel on his shinbones and to be banished forever.

About the latter end of the year a blazing-star appeared and after that two at once; the first was seen in the southeast for about two months, the other in the southwest, but their tails were opposite against one another. The court was so much alarmed at it that the king caused all the guards to be doubled in all his ports and aboard his ships. He also caused provisions to be carried into his stronghold, and store of ammunition. He made all his forces, both horse and foot, exercise every day, and expected nothing less than an invasion from some of his neighbors; insomuch that he forbid making any fire at night in those houses that might be seen from the sea. The common sort spent all they had, keeping only as much as would serve them poorly to subsist with rice, because they had seen the same signs in the heavens when the Tartars came to overrun their country. They also remembered that some such thing had appeared before the Japanese declared war against them.

Wherever we were they asked us what we judged were the consequences of comets in our country. We told them it denoted some signal judgment of God to follow, and generally the plague, war or famine, and sometimes all three. Having had experience of it, they agreed with our opinion.

We lived this and the ensuing year, 1665, enough at our ease, using all our endeavors to make ourselves masters of a barque, but without success. Sometimes we rowed in a little boat, which served us to get our living along the shore, and sometimes to round some small islands to see whether nothing would fall out to our purpose and which might forward our escape. Our companions that were in the two other towns came every now and then to see us and we repaid their visits oftener or seldomer, according as it pleased our governor, for some were more favorable than others. Yet we were patient under the greatest severities, thinking it a great mercy that God granted us our health and a subsistence during that long captivity.

The following year, 1666, we lost our protector and good friend; for, his time expiring, the king honored him with a better employment. It is incredible how much good he did to all sorts of people indifferently during his two years' government; and accordingly he was entirely beloved both in the city and country, and the king and nobility had a great esteem for his wisdom and good behavior. Whilst he was in his post he repaired public structures, cleared the coasts and maintained and increased the marine forces. The king was so well pleased at these actions of his that he preferred him to the prime dignities at court.

We were without a governor for three days after his departure, for it is enough, if he that quits has his place supplied the third day by his successor, these three days being allowed the new governor, that by the advice of some diviner he may choose a happy minute to enter upon his government. As soon as installed he thought it not enough to use us with all the severity the banished governor had done, but would oblige us continually to mold clay, which we refused to do, alleging that his predecessor had not imposed any such labor upon us; that our allowance being scarce enough to keep us alive, it was but reasonable to allow us what time we had to spare from our own affairs to get something to clothe us and supply our other wants; that the king had not sent us to work, or if we must be so used, it were better for us to quit his allowance and desire to be sent to Japan or some other place where there were any of our nation.

All the answer was, ordering us to be gone, threatening he would find a way to make us comply. But he was luckily prevented; for but few days after, he, being in a very pretty vessel, some fire accidentally fell into the powder and blew up the prow, killing five men. Here it must be observed that those people keep the powder in a powder-room before the mast. The governor, believing he could conceal that accident, gave no account of it to the intendant of the province; but he was mistaken, for the fire was seen by one of the spies the king keeps on the coasts, and even in the heart of the country, to be informed of all that happens. This spy having acquainted the intendant with it, he sent an account of it up to court, whither the governor was immediately summoned, and by sentence of the judges received fourscore and ten strokes on his shinbones and was banished forever.

Thus in July we had another governor, who, behaving himself towards us in all respects as the last had done, required of us every day a hundred fathom of mat. We gave him to understand that was impossible to be done and made the same remonstrances to him as we had done to his predecessors. This moved him no more than it had done them; for he told us that if we were not fit for that sort of work he would find other employment for us, which he had done but that he fell sick. His rigidness made us conclude that our misfortunes were beyond redress, because new officers rather add new burdens than take off those that are already laid on. Thus, besides our own affairs, we were obliged to pull up the grass in the square of Penigse and then to go cut and bring home wood fit for arrows.

These considerations made us resolve to take the advantage of our tyrant's indisposition and to get a barque at any rate whatsoever, choosing rather to hazard all than to groan any longer in captivity among idolaters and bear with all sorts of wrongs they would offer us. For the compassing of our design we decreed to make use of a Koresian our neighbor, who was very familiar with us and whom we had often relieved in his distress. We proposed to him to buy or cause a barque to be bought for us, pretending we wanted it to go beg cotton in the neighboring islands, promising him a good share when we came again. He performed what he was instructed with, bargaining very boldly for a fisherman's barque, and we presently gave him the money to pay for it. The seller perceiving it was for us, would have gone from his bargain at the instigation of some that told him it was to make our escape, and if we did so he would be put to death. This was really true; but we offering to pay double the value, he consented, making more account of the present profit than of the mischief that might ensue.

As soon as the two Koresians were gone we immediately furnished the barque with sails, an anchor, rigging, oars and all things we thought necessary, in order to set out at the first quarter of the moon, that being the fittest season. We kept two of our companions, whom their good fortune had brought to visit us, and who wanted not much courting; and understanding that John Peter, an able sailor, was at Siunschien, we went to desire him to come to us, telling him all things were in a readiness. The messenger, missing of him at Siunschien, went to look for him at Namman, which is sixteen leagues farther, and brought him away, having traveled above fifty long leagues in four days.

The day and hour being appointed to depart, which was the 4th of September as the moon was setting, though our neighbors had conceived some jealousy yet we forbore not at night, after eating a bit of what we had, to creep along under the city walls to carry the rest of our provisions, being rice, pots of water and a frying-pan. The moon being down, nobody saw us.

The first thing we did, we went over into a little island which was within cannon shot, where we filled a cask we found in the barque with fresh water. Thence, without making any noise, we made our way before the vessels belonging to the city and just opposite to the king's frigates, making out as far as we could into the channel. The calm which had continued till then ceasing, there started up a fair gale, which invited us to hoist sail, as we did, heartily calling upon God to assist us and resigning ourselves up to him. On the 5th of September in the morning, when we were almost out of the channel of the island, a fisherman hailed us but we would not answer, fearing it might be some advanced guard to the men of war that lie thereabouts. At sunrising the wind fell, which obliged us to lower our sails and row, to get farther off and prevent being discovered. About noon the weather began to freshen and at night we spread our sail, directing our course by guess southeast. The wind growing fresh at night, we cleared the point of Korea and were no longer apprehensive of being pursued, and the wind holding all night we made much way.

The sixth day in the morning we found ourselves very near the first of the islands of Japan; and the same gale still favoring us, we came without knowing it before the island of Firando, where we durst not put in because none of us had ever been at Japan and we were unacquainted with the road. Besides, the Koresians had often told us there were no isles to coast along in the way to Nagasaki. We therefore passed on to come up with an island that lay farther off, which appeared to us very small and near to us, and accordingly we left it astern that night.

The seventh day we held on our course with a cold wind and uncertain weather, running along abundance of islands, which seemed to us to be numberless; and being possessed there were no islands to be left behind, we endeavored to get above them. At night we thought to have touched at a small island and would have rid it out at anchor there but the sky seemed to look stormy; but we perceived such abundance of fires all about that we resolved to continue under sail, going before the wind, which was very cold.

The 8th, in the morning, we found ourselves in the same place whence we set forward at night, which we attributed to the force of some current. Hereupon we resolved to stand out to sea, but we had scarce sailed two leagues before there started up a contrary wind and blew so hard that it forced us in all haste to seek the shelter of the land. And the weather still growing more boisterous every moment, after crossing a bay we came to an anchor about noon, without knowing what country we were in. Whilst we were dressing some small matter to eat, the natives passed backwards and forwards close by us, without saying anything, or making any stay. About evening, the wind being somewhat fallen, we saw a barque with six men in it, who had each of them two knives at their girdle. They rowed close by us and landed a man opposite to the place where we were. This made us weigh and set sail as fast as we could, making use of our oars at the same time, to get out of the bay as soon as possible and gain the open sea. But that barque prevented us, for, setting out in pursuit of ours, it soon overtook us. True it is, if we would have made use of our long bamboos we could easily have prevented their coming aboard us; but seeing several other barques set out from the shore full of men, who by the description we had heard of them must be Japanese, we troubled ourselves no farther. They hailing us, and asking us by signs whither we would go, we let fly the colors with the arms of Orange, which we had provided for that purpose, crying, "Holland, Nagasaki!" Hereupon they made signs to us to strike our sail and go ashore, which we presently did. They carried one of our men into their barque and placed the rest in order before one of their pagodas.

Being come to an anchor and having placed barques about ours to guard it, they took another of our men and carried him to the first they had drawn out, asking them several questions, but neither understood the other. Our arrival alarmed all the coast and there was not a man to be seen but was armed with two swords; but what satisfied us was that they endeavored to show us Nagasaki and seemed to tell us there were some of our nation there. At night a great barque that brought the third man in dignity of the isle of Gotto came aboard us. That gentleman, perceiving we were Hollanders, gave us to understand by signs that we had six ships at Nagasaki, where he hoped to be with us in four or five days if we desired it. He signified to us that we were in the island of Gotto, subject to the emperor; and to satisfy his curiosity, desiring to know whence we came, we had a great deal of trouble to give him to understand that we came from Korea, and that it was thirteen years since we had been shipwrecked on an island belonging to that kingdom; that we desired nothing so earnestly at present as to get to Nagasaki to some of our countrymen, and that to gratify this our inclination we had exposed ourselves in a poor barque, in a sea unknown to us, where we had sailed forty leagues without a compass to reach Japan, not regarding all the Koresians had said to persuade us that the Japanese put all the strangers that came into their country to cruel deaths.

We continued the three following days well guarded in the same place aboard our barque, whither they brought us water, wood, flesh, and gave us a mat to cover us from the rain, which fell in great abundance all that time.

On the 12th they furnished us with provisions to go to Nagasaki, and that same night we anchored on the other side of the island where we spent the night.

On the 13th that gentleman we mentioned before weighed anchor, being attended by two large barques and two little ones. He carried some letters from the emperor and some goods. Our two companions were in one of those great barques and did not come to us again till we were at Nagasaki. About evening we saw the bay of that city and at midnight anchored before it, where we found five ships of ours. Several inhabitants of Gotto and even some of the chief men did us many kindnesses without taking anything of us.

On the 14th we were all carried ashore, where interpreters received us. When they had writ down all the answers we made to their several questions they carried us to the governor's house, and about noon we were brought before him. When we had satisfied his curiosity he much commended our action in overcoming so many dangers and difficulties to recover our liberty. Then he ordered the interpreters to conduct us to our commandant, Min Heer William Volguers, who received us very kindly. Min Heer Nicholas le Roy, his deputy, was also very friendly, and so was all the nation in general. When we went thence they caused us to be habited after our own fashion.

On the first of October Min Heer Volguers left the island, and on the 23rd sailed out of the bay with seven ships. The governor of Nagasaki, who would have kept us a year, caused us to be brought before him on the 25th of the month, and after examining us over again restored us to the company's director, who lodged us in his own house, whence we sailed some days after for Batavia. Where we arrived on the 20th of November and at our landing delivered our journal to the general, who, after a very favorable reception, promised to put us aboard the ships that were to sail from thence on the 28th of December. These ships, after some storms, arrived at Amsterdam on the 20th of July 1668, where we returned thanks to God for having delivered us from a captivity of thirteen years and twenty-eight days, beseeching him to have mercy on our poor companions who were left behind.

1708 *Providence Displayed:*

being an excerpt of the journal written by Woodes Rogers in his voyage round the world.

FEBRUARY 2. We stood on the back side along the south end of the island [of Juan Fernandez] in order to lay in with the first southerly wind, which Captain Dampier told us generally blows there all day long. In the morning, being past the island, we tacked to lay it in close aboard the land; and about ten o'clock opened the south end of the island and ran close aboard the land that begins to make the northeast side.

The flaws came heavy offshore, and we were forced to reef our topsails when we opened the middle bay, where we expected to find our enemy, but saw all clear and no ships in that nor the other bay next the northwest end. These two bays are all that ships ride in which recruit on this island, but the middle bay is by much the best. We guessed there had been ships there but that they were gone on sight of us.

We sent our yawl ashore about noon with Captain Dover, Mr. Frye and six men, all armed; meanwhile we and the Dutchess kept turning to get in, and such heavy flaws came off the land that we were forced to let fly our topsail's sheet, keeping all hands to stand by our sails for fear of the wind's carrying 'em away; but when the flaws were gone, we had little or no wind. These flaws proceeded from the land, which is very high in the middle of the island. Our boat did not return, so we sent our pinnace, with the men armed, to see what was the occasion of the yawl's stay; for we were afraid that the

Spaniards had a garrison there and might have seized 'em. We put out a signal for our boat, and the Dutchess showed a French ensign.

Immediately our pinnace returned from the shore and brought abundance of crawfish, with a man clothed in goatskins, who looked wilder than the first owners of them.

He had been on the island four years and four months, being left there by Captain Stradling in the Cinque-Ports. His name was Alexander Selkirk, a Scotchman, who had been master of the Cinque-Ports, a ship that came here last with Captain Dampier, who told me that this was the best man in her. So I immediately agreed with him to be a mate on board our ship. 'Twas he that made the fire last night when he saw our ships, which he judged to be English. During his stay here he saw several ships pass by, but only two came in to anchor. As he went to view them he found 'em to be Spaniards and retired from 'em, upon which they shot at him. Had they been French he would have submitted; but chose to risk his dying alone on the island rather than fall into the hands of the Spaniards in these parts, because he apprehended they would murder him or make a slave of him in the mines, for he feared they would spare no stranger that might be capable of discovering the South Sea.

The Spaniards had landed before he knew what they were and they came so near him that he had much ado to escape; for they not only shot at him but pursued him into the woods, where he climbed to the top of a tree, at the foot of which they made water and killed several goats just by, but went off again without discovering him.

He told us that he was born at Largo in the County of Fife in Scotland and was bred a sailor from his youth. The reason of his being here was a difference betwixt him and his captain; which, together with the ship's being leaky, made him willing rather to stay here than go along with him at first; and when he was at last willing the captain would not receive him. He had been in the island before to wood and water, when two of the ship's company were left upon it for six months till the ship returned, being chased thence by two French South Sea ships.

He had with him his clothes and bedding, with a firelock, some powder, bullets and tobacco, a hatchet, a knife, a kettle, a Bible, some practical pieces and his mathematical instruments and books. He diverted and provided for himself as well as he could; but for the first eight months had much ado to bear up against melancholy and the terror of being left alone in such a desolate place. He built two huts with piemento trees, covered them with long grass and lined them with the skins of goats, which he killed with his gun as he wanted so long as his powder lasted, which was but a pound; and that being near spent he got fire by rubbing two sticks of piemento wood together upon his knee. In the lesser hut, at some distance from the other, he dressed his victuals and in the larger he slept and employed himself in reading, singing psalms and praying; so that he said he was a better Christian while in this solitude than ever he was before, or than, he was afraid, he should ever be again. At first he never eat anything till hunger constrained him, partly for grief and partly for want of bread and salt; nor did he go to bed till he could watch no longer. The piemento wood, which burnt very clear, served him both for firing and candle, and refreshed him with its fragrant smell.

He might have had fish enough but could not eat 'em for want of salt, because they occasioned a looseness; except crawfish, which are there as large as our lobsters and very good. These he sometimes boiled and at other times broiled, as he did his goats' flesh, of which he made very good broth, for they are not so rank as ours. He kept an account of five hundred that he killed while there, and caught as many more, which he marked on the ear and let go. When his powder failed, he took them by speed of foot; for his way of living and continual exercise of walking and running cleared him of all gross humors, so that he ran with wonderful swiftness through the woods and up the rocks and hills, as we perceived when we employed him to catch goats for us. We had a bulldog, which we sent with several of our nimblest runners to help him in catching goats; but he distanced and tired both the dog and the men, catched the goats and brought 'em to us on his back. He told us that his agility in pursuing a goat had once like to have cost him his life; he pursued it with so much eagerness that he catched hold of it on the brink of a precipice of which he was not aware, the bushes having hid it from him; so that he fell with the goat down the said precipice a great height, and was so stunned and bruised with the fall that he narrowly escaped with his life. And when he came to his senses he found the goat dead under him. He lay there about twenty-four hours and was scarce able to crawl to his hut, which was about a mile distant, or to stir abroad again in ten days.

He came at last to relish his meat well enough without salt or bread and in the season had plenty of good turnips, which had been sowed there by Captain Dampier's men and have now overspread some acres of ground. He had enough of good cabbage from the cabbage trees and seasoned his meat with the fruit of the piemento trees, which is the same as the Jamaica pepper and smells deliciously. He found there also a black pepper called *Malagita,* which was very good to expel wind and against griping of the guts.

He soon wore out all his shoes and clothes by running through the woods and at last, being forced to shift without them, his feet became so hard that he ran everywhere without annoyance. And it was some time before he could wear shoes after we found him; for not being used to any so long, his feet swelled when he came first to wear 'em again.

After he had conquered his melancholy he diverted himself sometimes by cutting his name on the trees and the time of his being left and continuance there. He was at first much pestered with cats and rats that had bred in great numbers from some of each species which had got ashore from ships that put in there to wood and water. The rats gnawed his feet and clothes while asleep, which obliged him to cherish the cats with his goats' flesh; by which many of them became so tame that they would lie about him in hundreds and soon delivered him from the rats. He likewise tamed some kids and, to divert himself, would now and then sing and dance with them and his cats; so that by the care of Providence and vigor of his youth, being now but about thirty years old, he came at last to conquer all the inconveniences of his solitude and to be very easy. When his clothes wore out he made himself a coat and cap of goatskins, which he stitched together with little thongs of the same, that he cut with his knife. He had no other needle but a nail; and when his knife was wore to the back he made others as well as he could of some iron hoops that were left ashore, which he beat thin and ground upon stones. Having some linen cloth by him, he sewed himself shirts with a nail and stitched 'em with the worsted of his old stockings, which he pulled out on purpose. He had his last shirt on when we found him in the island.

At his first coming on board us he had so much forgot his language for want of use that we could scarce understand him, for he seemed to speak his words by halves. We offered him a dram but he would not touch it, having drank nothing but water since his being there, and 'twas some time before he could relish our victuals.

He could give us an account of no other product of the island than what we have mentioned, except small black plums, which are very good but hard to come at, the trees which bear 'em growing on high mountains and rocks. Piemento trees are plenty here, and we saw some of sixty foot high and about two yards thick; and cotton trees higher and near four fathom round in the stock.

The climate is so good that the trees and grass are verdant all the year. The winter lasts no longer than June and July and is not then severe, there being only a small frost and a little hail, but sometimes great rains. The heat of the summer is equally moderate and there's not much thunder or tempestuous weather of any sort. He saw no venomous or savage creature on the island, nor any other sort of beast but goats, etc., as above-mentioned; the first of which had been put ashore here on purpose for a breed by Juan Fernando, a Spaniard, who settled there with some families for a time, till the continent of Chili began to submit to the Spaniards; which being more profitable, tempted them to quit this island, which is capable of maintaining a good number of people and of being made so strong that they could not be easily dislodged.

Ringrose, in his account of Captain Sharp's voyage and other buccaneers, mentions one who had escaped ashore here out of a ship which was cast away with all the rest of the company, and says he lived five years alone before he had the opportunity of another ship to carry him off. Captain Dampier talks of a Mosquito Indian that belonged to Captain Watlin, who being ahunting in the woods when the captain left the island, lived there three years alone and shifted much in the same manner as Mr. Selkirk did, till Captain Dampier came hither in 1684 and carried him off. The first that went ashore was one of his countrymen, and they saluted one another first by prostrating themselves by turns on the ground and then embracing. But whatever there is in these stories, this of Mr. Selkirk I know to be true; and his behavior afterwards gives me reason to believe the account he gave me how he spent his time and bore up under such an affliction, in which nothing but the Divine Providence could have supported any man.

By this one may see that solitude and retirement from the world is not such an unsufferable state of life as most men imagine, especially when people are fairly called or thrown into it unavoidably, as this man was; who in all probability must otherwise have perished in the seas, the ship which left him being cast away not long after and few of the company escaped. We may perceive by this story the truth of the maxim that necessity is the mother of invention, since he found means to supply his wants in a very natural manner, so as to maintain his life, though not so conveniently yet as effectually as we are able to do with the help of all our arts and society. It may likewise instruct us how much a plain and temperate way of living conduces to the health of the body and the vigor of the mind, both which we are apt to destroy by excess and plenty, especially of strong liquor and the variety as well as the nature of our meat and drink; for this man, when he came to our ordinary method of diet and life, though he was sober enough, lost much of his strength and agility. But I must quit these reflections, which are more proper for a philosopher and divine than a mariner, and return to my own subject. . . .

1708 The Englishman:

being the twenty-sixth in a magazine series written
and edited by Richard Steele; this particular issue, of
December 1, 1713, devoted to the adventures of the
famous Mr. Selkirk.

UNDER the title of this paper I do not think it
foreign to my design to speak of a man born in Her Majesty's dominions and relate an adventure in his life so uncommon that it's doubt-
ful whether the like has happened to any other of human race. The
person I speak of is Alexander Selkirk, whose name is familiar to men
of curiosity, from the fame of his having lived four years and four
months alone in the island of Juan Fernandez. I had the pleasure
frequently to converse with the man soon after his arrival in England,
in the year 1711. It was matter of great curiosity to hear him, as he
is a man of good sense, give an account of the different revolutions
in his own mind in that long solitude. When we consider how painful
absence from company for the space of but one evening is to the
generality of mankind we may have a sense how painful this necessary
and constant solitude was to a man bred a sailor and ever accustomed
to enjoy and suffer, eat, drink and sleep, and perform all offices of
life in fellowship and company. He was put ashore from a leaky
vessel, with the captain of which he had had an irreconcilable difference; and he chose rather to take his fate in this place than in a
crazy vessel under a disagreeable commander. His portion were a
sea chest, his wearing clothes and bedding, a firelock, a pound of
gunpowder, a large quantity of bullets, a flint and steel, a few pounds
of tobacco, a hatchet, a knife, a kettle, a Bible and other books of

devotion, together with pieces that concerned navigation, and his mathematical instruments. Resentment against his officer, who had ill-used him, made him look forward on this change of life as the more eligible one, till the instant in which he saw the vessel put off; at which moment, his heart yearned within him and melted at the parting with his comrades and all human society at once.

He had in provisions for the sustenance of life but the quantity of two meals, the island abounding only with wild goats, cats and rats. He judged it most probable that he should find more immediate and easy relief by finding shellfish on the shore than seeking game with his gun. He accordingly found great quantities of turtles, whose flesh is extremely delicious and of which he frequently eat very plentifully on his first arrival, till it grew disagreeable to his stomach except in jellies. The necessities of hunger and thirst were his greatest diversions from the reflection on his lonely condition. When those appetites were satisfied the desire of society was as strong a call upon him and he appeared to himself least necessitous when he wanted everything; for the supports of his body were easily attained, but the eager longings for seeing again the face of man during the interval of craving bodily appetites were hardly supportable. He grew dejected, languid and melancholy, scarce able to refrain from doing himself violence, till by degrees, by the force of reason and frequent reading of the Scriptures and turning his thoughts upon the study of navigation, after the space of eighteen months he grew thoroughly reconciled to his condition. When he had made this conquest, the vigor of his health, disengagement from the world, a constant, cheerful, serene sky and a temperate air made his life one continual feast, and his being much more joyful than it had before been irksome. He, now taking delight in everything, made the hut in which he lay, by ornaments which he cut down from a spacious wood, on the side of which it was situated, the most delicious bower fanned with continual breezes and gentle aspirations of wind, that made his repose after the chase equal to the most sensual pleasures.

I forgot to observe that during the time of his dissatisfaction monsters of the deep, which frequently lay on the shore, added to the terrors of his solitude; the dreadful howlings and voices seemed too terrible to be made for human ears. But upon the recovery of his temper he could with pleasure not only hear their voices but approach the monsters themselves with great intrepidity. He speaks of sea lions whose jaws and tails were capable of seizing or breaking the limbs of a man if he approached them. But at that time his spirits and life were so high that he could act so regularly and unconcerned that merely from being unruffled in himself he killed them with the greatest ease imaginable. For observing that though their jaws and tails were so terrible, yet the animals being mighty slow in working themselves round, he had nothing to do but place himself exactly opposite to their middle and as close to them as possible, and he dispatched them with his hatchet at will.

The precautions which he took against want, in case of sickness, was to lame kids when very young, so as that they might recover their health but never be capable of speed. These he had in great numbers about his hut; and when he was himself in full vigor he could take at full speed the swiftest goat running up a promontory and never failed of catching them but on a descent.

His habitation was extremely pestered with rats, which gnawed his clothes and feet when sleeping. To defend him against them he fed and tamed numbers of young kitlings, who lay about his bed and preserved him from the enemy. When his clothes were quite worn out he dried and tacked together the skins of goats, with which he clothed himself, and was inured to pass through woods, bushes and brambles with as much carelessness and precipitance as any other animal. It happened once to him that running on the summit of a hill he made a stretch to seize a goat, with which under him he fell down a precipice and lay senseless for the space of three days, the length of which time he measured by the moon's growth since his last observation. This manner of life grew so exquisitely pleasant that he never had a moment heavy upon his hands; his nights were untroubled and his days joyous from the practice of temperance and exercise. It was his manner to use stated hours and places for exercises of devotion, which he performed aloud in order to keep up the faculties of speech and to utter himself with greater energy.

When I first saw him I thought, if I had not been let into his character and story I could have discerned that he had been much separated from company, from his aspect and gesture; there was a strong but cheerful seriousness in his look, and a certain disregard to the ordinary things about him, as if he had been sunk in thought. When the ship which brought him off the island came in he received them with the greatest indifference with relation to the prospect of going off with them, but with great satisfaction in an opportunity to refresh and help them. The man frequently bewailed his return to the world, which could not, he said, with all its enjoyments, restore him to the tranquillity of his solitude. Though I had frequently conversed with him, after a few months' absence he met me in the street, and though he spoke to me I could not recollect that I had seen him; familiar converse in this town had taken off the loneliness of his aspect and quite altered the air of his face.

This plain man's story is a memorable example that he is happiest who confines his wants to natural necessities, and he that goes further in his desires increases his wants in proportion to his acquisitions; or to use his own expression, "I am now worth eight hundred pounds, but shall never be so happy as when I was not worth a farthing."

1710   The Preservation of Captain John Dean

THE Nottingham Galley, of and from London, 120 tons, 10 guns and 14 men, John Dean, Commander, having taken in cordage in England and butter and cheese, etc., in Ireland, sailed for Boston in New England the 25th of September, 1710. But meeting with contrary winds and bad weather, 'twas the beginning of December when first made land to the eastward of Piscataqua and hailing southerly for the Massachusetts Bay, under a hard gale of wind at northeast, accompanied with rain, hail and snow, having no observation for ten or twelve days. We on the eleventh handed all our sails except our foresail and maintopsail double reefed, ordering one hand forward to look out. Between eight and nine, going forward myself, I saw the breakers ahead, whereupon I called out to put the helm hard a starboard, but ere the ship could veer we struck upon the east end of the rock called Boon Island, four leagues to the eastward of Piscataqua.

The second or third sea heaved the ship alongside of it, running likewise so very high and the ship laboring so excessively that we were not able to stand upon deck, and notwithstanding it was not above thirty or forty yards, yet the weather was so thick and dark we could not see the rock, so that we were justly thrown into a consternation at the sad prospect of immediately perishing in the sea. I presently called down all hands to the cabin, where we continued a few minutes earnestly supplicating mercy; but, knowing prayers without endeavors are vain, I ordered all up again to cut the masts by the board; but several sunk so under racks of conscience that they were not able to stir. However, we upon deck cut the weather-most shrouds, and the ship heeling towards the rock, the force of the sea soon broke the masts so that they fell right towards the shore.

One of the men went out on the boltspright and, returning, told me he saw something black ahead and would adventure to get on shore, accompanied with any other person; upon which I desired some of the best swimmers (my mate and one more) to go with him, and if they recovered the rock to give notice by their calls and direct us to the most secure place. And remembering some money and papers that might be of use, also ammunition, brandy, etc., I went down and opened the place in which they were; but the ship bulging, her decks opening, her back broke, and beams giving way, so that the stern sunk almost under water, I was obliged to hasten forward to prevent immediate perishing. And, having heard nothing of the men gone before, concluded them lost; yet, notwithstanding, I was under a necessity to make the same adventure upon the foremast, moving gradually forward betwixt every sea till, at last quitting it, I cast myself with all the strength I had toward the rock, and it being dead low water and the rock exceeding slippery I could get no hold but tore my fingers, hands and arms in a most lamentable manner, every wash of the sea fetching me off again, so that it was with the utmost peril and difficulty that I got safe on shore at last. The rest of the men ran the same hazard yet through mercy we all escaped with our lives.

After endeavoring to discharge the salt water, and creeping a little way up the rock, I heard the three men mentioned before, and by ten all met together; where with joyful hearts we returned humble thanks to Providence for our deliverance from so eminent a danger. We then endeavored to gain shelter to the leeward of the rock but found it so small and inconsiderable that it would afford none (being but about a hundred yards long and fifty broad) and so very craggy that we could not walk to keep ourselves warm, the weather still continuing extreme cold, with snow and rain.

As soon as daylight appeared I went towards the place where we came on shore, not questioning but we should meet with provisions enough from the wreck for our support; but found only some pieces of the masts and yards amongst some old junk and cables congered together, which the anchors had prevented from being carried away and kept moving about the rock at some distance. Part of the ship's stores, with some pieces of plank and timber, old sails and canvas, etc., drove on shore, but nothing to eat except some small pieces of cheese we picked up from the rockweed (in the whole to the quantity of three small cheeses).

We used our utmost endeavor to get fire (having a steel and flint with us, also by a drill with a very swift motion); but, having nothing but what had been long water-soaked, we could not effect it.

At night we stowed one upon another under our canvas in the best manner possible to keep each other warm; and the next day, the weather a little clearing and inclining to frost, I went out; and, seeing the mainland, knew where we was, therefore encouraged my men with hopes of being discovered by fishing shallops, requiring them to go about and fetch up what planks they could get, as also carpenter's tools and stores, in order to build a tent and a boat. The cook then complaining he was almost starved, and his countenance discovering his illness, I ordered him to remain with two or three more the frost had seized. About noon the men acquainted me that he was dead, so laid him in a convenient place for the sea to carry him away, none mentioning eating of him, though several with myself afterwards acknowledged had thoughts of it.

After we had been there two or three days the frost being very severe and the weather extremely cold, it seized most of our hands and feet to such a degree as to take away the sense of feeling and render them almost useless; so benumbing and discoloring them as gave us just reason to fear mortifications. We pulled off our shoes and cut off our boots, but in getting off our stockings many whose legs were blistered pulled off skin and all and some the nails of their toes. We wrapped up our legs and feet as warm as we could in oakum and canvas.

We now began to build our tent in a triangular form, each angle about eight foot, covered with what sails and old canvas came on shore, having just room for all to lie down each on one side, so that none could turn except all turned, which was about every two hours, upon notice given. We also fixed a staff to the top of our tent, upon which (as often as weather would permit) we hoisted a piece of cloth in the form of a flag in order to discover ourselves to any vessels that might come near.

We began now to build our boat of plank and timber belonging to the wreck, our tools the blade of a cutlass (made into a saw with our knives), a hammer and a caulking mallet. Some nails we found in the clefts of the rock, others we got from the sheathing. We laid three planks flat for the bottom and two up each side fixed to stanchions and let into the bottom timbers, with two short pieces at each end, also one breadth of new Holland duck round the sides to keep out the spray of the sea. We corked all we could with oakum drawn from the old junk and in other places, filled up the distances with long pieces of canvas, all which we secured in the best manner possible. We found also some sheet lead and pump leather, which proved of use. We fixed a short mast and square sail, with seven paddles to row, and another longer to steer. But our carpenter, who now should have been of most use to us, was by reason of illness scarce able to afford us either assistance or advice; and all the rest benumbed and feeble as not able to stir, except myself and two more, also the weather so extreme cold that we could seldom stay out of the tent above four hours in the day, and some days do nothing at all.

When we had been there about a week without any manner of provisions except the cheese before-mentioned and some beef bones, which we eat (first beating them to pieces), we saw three boats about five leagues from us, which may be easily imagined rejoiced us not a little, believing our deliverance was now come. I made all creep out of the tent and hollo together so well as our strength would allow, making also all the signals we could; but alas, all in vain, they neither hearing nor otherwise discovering us. However, we received no small encouragement from the sight of 'em; they coming from southwest, and the wind at northeast when we were cast away, gave us reason to conclude our distress might be known by the wreck driving on shore, and to presume were come out in search of us and that they would daily do so when weather would permit. Thus we flattered ourselves in hopes of deliverance though in vain.

Just before we finished our boat, Providence so ordered it that the carpenter's ax was cast on the rock to us, whereby we were enabled to complete our work. But then we had scarce strength enough to get her into the water.

About the 21st December, the boat just perfected, a fine day, and the water smoother than I had ever yet seen it since we came there, we consulted who should attempt getting on shore, I offering myself as one to adventure, which they agreed to because I was the strongest and therefore fittest to undergo the extremities we might be reduced to. My mate also offering himself and desiring to accompany me, I was allowed him with my brother and four more. So, committing our enterprise to Divine Providence, all that were able came out and with much difficulty we got our poor patched-up boat to the water's side. And the surf running very high, was obliged to wade very deep to launch her, which being done and myself and one more got into her, the swell of the sea heaved her alongshore and overset her upon us, whereby we again narrowly escaped drowning, and staved our poor boat all to pieces, totally disappointing our enterprise and destroying all our hopes at once.

We lost with our boat both our ax and hammer, which would have been of great use to us if we should hereafter attempt to build a raft, yet had we reason to admire the goodness of God in overruling our disappointment for our safety, for that afternoon the wind, springing up, it blew very hard, so that had we been at sea in that imitation of a boat, in all probability we must have perished and the rest left behind had no better fare because unable to help themselves.

We were now reduced to the most deplorable and melancholy circumstance imaginable, almost every man but myself weak to an extremity and near starved with hunger and cold, their hands and feet frozen and mortified, with large and deep ulcers in their legs, the very smell offensive, and nothing to dress them with but a piece of linen that was cast on the shore. No fire, and the weather extreme cold; our small stock of cheese spent and nothing to support our feeble bodies but rockweed and a few mussels, scarce and difficult to get (at most not above two or three for each man a day). So that we had our miserable bodies perishing and our poor disconsolate spirits overpowered with the deplorable prospect of starving, without any appearance of relief. Besides, to heighten if possible the aggravation, we had to apprehend lest the approaching spring tide (if accompanied with high winds) should totally overflow us. How dismal such a circumstance must be is impossible to express: the pinching cold and hunger, extremity of weakness and pain, racks and horror of conscience (to many) and foresight of certain and painful but lingering death, without any (even the most remote) views of deliverance.

The last method of safety we could possibly propose was the fixing a raft that might carry two men, which was mightily urged by one of our men, a Swede, a stout brave fellow, but had since lost both his feet by the frost. He frequently importuned me to attempt our deliverance in that way, offering himself to accompany me, or if I refused him to go alone. After deliberate thoughts and consideration we resolved upon a raft but found abundance of labor and difficulty in clearing the foreyard (of which it was chiefly to be made) from the junk, by reason our working hands were so few and weak.

That done, we split the yard and with the two parts made side pieces, fixing others and adding some of the lightest plank we could get, first spiking and afterwards seizing them firm, in breadth four foot. We likewise fixed a mast, and of two hammocks that were drove on shore we made a sail, with a paddle for each man and a spare one in case of necessity. This difficulty thus surmounted and brought to a period, he would frequently ask me whether I designed to accompany him, giving me also to understand that if I declined there was another ready to embrace the offer.

About this time we saw a sail come out of Piscataqua River, about seven leagues to the westward. We again made all the signal we could, but the wind being at northwest and the ship standing to the eastward, was presently out of sight without ever coming near us, which proved a very great mortification to our hopes. But the next day being moderate, and in the afternoon a small breeze right on shore, also the raft finished, the two men were very solicitous to have it launched, and the mate as strenuously opposed it on account 'twas so late (being two in the afternoon); but they, urging the light nights, begged of me to have it done, to which at last I agreed, first committing the enterprise to God's blessing. They both got upon it and, the swell rolling very high, soon overset them as it did our boat. The Swede, not minding it, swam on shore, but the other (being no swimmer) continued some time under water, and as soon as he appeared, I caught hold of him and saved him but he was so discouraged that he was afraid to make a second attempt.

I desired the Swede to wait a more favorable opportunity, but he, continuing resolute, begged of me to go with him or help him to turn the raft and would go himself alone.

By this time another man came down and offered to adventure; so, getting upon the raft, I launched 'em off, they desiring us to go to prayers, also to watch what became of them. I did so, and by sunset judged them half way to the main, and that they might reach the shore by two in the morning. But I suppose they fell in with some breakers, or the violence of the sea overset them and they perished; for, two days after, the raft was found on shore and one man dead about a mile from it, with a paddle fastened to his wrist; but the Swede who was so very forward to adventure was never heard of more.

At our first coming, saw several seals upon the rock and, supposing they might harbor there in the night, I walked round at midnight but could never get anything. We also saw a great many fowls, but they perceiving us daily there would never come on the rock to lodge, so that we caught none.

Which disappointment was very grievous and still served to irritate our miseries, but it was more especially afflicting to a brother I had with me and another young gentleman, who had never either of 'em been at sea or endured any severities before, but were now reduced to the last extremities, having no assistance but what they received from me.

Part of a green hide being thrown up by the sea, fastened to a piece of the mainyard, the men importuned me to bring it to the tent, which being done we minced it small and swallowed it down.

About this time I set the men to open junk, and with the rope-yarn (when weather would permit) I thatched the tent in the best manner my strength would allow, that it might the better shelter us from extremities of weather.

About the latter end of this month our carpenter (a fat man and naturally of a dull, heavy, phlegmatic constitution and disposition, aged about 47) who from our first coming on shore had been always very ill and lost the use of his feet, complained of an excessive pain in his back and stiffness in his neck; being likewise almost choked with phlegm for want of strength to discharge it, so that to our apprehension he drew near his end. We prayed over him and used our utmost endeavors to be serviceable to him in his last moments. He showed himself sensible though speechless and that night died. We suffered the body to remain with us till morning, when I desired them who were best able to remove it, creeping out myself to see if Providence had yet sent us anything to satisfy our extremely craving appetites. Before noon, returning and not seeing the dead body without, I asked why they had not removed it. And received for answer, they were not all of them able. Whereupon fastening a rope to the body, I gave the utmost of my assistance, and with some difficulty we got it out of the tent. But the fatigue and consideration of our misery together so overcame my spirits that, being ready to faint, I crept into the tent and was no sooner got in there but (as the highest addition of trouble) the men began to request of me the dead body to eat, the better to support their lives.

This, of all I had met with, was the most grievous and shocking to me, to see myself and company, who came thither laden with provisions but three weeks before, now reduced to such a deplorable circumstance as to have two of us absolutely starved to death, other two we knew not what was become of, and the rest of us at the last extremity and though still living yet requiring to eat the dead for support.

After abundance of mature thought and consultation about the lawfulness or sinfulness on the one hand and absolute necessity on the other, judgment, conscience, etc., were obliged to submit to the more prevailing arguments of our craving appetites, so that at last we determined to satisfy our hunger and support our feeble bodies with the carcass in possession. First I ordered his skin, head, hands, feet and bowels to be buried in the sea and the body to be quartered for convenience of drying and carriage, to which I again received for answer that they were not all of them able but entreated I would perform it for them. A task very grievous, and not readily complied with, but their incessant prayers and entreaties at last prevailed and by night I had performed my labor.

I then cut part of the flesh in thin slices and, washing it in salt water, brought it to the tent and obliged the men to eat rockweed along with it, to serve instead of bread.

My mate and two others refused to eat any that night, but next morning complied and earnestly desired to partake with the rest.

I found they all eat abundance and with the utmost greediness, so that I was constrained to carry the quarters farther from the tent, quite out of their reach, lest they should prejudice themselves by overmuch eating, as also expend our small stock too soon.

I also limited each man to an equal proportion, that none might quarrel or entertain hard thoughts of myself or one another, and I was the more obliged to this method because I found in a few days their very natural dispositions changed, and that affectionate, peaceable temper they had all along discovered totally lost, their eyes staring and looking wild, their countenances fierce and barbarous, and instead of obeying my commands as they had universally and readily done before, I found all I could say, even prayers and entreaties, vain and fruitless, nothing now being to be heard but brutish quarrels, with horrid oaths and imprecations, instead of that quiet submissive spirit of prayer and supplication we had before enjoyed.

This, together with the dismal prospect of future want, obliged me to keep a strict watch over the rest of the body, lest any of 'em should if able get to it, and this being spent we be forced to feed upon the living, which we must certainly have done had we stayed a few days longer.

But now the goodness of God began to appear and make provision for our deliverance by putting it in the hearts of the good people on shore, where our raft drove, to come out in search of us; which they did the 2nd of January in the morning.

Just as I was creeping out of the tent I saw a shallop halfway from shore, standing directly towards us, which may be easily imagined was life from the dead. How great our joys and satisfactions were at the prospect of so speedy and unexpected deliverance no tongue is able to express nor thoughts to conceive.

Our good and welcome friends came to an anchor to the southwest at about 100 yards distance, the swell not suffering them to come nearer. But their anchor coming home, obliged them to stand off till about noon, waiting for smoother water upon the flood. Meantime our passions were differently moved, our expectations of deliverance and fears of miscarriage hurried our weak and disordered spirits strangely.

I gave them account of our miseries in every respect except the want of provisions (which I did not mention, lest I should not get them on shore for fear of being constrained by the weather to tarry with us). I earnestly entreated them to attempt our immediate deliverance, or at least if possible to furnish us with fire, which with the utmost hazard and difficulty they at last accomplished, by sending a small canoe with one man, who with abundance of labor got on shore.

After helping him up with his canoe and seeing nothing to eat I asked him if he could give us fire. He answered in the affirmative but was so affrighted, seeing me look so thin and meager that could hardly at first return me an answer. But recollecting himself, after several questions asked on both sides, he went with me to the tent, where was surprised to see so many of us in so deplorable condition, our flesh so wasted and our looks so ghastly and frightful that it was really a very dismal prospect.

With some difficulty we made a fire, determining to go myself with the man on board and after to send for the rest, one or two at a time, and accordingly got both into the canoe, but the sea immediately drove it with such violence against the rock, that overset us into the water; and I being very weak, 'twas a great while before I could recover myself, so that I had a very narrow escape from drowning.

The good man with very great difficulty got on board himself without me, designing to return the next day with better conveniences if weather would permit.

'Twas a very uncomfortable sight to see our worthy friends in the shallop stand away from the shore without us. But God, who orders all our affairs by unseen movements for the best, had doubtless designs of preservation towards us in denying us that appearance of present deliverance. For that night the wind coming about to southeast, blowing hard and being dark weather, our good friends lost their shallop and with extreme difficulty saved their lives. But, in all probability, had we been with them we must have perished, not having strength sufficient to help ourselves.

Immediately after their getting on shore they sent an express to Portsmouth in Piscataqua, where the good people made no delay in hastening to our deliverance as soon as weather would allow. But to our great sorrow and for further trial of our patience, the next day continued very stormy, so that though we doubted not but the people on shore knew our condition and would assist us as soon as possible, yet our flesh being near spent, no fresh water, nor any certainty how long the weather might continue thus, rendered our circumstance still miserable though much advanced by the fire, for now we could both warm ourselves and broil our meat.

The next day, our men urging me vehemently for flesh, I gave them a little more than usual, but not to their satisfaction, for they would certainly have eat up the whole at once had I not carefully watched 'em, designing to share the rest next morning if the weather continued bad. But it pleased God that night the wind abated, and early next morning a shallop came for us, with my much esteemed friends Captain Longland and Captain Purver and three more men, who brought a large canoe; and in two hours' time got us all on board to their satisfaction and our great comfort, being forced to carry almost all the men on their backs from the tent to the canoe and fetch us off by two or three at a time.

When we first came on board the shallop each of us eat a bit of bread and drank a dram of rum, and most of us were extremely seasick; but after we had cleansed our stomachs and tasted warm nourishing food we became so exceeding hungry and ravenous that had not our worthy friends dieted us and limited the quantity for about two or three days we should certainly have destroyed ourselves with eating.

We had also two other vessels come off for our assistance if there had been any necessity (so generous and charitable were the good people of New England in our distress); but, seeing us all on board the shallop, made the best of their way home again.

At eight at night we came on shore, where we were kindly entertained myself and another at a private house (having credit sufficient to help us), all the rest at the charge of the government, who took such care that the poor men knew not the least want of anything their necessities called for or the kind and generous gentlemen could furnish them with (the care, industry and generosity of my much honored friends John Plaisted, Esq., and Captain John Wentworth, in serving both myself and these poor men being particularly eminent), providing them a good surgeon and nurses till well, bearing the charge and afterwards allowing each man sufficient clothing; behaving themselves in the whole with so much freedom, generosity and Christian temper that was no small addition to their other services, and rendered the whole worthy both of admiration and imitation; and likewise was of the last consequence to the poor men in their distress.

Two days after we came on shore my apprentice lost a great part of one foot; the rest all recovered their limbs but not their perfect life, very few besides myself escaping without losing the benefit of fingers or toes, though thank God all otherwise in perfect health.

1722 *Philip Ashton's Own Account,*

who, after escaping from pirates, lived sixteen months in solitude on a desolate island.

UPON Friday the 15th of June, 1722, after being out some time in a schooner with four men and a boy off Cape Sable, I stood in for Port Rossaway, designing to lie there all Sunday. Having arrived at four in the afternoon, we saw, among other vessels which had reached the port before us, a brigantine supposed to be inward bound from the West Indies. After remaining three or four hours at anchor, a boat from the brigantine came alongside with four hands, who leaped on deck and, suddenly drawing out pistols and brandishing cutlasses, demanded the surrender both of ourselves and our vessel. All remonstrance was vain; nor indeed, had we known who they were before boarding us, could we have made any effectual resistance, being only five men and a boy; and were thus under the necessity of submitting at discretion. We were not single in misfortune, as thirteen or fourteen fishing vessels were in like manner surprised the same evening.

When carried on board the brigantine I found myself in the hands of Ned Low, an infamous pirate, whose vessel had two great guns, four swivels and about forty-two men. I was strongly urged to sign the articles of agreement among the pirates and to join their number, which I steadily refused, and suffered much bad usage in consequence. At length, being conducted along with five of the prisoners to the quarterdeck, Low came up to us with pistols in his hand and loudly demanded, "Are any of you married men?"

This unexpected question added to the sight of the pistol, struck us all speechless. We were alarmed lest there was some secret meaning in his words and that he would proceed to extremities; therefore none could reply. In a violent passion he cocked a pistol and, clapping it to my head, cried out, "You dog, why don't you answer?" swearing vehemently at the same time that he would shoot me through the head. I was sufficiently terrified by his threats and fierceness, but rather than lose my life in so trifling a matter I ventured to pronounce, as loud as I durst speak, that I was not married. Hereupon he seemed to be somewhat pacified and turned away.

It appeared that Low was resolved to take no married men whatever, which often seemed surprising to me until I had been a considerable time with him. But his own wife had died lately before he became a pirate, and he had a young child at Boston for whom he entertained such tenderness, on every lucid interval from drinking and reveling, that, on mentioning it, I have seen him sit down and weep plentifully. Thus I concluded that his reason for taking only single men was probably that they might have no ties such as wives and children to divert them from his service and render them desirous of returning home.

The pirates, finding force of no avail in compelling us to join them, began to use persuasion instead of it. They tried to flatter me into compliance by setting before me the share I should have in their spoils and the riches which I should become master of; and all the time eagerly importuned me to drink along with them. But I still continued to resist their proposals, whereupon Low, with equal fury as before, threatened to shoot me through the head; and though I earnestly entreated my release he and his people wrote my name and that of my companions in their books.

On the 19th of June the pirates changed the privateer, as they called their vessel, and went into a new schooner belonging to Marblehead, which they had captured. They then put all the prisoners whom they designed sending home on board of the brigantine and sent her to Boston, which induced me to make another unsuccessful attempt for liberty; but though I fell on my knees to Low he refused to let me go. Thus I saw the brigantine depart with all the captives excepting myself and seven more.

A very short time before she departed I had nearly effected my escape; for a dog belonging to Low being accidentally left on shore, he ordered some hands into a boat to bring it off. Thereupon two young men, captives, both belonging to Marblehead, readily leapt into the boat, and I, considering that if I could once get on shore means might be found of effecting my escape, endeavored to go along with them. But the quartermaster, called Russel, catching hold of my shoulder, drew me back. As the young men did not return he thought I was privy to their plot and, with the most outrageous oaths, snapped his pistol on my denying all knowledge of it. The pistol missing fire, however, only served to enrage him the more. He snapped it three times again, and as often it missed fire; on which he held it overboard and then it went off. Russel on this drew his cutlass and was about to attack me in the utmost fury, when I leapt down into the hold and saved myself.

Off St. Michael's the pirates took a large Portuguese pink, laden with wheat, coming out of the road; and, she being a good sailer and carrying fourteen guns, transferred their company into her. It afterwards became necessary to careen her, whence they made three islands, called the Triangles, lying about forty leagues to the eastward of Surinam.

In heaving down the pink, Low had ordered so many men to the shrouds and yards that the ports, by her heeling, got under water and, the sea rushing in, she overset. He and the doctor were then in the cabin, and as soon as he observed the water gushing in he leaped out of one of the stern ports while the doctor attempted to follow him. But the violence of the sea repulsed the latter, and he was forced back into the cabin. Low, however, contrived to thrust his arm into the port and, dragging him out, saved his life. Meanwhile the vessel completely overset. Her keel turned out of the water but as the hull filled she sank, in the depth of about six fathoms.

The yardarms, striking the ground, forced the masts somewhat above the water. As the ship overset, the people got from the shrouds and yards upon the hull and as the hull went down they again resorted to the rigging, rising a little out of the sea.

Being an indifferent swimmer, I was reduced to great extremity; for, along with other light lads, I had been sent up to the main topgallant yard; and the people of a boat who were now occupied in preserving the men refusing to take me in, I was compelled to attempt reaching the buoy. This I luckily accomplished and as it was large secured myself there until the boat approached. I once more requested the people to take me in but they still refused, as the boat was full. I was uncertain whether they designed leaving me to perish in the situation. However, the boat, being deeply laden, made way very slowly, and one of my own comrades, captured at the same time with myself, calling to me to forsake the buoy and swim towards her, I assented, and, reaching the boat, he drew me on board. Two men, John Bell and Zana Gourdon, were lost in the pink.

Though the schooner in company was very near at hand, her people were employed mending their sails under an awning and knew nothing of the accident until the boat, full of men, got alongside.

The pirates, having thus lost their principal vessel and the greatest part of their provisions and water, were reduced to great extremities for want of the latter. They were unable to get a supply at the Triangles nor, on account of calms and currents, could they make the island of Tobago. Thus they were forced to stand for Grenada, which they reached after being on short allowance for sixteen days together.

Grenada was a French settlement, and Low, on arriving, after having sent below all his men except a sufficient number to maneuver the vessel, said he was from Barbadoes, that he had lost the water on board and was obliged to put in here for a supply.

The people entertained no suspicion of his being a pirate, but afterwards, supposing him a smuggler, thought it a good opportunity to make a prize of his vessel. Next day, therefore, they equipped a large sloop of seventy tons and four guns, with about thirty hands, as sufficient for the capture, and came alongside, while Low was quite unsuspicious of their design. But this being evidently betrayed by their number and actions, he quickly called ninety men on deck and, having eight guns mounted, the French sloop became an easy prey.

Provided with these two vessels, the pirates cruised about in the West Indies, taking seven or eight prizes, and at length arrived at the island of Santa Cruz, where they captured two more. While lying there Low thought he stood in need of a medicine chest and in order to procure one sent four Frenchmen in a ship he had taken to St. Thomas', about twelve leagues distant, with money to purchase it, promising them liberty and the return of all their vessels for the service. But he declared, at the same time, if it proved otherwise he would kill the rest of the men and burn the vessels. In little more than twenty-four hours the Frenchmen returned with the object of their mission, and Low punctually performed his promise by restoring the vessels.

Having sailed for the Spanish American settlements, the pirates described two large ships about halfway between Carthagena and Portobello, which proved to be the Mermaid, an English man-of-war, and a Guineaman. They approached in chase until discovering the man-of-war's great range of teeth, when they immediately put about and made the best of their way off. The man-of-war then commenced the pursuit and gained upon them apace, and I confess that my terrors were now equal to any that I had previously suffered; for I concluded that we should certainly be taken and that I should no less certainly be hanged for company's sake; so true are the words of Solomon, "A companion of fools shall be destroyed." But the two pirate vessels, finding themselves outsailed, separated; and Farrington Spriggs, who commanded the schooner in which I was, stood in for the shore. The Mermaid, observing the sloop with Low himself to be the larger of the two, crowded all sail and continued gaining still more, indeed until her shot flew over; but one of the sloop's crew showed Low a shoal which he could pass, and in the pursuit the man-of-war grounded. Thus the pirates escaped hanging on this occasion.

Spriggs and one of his chosen companions, dreading the consequences of being captured and brought to justice, laid their pistols beside them in the interval and, pledging a mutual oath in a bumper of liquor, swore if they saw no possibility of escape to set foot to foot and blow out each other's brains. But, standing towards the shore, they made Pickeroon Bay and escaped the danger.

Next we repaired to a small island called Utilla, about seven or eight leagues to leeward of the island of Roatan, in the Bay of Honduras, where the bottom of the schooner was cleaned. There were now twenty-two persons on board, and eight of us engaged in a plot to overpower our masters and make our escape. Spriggs proposed sailing for New England in quest of provisions and to increase his company; and we intended, on approaching the coast, when the rest had indulged freely in liquor and fallen sound asleep, to secure them under the hatches and then deliver ourselves up to government.

Although our plot was carried on with all possible privacy Spriggs had somehow or other got intelligence of it; and, having fallen in with Low on the voyage, went on board his ship to make a furious declaration against us. But Low made little account of his information, otherwise it might have been fatal to most of our number. Spriggs, however, returned raging to the schooner, exclaiming that four of us should go forward to be shot, and to me in particular he said, "You dog Ashton, you deserve to be hanged up to the yardarm for designing to cut us off." I replied that I had no intention of injuring any man on board but I should be glad if they would allow me to go away quietly. At length this flame was quenched and through the goodness of God I escaped destruction.

Roatan harbor, as all about the Bay of Honduras, is full of small islands which pass under the general name of keys; and, having got in here, Low with some of his chief men landed on a small island which they called Port Royal Key. There they erected huts and continued carousing, drinking and firing, while the different vessels of which they now had possession were repairing.

On Saturday the 9th of March, 1723, the cooper, with six hands, was going ashore for water; and, coming alongside of the schooner, I requested to be of the party. Seeing him hesitate, I urged that I had never hitherto been ashore and thought it hard to be so closely confined, when everyone besides had the liberty of landing as there was occasion. Low had before told me, on requesting to be sent away in some of the captured vessels which he dismissed, that I should go home when he did and swore that I should never previously set my foot on land. But now I considered if I could possibly once get on terra firma, though in ever such bad circumstances, I should account it a happy deliverance, and resolved never to embark again.

The cooper at length took me into the longboat while Low and his chief people were on a different island from Roatan, where the watering place lay. My only clothing was a frock and trousers, a milled cap, but neither shirt, shoes, stockings nor anything else.

When we first landed I was very active in assisting to get the casks out of the boat and in rolling them to the watering place. Then, taking a hearty draught of water, I strolled along the beach, picking up stones and shells; but on reaching the distance of a musketshot from the party, I began to withdraw towards the skirts of the woods. In answer to a question by the cooper of whither I was going I replied, "for coconuts," as some coco trees were just before me; and as soon as I was out of sight of my companions I took to my heels, running as fast as the thickness of the bushes and my naked feet would admit. Notwithstanding I had got a considerable way into the woods, I was still so near as to hear the voices of the party if they spoke loud, and I lay close in a thicket where I knew they could not find me.

After my comrades had filled their casks and were about to depart the cooper called on me to accompany them; however, I lay snug in the thicket and gave him no answer, though his words were plain enough. At length, after hallooing, I could hear them say to one another, "the dog is lost in the woods and cannot find the way out again." Then they hallooed once more and cried, "He has run away and won't come to us," and the cooper observed that had he known my intentions he would not have brought me ashore. Satisfied of their inability to find me among the trees and bushes, the cooper at last, to show his kindness, exclaimed, "If you do not come away presently I shall go off and leave you alone." Nothing, however, could induce me to discover myself; and my comrades, seeing it vain to wait any longer, put off without me.

Thus I was left on a desolate island, destitute of all help and remote from the track of navigators; but, compared with the state and society I had quitted, I considered the wilderness hospitable and the solitude interesting.

When I thought they were all gone I emerged from my thicket and came down to a small run of water about a mile from the place where our casks were filled and there sat down to observe the proceedings of the pirates. To my great joy, in five days their vessels sailed, and I saw the schooner part from them to shape a different course.

I then began to reflect on myself and my present condition. I was on an island which I had no means of leaving; I knew of no human being within many miles; my clothing was scanty and it was impossible to procure a supply. I was altogether destitute of provision, nor could tell how my life was to be supported. This melancholy prospect drew a copious flood of tears from my eyes; but, as it had pleased God to grant my wishes in being liberated from those whose occupation was devising mischief against their neighbors, I resolved to account every hardship light. Yet Low would never suffer his men to work on the Sabbath, which was more devoted to play; and I have even seen some of them sit down to read in a good book.

In order to ascertain how I was to live in time to come I began to range over the island, which proved ten or eleven leagues long and lay in about sixteen degrees, thirty minutes north latitude. But I soon found that my only companions would be the beasts of the earth and fowls of the air; for there were no indications of any habitations on the island, though every now and then I found some shreds of earthenware scattered in a lime walk, said by some to be the remains of Indians formerly dwelling here.

The island was well watered, full of high hills and deep valleys. Numerous fruit trees, such as figs, vines and coconuts, are found in the latter; and I found a kind larger than an orange, oval-shaped, of a brownish color without and red within. Though many of these had fallen under the trees I could not venture to take them until I saw the wild hogs feeding with safety, and then I found them very delicious fruit.

Store of provisions abounded here, though I could avail myself of nothing but the fruit; for I had no knife or iron implement, either to cut up a tortoise on turning it, or weapon wherewith to kill animals, nor had I any means of making a fire to cook my capture even if I were successful.

Sometimes I entertained thoughts of digging pits and covering them over with small branches of trees for the purpose of taking hogs or deer; but I wanted a shovel and every substitute for the purpose and I was soon convinced that my hands were insufficient to make a cavity deep enough to retain what should fall into it. Thus I was forced to rest satisfied with fruit, which was to be esteemed very good provision for anyone in my condition.

In process of time, while poking among the sand with a stick in quest of tortoise's eggs, which I had heard were laid in the sand, part of one came up adhering to it; and, on removing the sand, I found nearly a hundred and fifty, which had not lain long enough to spoil. Therefore, taking some, I ate them and strung others on a strip of palmetto, which, being hung up in the sun, became thick and somewhat hard, so that they were more palatable. After all they were not very savory food, though one who had nothing but what fell from the trees behoved to be content. Tortoises lay their eggs in the sand in holes about a foot or a foot and a half deep, and smooth the surface over them so that there is no discovering where they lie. According to the best of my observation the young are hatched in eighteen or twenty days and then immediately take to the water.

Many serpents are on this and the adjacent islands; one, about twelve or fourteen feet long, is as large as a man's waist but not poisonous. When lying at length they look like old trunks of trees covered with short moss, though they more usually assume a circular position. The first time I saw one of these serpents I had approached very near before discovering it to be a living creature. It opened its mouth wide enough to have received a hat and breathed on me. A small black fly creates such annoyance that even if a person possessed ever so many comforts his life would be oppressive to him unless for the possibility of retiring to some small quay, destitute of wood and bushes, where multitudes are dispersed by the wind.

To this place, then, was I confined during nine months without seeing a human being. One day after another was lingered out, I know not how, void of occupation or amusement except collecting food, rambling from hill to hill and from island to island and gazing on sky and water. Although my mind was occupied by many regrets I had the reflection that I was lawfully employed when taken, so that I had no hand in bringing misery on myself. I was also comforted to think that I had the approbation and consent of my parents in going to sea, and I trusted that it would please God in his own time and manner to provide for my return to my father's house. Therefore I resolved to submit patiently to my misfortune.

It was my daily practice to ramble from one part of the island to another, though I had a more special home near the waterside. Here I built a hut to defend me against the heat of the sun by day and the heavy dews by night. Taking some of the best branches that I could find fallen from the trees, I contrived to fix them against a low-hanging bough by fastening them together with split palmetto leaves. Next I covered the whole with some of the largest and most suitable leaves that I could get. Many of those huts were constructed by me generally near the beach, with the open part fronting the sea, to have the better look-out and the advantage of the sea breeze, which both the heat and the vermin required.

But the insects were so troublesome that I thought of endeavoring to get over to some of the adjacent keys in hopes of enjoying rest. However, I was, as already said, a very indifferent swimmer. I had no canoe nor any means of making one. At length, having got a piece of bamboo, which is hollow like a reed and light as cork, I ventured, after frequent trials with it under my breast and arms, to put off for a small key about a gunshot distant, which I reached in safety.

My new place of refuge was only about three or four hundred feet in circuit, being very low, and clear of woods and brush. From exposure to the wind it was quite free of vermin, and I seemed to have got into a new world, where I lived infinitely more at ease. Hither I retired, therefore, when the heat of the day rendered the insect tribe most obnoxious; yet I was obliged to be much on Roatan to procure food and water, and at night on account of my hut.

When swimming back and forward between the two islands I used to bind my frock and trousers about my head and, if I could have carried over wood and leaves whereof to make a hut with equal facility, I should have passed more of my time on the smaller one.

Yet these excursions were not unattended with danger. Once, I remember, when passing from the larger island, the bamboo, before I was aware, slipped from under me, and the tide or current set down so strong that it was with great difficulty I could reach the shore. At another time, when swimming over to the small island, a shovel-nosed shark, which, as well as alligators, abound in those seas, struck me in the thigh, just as my foot could reach the bottom, and grounded itself from the shallowness of the water, as I suppose, so that its mouth could not get round towards me. The blow I felt some hours after making the shore. By repeated practice I at length became a pretty dexterous swimmer and amused myself by passing from one island to another among the keys.

I suffered very much from being barefoot. So many deep wounds were made in my feet from traversing the woods, where the ground was covered with sticks and stones, and on the hot beach over sharp broken shells, that I was scarce able to walk at all. Often, when treading with all possible caution, a stone or shell on the beach or a pointed stick in the woods would penetrate the old wound and the extreme anguish would strike me down as suddenly as if I had been shot. Then I would remain for hours together with tears gushing from my eyes from the acuteness of the pain. I could travel no more than absolute necessity compelled me in quest of subsistence and I have sat, my back leaning against a tree, looking out for a vessel during a complete day.

Once, while faint from such injuries, as well as smarting under the pain of them, a wild boar rushed towards me. I knew not what to do, for I had not strength to resist his attack. Therefore as he drew nearer I caught the bough of a tree and half suspended myself by means of it. The boar tore away part of my ragged trousers with his tusks and then left me. This, I think, was the only time that I was attacked by any wild beast, and I considered myself to have had a very great deliverance.

As my weakness continued to increase I often fell to the ground insensible and then, as also when I laid myself to sleep, I thought I should never awake again, or rise in life. Under this affliction I first lost count of the days of the week. I could not distinguish Sunday, and as my illness became more aggravated I became ignorant of the month also.

All this time I had no healing balsam for my feet nor any cordial to revive my drooping spirits. My utmost efforts could only now and then procure some figs and grapes. Neither had I fire; for, though I had heard of a way to procure it by rubbing two sticks together, my attempts in this respect, continued until I was tired, proved abortive. The rains having come on, attended with chill winds, I suffered exceedingly.

While passing nine months in this lonely, melancholy and irksome condition my thoughts would sometimes wander to my parents; and I reflected that, notwithstanding it would be consolatory to myself if they knew where I was, it might be distressing to them. The nearer my prospect of death, which I often expected, the greater my penitence became.

Sometime in November 1723 I descried a small canoe approaching with a single man. But the sight excited little emotion. I kept my seat on the beach, thinking I could not expect a friend and knowing that I had no enemy to fear nor was I capable of resisting one. As the man approached he betrayed many signs of surprise; he called me to him and I told him he might safely venture ashore, for I was alone and almost expiring. Coming close up, he knew not what to make of me; my garb and countenance seemed so singular that he looked wild with astonishment. He started back a little and surveyed me more thoroughly; but, recovering himself again, came forward and, taking me by the hand, expressed his satisfaction at seeing me.

This stranger proved to be a native of North Britain. He was well advanced in years, of a grave and venerable aspect and of a reserved temper. His name I never knew; he did not disclose it and I had not inquired during the period of our acquaintance. But he informed me he had lived twenty-two years with the Spaniards, who now threatened to burn him though I know not for what crime. Therefore he had fled hither as a sanctuary, bringing his dog, gun and ammunition, as also a small quantity of pork, along with him. He designed spending the remainder of his days on the island, where he could support himself by hunting.

I experienced much kindness from the stranger. He was always ready to perform any civil offices and assist me in whatever he could, though he spoke little; and he gave me a share of his pork.

On the third day after his arrival he said he would make an excursion in his canoe among the neighboring islands for the purpose of killing wild hogs and deer, and wished me to accompany him. Though my spirits were somewhat recruited by his society, the benefit of the fire, which I now enjoyed, and dressed provisions, my weakness and the soreness of my feet precluded me; therefore he set out alone, saying he would return in a few hours. The sky was serene and there was no prospect of any danger during a short excursion, seeing he had come nearly twelve leagues in safety in his canoe. But, when he had been absent about an hour, a violent gust of wind and rain arose, in which he probably perished, as I never heard of him more.

Thus, after having the pleasure of a companion almost three days, I was reduced to my former lonely state as unexpectedly as I had been relieved from it. Yet, through God's goodness, I was myself preserved from having been unable to accompany him, and I was left in better circumstances than those in which he had found me; for now I had about five pounds of pork, a knife, a bottle of gunpowder, tobacco, tongs, and flint, by which means my life could be rendered more comfortable. I was enabled to have fire, extremely requisite at this time, being the rainy months of winter. I could cut up a tortoise and have a delicate broiled meal. Thus, by the help of the fire and dressed provisions, through the blessing of God I began to recover strength, though the soreness of my feet remained. But I had, besides, the advantage of being able now and then to catch a dish of crayfish, which, when roasted, proved good eating. To accomplish this I made up a small bundle of old broken sticks, nearly resembling pitch-pine or candle-wood; and having lighted one end, waded with it in my hand up to the waist in water. The crayfish, attracted by the light, would crawl to my feet and lie directly under it; when, by means of a forked stick, I could toss them ashore.

Between two and three months after the time of losing my companion I found a small canoe while ranging along the shore. The sight of it revived my regret for his loss, for I judged that it had been his canoe; and from being washed up here, a certain proof of his having been lost in the tempest. But, on examining it more narrowly, I satisfied myself that it was one which I had never seen before.

Master of this little vessel, I began to think myself admiral of the neighboring seas as well as sole possessor and chief commander of the islands. Profiting by its use, I could transport myself to the places of retreat more conveniently than by my former expedient of swimming.

In process of time I projected an excursion to some of the larger and more distant islands, partly to learn how they were stored or inhabited and partly for the sake of amusement. Laying in a stock of figs and grapes, therefore, as also some tortoise to eat, and carrying my implements for fire, I put off to steer for the island of Bonacco, which is about four or five leagues long and situated five or six from Roatan.

In the course of the voyage, observing a sloop at the east end of the island, I made the best of my way to the west, designing to travel down by land, both because a point of rocks ran far into the sea, beyond which I did not care to venture in the canoe, as was necessary to come ahead of the sloop, and because I wished to ascertain something concerning her people before I was discovered. Even in my worst circumstances I never could brook the thoughts of returning on board of my piratical vessel, and resolved rather to live and die in my present situation. Hauling up the canoe and making it fast as well as I was able, I set out on the journey. My feet were yet in such a state that two days and the best part of two nights were occupied in it. Sometimes the woods and the bushes were so thick that it was necessary to crawl half a mile together on my hands and knees, which rendered my progress very slow.

When within a mile or two of the place where I supposed the sloop might lie I made for the water side and approached the sea gradually, that I might not too soon disclose myself to view; however, on reaching the beach, there was no appearance of the sloop, whence I judged that she had sailed during the time spent by me in traveling.

Being much fatigued with the journey, I rested myself against the stump of a tree with my face towards the sea, where sleep overpowered me. But I had not slumbered long before I was suddenly awakened by the noise of firing. Starting up in affright, I saw nine periaguas or large canoes full of men firing upon me from the sea; whence I soon turned about and ran among the bushes as fast as my sore feet would allow, while the men, who were Spaniards, cried after me, "O Englishman, we will give you good quarter." However, my astonishment was so great and I was so suddenly roused from sleep that I had no self-command to listen to their offers of quarter, which, it may be, at another time, in my cooler moments, I might have done. Thus I made into the woods, and the strangers continued firing after me to the number of 150 bullets at least, many of which cut small twigs of the bushes close by my side. Having gained an extensive thicket beyond reach of the shot, I lay close several hours until, observing by the sound of their oars that the Spaniards were departing, I crept out. I saw the sloop under English colors sailing away with the canoes in tow, which induced me to suppose she was an English vessel which had been at the Bay of Honduras and taken there by the Spaniards.

Next day I returned to the tree where I had been so nearly surprised, and was astonished to find six or seven shot in the trunk within a foot or less of my head. Yet through the wonderful goodness of God, though having been as a mark to shoot at, I was preserved.

After this I traveled to recover my canoe at the western end of the island, which I reached in three days, but suffering severely from the soreness of my feet and the scantiness of provision. This island is not so plentifully stored as Roatan, so that during the five or six days of my residence I had difficulty in procuring subsistence. And the insects were, besides, infinitely more numerous and harassing than at my old habitation. These circumstances deterred me from further exploring the island; and, having reached the canoe very tired and exhausted, I put off for Roatan, which was a royal palace to me compared with Bonacco, and arrived at night in safety.

Here I lived, if it may be called living, alone for about seven months after losing my North British companion. My time was spent in the usual manner, hunting for food and ranging among the islands.

Some time in June 1724, while on the small quay, whither I often retreated to be free from the annoyance of insects, I saw two canoes making for the harbor. Approaching nearer, they observed the smoke of a fire which I had kindled and, at a loss to know what it meant, they hesitated on advancing. What I had experienced at Bonacco was still fresh in my memory and, loath to run the risk of such another firing, I withdrew to my canoe, lying behind the quay, not above 100 yards distant, and immediately rowed over to Roatan. There I had places of safety against an enemy and sufficient accommodation for any ordinary number of friends.

The people in the canoes observed me cross the sea to Roatan, the passage not exceeding a gunshot over; and, being as much afraid of pirates as I was of Spaniards, approached very cautiously towards the shore. I then came down to the beach, showing myself openly; for their conduct led me to think that they could not be pirates, and I resolved, before being exposed to the danger of their shot, to inquire who they were. If they proved such as I did not like, I could easily retire. But before I spoke, they, as full of apprehension as I could be, lay on their oars and demanded who I was and whence I came. To which I replied that I was an Englishman and had run away from pirates. On this they drew somewhat nearer, inquiring who was there besides myself, when I assured them in return that I was alone. Next, according to my original purpose, having put similar questions to them, they said they had come from the Bay of Honduras. Their words encouraged me to bid them row ashore, which they did accordingly, though at some distance; and one man landed, whom I advanced to meet. But he started back at the sight of a poor, ragged, wild, forlorn, miserable object so near him. Collecting himself, however, he took me by the hand and we began embracing each other, he from surprise and wonder and I from a sort of ecstasy of joy. When this was over he took me in his arms and carried me down to the canoes, where all his comrades were struck with astonishment at my appearance; but they gladly received me and I experienced great tenderness from them.

I gave the strangers a brief account of my escape from Low and my lonely residence for sixteen months, the hardships I had suffered and the dangers to which I had been exposed. They stood amazed at the recital. They wondered I was alive and expressed much satisfaction at being able to relieve me. Observing me very weak and depressed, they gave me about a spoonful of rum to recruit my fainting spirits. But even this small quantity, from my long disuse of strong liquors, threw me into violent agitation and produced a kind of stupor, which at last ended in privation of sense. Some of the party, perceiving a state of insensibility come on, would have administered more rum, which those better skilled among them prevented; and, after lying a short time in a fit, I revived.

Then I ascertained that the strangers were eighteen in number, the chief of them named John Hope, an old man called Father Hope by his companions, and John Ford, and all belonging to the Bay of Honduras. The cause of their coming hither was an alarm for an attack from the sea by the Spaniards while the Indians should make descent by land and cut off the Bay; thus they had fled for safety. On a former occasion the two persons above named had for the like reason taken shelter among these islands and lived four years at a time on a small one named Barbarat, about two leagues from Roatan. There they had two plantations, as they called them; and now they brought two barrels of flour, with other provisions, firearms, dogs for hunting and nets for tortoises; and also an Indian woman to dress their provisions. Their principal residence was a small key about a quarter of a mile round lying near to Barbarat and named by them the Castle of Comfort, chiefly because it was low and clear of woods and bushes, so that the free circulation of the wind could drive away the pestiferous mosquitoes and other insects. Hence they sent to the surrounding islands for wood, water and materials to build two houses, such as they were, for shelter.

I now had the prospect of a much more agreeable life than I had spent during the sixteen months past. For besides having company, the strangers treated me with a great deal of civility in their way. They clothed me and gave me a large wrapping gown as a defense against the nightly dews until their houses were covered; and there was plenty of provisions. Yet after all they were bad society; and, as to their common conversation, there was little difference between them and pirates. However, it did not appear that they were now engaged in any such evil design as rendered it unlawful to join them or be found in their company.

In process of time and with the assistance afforded by my companions I gathered so much strength as sometimes to be able to hunt along with them. The islands abounded with wild hogs, deer and tortoise; and different ones were visited in quest of game. This was brought home, where instead of being immediately consumed it was hung up to dry in smoke, so as to be a ready supply at all times.

I now considered myself beyond the reach of danger from an enemy; for, independent of supposing that nothing could bring anyone here, I was surrounded by a number of men with arms constantly in their hands. Yet, at the very time that I thought myself most secure, I was very nearly again falling into the hands of pirates.

Six or seven months after the strangers joined me, three of them, along with myself, took a four-oared canoe for the purpose of hunting and killing tortoise on Bonacco. During our absence the rest repaired their canoes and prepared to go over to the Bay of Honduras to examine how matters stood there and bring off their remaining effects in case it were dangerous to return. But before they had departed we were on our voyage homewards, having a full load of pork and tortoise, as our object was successfully accomplished. While entering the mouth of the harbor, in a moonlight evening we saw a great flash and heard a report much louder than that of a musket proceed from a large periagua, which we observed near the Castle of Comfort. This put us in extreme consternation and we knew not what to consider; but in a minute or two we heard a volley from eighteen or twenty small arms discharged towards the shore and also some returned from it. Satisfied that an enemy, either Spaniards or pirates, was attacking our people, and being intercepted from them by periaguas lying between us and the shore, we thought the safest plan was trying to escape. Therefore, taking down our little mast and sail, that they might not betray us, we rowed out of the harbor as fast as possible towards an island about a mile and a half distant, trusting to retreat undiscovered. But the enemy, having either seen us before lowering our sail or heard the noise of the oars, followed with all speed in an eight- or ten-oared periagua. Observing her approach and fast gaining on us, we rowed with all our might to make the nearest shore. However, she was at length enabled to discharge a swivel, the shot from which passed over our canoe. Nevertheless we contrived to reach the shore before being completely within the range of small arms, which our pursuers discharged on us while landing.

They were now near enough to cry aloud that they were pirates and not Spaniards and that we need not dread them, as we should get good quarter; thence supposing that we should be the easier induced to surrender. Yet nothing could have been said to discourage me more from putting myself in their power. I had the utmost dread of a pirate; and my original aversion was now enhanced by the apprehension of being sacrificed by my former desertion. Thus, concluding to keep as clear of them as I could, and the Honduras Bay men having no great inclination to do otherwise, we made the best of our way to the woods. Our pursuers carried off the canoe with all its contents, resolving, if we would not go to them, to deprive us as far as possible of all means of subsistence where we were. But it gave me, who had known both want and solitude, little concern now that

I had company and there were arms among us to procure provision and also fire wherewith to dress it.

Our assailants were some men belonging to Spriggs, my former commander, who had thrown off his allegiance to Low, and set up for himself at the head of a gang of pirates, with a good ship of twenty-four guns and a sloop of twelve, both presently lying in Roatan harbor. He had put in for fresh water and to refit at the place where I first escaped; and, having discovered my companions at the small island of their retreat, sent a periagua full of men to take them. Accordingly they carried all ashore, as also a child and an Indian woman, the last of whom they shamefully abused. They killed a man after landing and, throwing him into one of the canoes containing tar, set it on fire and burnt his body in it. Then they carried the people on board of their vessels, where they were barbarously treated. One of them turned pirate, however, and told the others that John Hope had hid many things in the woods; therefore they beat him unmercifully to make him disclose his treasure, which they carried off with them.

After the pirates had kept these people five days on board of their vessels they gave them a flat of five or six tons to carry them to the Bay of Honduras, but no kind of provision for the voyage; and further, before dismissal, compelled them to swear that they would not come near me and my party, who had escaped to another island.

While the vessels rode in the harbor we kept a good lookout but were exposed to some difficulties from not daring to kindle a fire to dress our victuals, lest our residence should be betrayed. Thus we lived for five days on raw provisions. As soon as they sailed, however, Hope, little regarding the oath extorted from him, came and informed us of what had passed; and I could not, for my own part, be sufficiently grateful to Providence for escaping the hands of the pirates, who would have put me to a cruel death.

Hope and all his people except John Symonds now resolved to make their way to the Bay. Symonds, who had a Negro, wished to remain some time for the purpose of trading with the Jamaica men on the main. But, thinking my best chance of getting to New England was from the Bay of Honduras, I requested Hope to take me with him. The old man, though he would have gladly done so, advanced many objections, such as the insufficiency of the flat to carry so many men seventy leagues; that they had no provision for the passage, which might be tedious; and the flat was, besides, ill-calculated to stand the sea; as also that it was uncertain how matters might turn out at the Bay. Thus he thought it better for me to remain; yet, rather than I should be in solitude, he would take me in.

Symonds, on the other hand, urged me to stay and bear him company, and gave several reasons why I should more likely obtain a passage from the Jamaica men to New England than by the Bay of Honduras. As this seemed a fairer prospect of reaching my home, which I was extremely anxious to do, I assented; and, having thanked Hope and his companions for their civilities, I took leave of them and they departed.

Symonds was provided with a canoe, firearms and two dogs, in addition to his Negro, by which means he felt confident of being able to provide all that was necessary for our subsistence. We spent two or three months after the usual manner, ranging from island to island, but the prevalence of the winter rains precluded us from obtaining more game than we required.

When the season for the Jamaica traders approached, Symonds proposed repairing to some other island to obtain a quantity of tortoise-shell, which he could exchange for clothes and shoes; and, being successful in this respect, we next proceeded to Bonacco, which lies nearer the main, that we might thence take a favorable opportunity to run over.

Having been a short time at Bonacco, a furious tempest arose and continued for three days, when we saw several vessels standing in for the harbor. The largest of them was anchored at a great distance, but a brigantine came over the shoals opposite to the watering place and sent her boat ashore with casks. Recognizing three people who were in the boat by their dress and appearance for Englishmen, I concluded they were friends and showed myself openly on the beach before them. They ceased rowing immediately on observing me and, after answering their inquiries of who I was, I put the same question, saying they might come ashore with safety. They did so and a happy meeting it was for me.

I now found that the vessels were a fleet under convoy of the Diamond, man-of-war, bound for Jamaica; but many ships had parted company in the storm. The Diamond had sent in the brigantine to get water here, as the sickness of her crew had occasioned a great consumption of that necessary article.

Symonds, who had kept at a distance lest the three men might hesitate to come ashore, at length approached to participate in my joy, though at the same time testifying considerable reluctance at the prospect of my leaving him. The brigantine was commanded by Captain Dove, with whom I was acquainted, and she belonged to Salem, within three miles of my father's house. Captain Dove not only treated me with great civility and engaged to give me a passage home, but took me into pay, having lost a seaman, whose place he wanted me to supply. Next day, the Diamond having sent her long-boat ashore with casks for water, they were filled; and, after taking leave of Symonds, who shed tears at parting, I was carried on board of the brigantine.

We sailed along with the Diamond, which was bound for Jamaica, in the latter end of March 1725, and kept company until the first of April. By the providence of Heaven we passed safely through the gulf of Florida and reached Salem Harbor on the first of May, two years, ten months and fifteen days after I was first taken by pirates, and two years and nearly two months after making my escape from them on Roatan Island. That same evening I went to my father's house, where I was received as one risen from the dead.

1725   The Just Vengeance of Heaven,

exemplified in a journal found by Captain Mawson
(Commander of the ship Compton), on the Island
of Ascension, as he was homeward bound from
India. In which is a full and exact relation of the
author's being set on shore there by order of the
commodore and captains of the Dutch fleet, for a
most enormous crime he had been guilty of, and the
extreme and unparalleled hardships, sufferings and
misery he endured from the time of his being left
there to that of his death. All wrote with his own
hand and found lying near the skeleton.

BY ORDER of the commodore and captains of
the Dutch fleet I was set on shore the 5th of May, 1725, upon the
Island of Ascension, which struck me with great dread and uneasiness, having no hopes remaining but that the Almighty God would
be my protector. They put on shore with me a cask of water, a
hatchet, two buckets, an old frying pan, a fowling piece, teakettle,
tarpaulin, onions, pease, calivances,* rice, etc. I pitched my tent on
the beach and put some of my clothes on the sand near a rock, that
I might the better know where to find them again.

On Sunday, the 6th, I went to the top of a hill to see whether I
could discover any living creatures that were good for food, or any
greens whereby I might satisfy my raging hunger; but to my great
sorrow and confusion found nothing. I began then seriously to reflect
upon my misspent life and the justice of the Almighty, who had
thought fit to punish me in so exemplary a manner for the foul

* chick-peas

121

crimes I had committed; and sincerely wished that some unforeseen accident would put a period to those days which my malpractices had rendered miserable.

In the evening I returned to my tent with much difficulty, not being acquainted with the way, walking very melancholy along the sand, praying to God to further my escape from this desolate island. When I was arrived at my tent I fortified it with stones and covered it with a tarpaulin to screen me from the weather. About four or five o'clock I killed three birds, called boobies, which I skinned, salted and put in the sun to dry, and were the first birds I killed upon the island.

On the 7th in the morning I went to my water cask, which was full half a league from my tent, and broached it, by which I lost a great quantity of water; but afterwards turning the cask upon its head, with much difficulty I saved the rest. I then made a white flag out of one of my old shirts, which I placed on the top of a hill very near the sea, making my fowling piece as part of the standard, having nothing proper, it being rendered entirely useless for want of powder and shot; and employed myself for the remaining part of the evening in carrying stones to make my tent the stronger.

On the 8th early in the morning I took down my flag in order to place it on a hill the other side of the island. In my way thither I found a turtle, which I killed with the butt end of my piece, and returned back to my tent to rest my limbs, still flattering myself that some ship or other would speedily come to my deliverance. At night I removed my tent to the other side of the rock, being apprehensive of the destruction threatened by the moldering stones that were impending and unwilling to be accessory to my own death, trusting that the Omnipotent would still permit me to see better days. There was not a more commodious place on the whole island where I could have pitched my tent, which was no small satisfaction to one who labored under such deplorable circumstances. And what illustrated more the beauty of divine Providence, I still enjoyed my health. In the evening I killed more birds.

On the 9th in the morning I went to search for the turtle I had killed the day before, carrying my ax with me and split it down the back, it being so large that I could not turn it whole: cut some of the flesh from off the forefin which I carried to my tent, salted and dried in the sun; and having a second time screened my tent with a tarpaulin, I began to build my bulwark of stones about it.

On the 10th in the morning I took four or five onions and a few pease and carried them to the south part of the island to find a proper place for them, looking carefully all the way on the sand in order to discover a rivulet of water or the footsteps of some beast, by whose track I might in time find out the place where they drank. I also diligently sought after some herbage, and after a tedious walk over barren sands, hills and rock, almost inaccessible, I discovered a little purslane, part of which I eat for my refreshment. And being both weary and thirsty and having no water to drink, put the remainder into a sack which I had with me. In returning to my tent I found some other greens, but not knowing what they were did not dare to eat of them.

On the 11th in the morning I went into the country again and found some roots which had a taste not unlike that of potatoes, but was apprehensive they were not wholesome. I endeavored to make other necessary discoveries but to no purpose, which made me very disconsolate. Being almost choked with thirst, I returned to my tent, which was situated on the side of a hill, near which was another hill of a larger size, and adjacent to that a sandy bay. Upon the largest hill in the evening I boiled some rice, being much disordered in mind and body.

On the 12th in the morning I boiled some rice again and, having eat a small quantity, offered my prayers to God for a speedy deliverance. I then went towards the shore in hopes of seeing some friendly vessel approaching but found none; then walking on the beach till I was weary, seeing nothing but empty shells, returned to my tent. It was my usual custom to walk out every day in hopes of a distant view of ships upon the ocean, forced by stress of weather to make towards this desolate island to repair their damages. Afterwards I read till I was tired and employed the remainder of the day in mending my clothes and the chief part of the night in meditations and dismal reflections on my unhappy state.

On the 13th in the afternoon I put the onions, together with some pease and calivances, into the ground near my tent, to try if they would grow. The 13th early in the morning went in search of some sea fowls but found none. In my return back I found a turtle, with whose eggs and flesh I made an excellent dinner, boiling them with some rice, and buried the remainder that could not be immediately used, for fear the stench should offend me, the turtles being of so large a size that it is impossible for one man to eat a whole one whilst sweet. I also found some nests of turtle eggs, which I boiled, melting some of the fat of the turtle to mingle with them, burning the remainder of it in the night in a saucepan, not having a lamp. On the 14th after prayers I took my walk as usual, but finding nothing new returned to my tent, mended my clothes and continued writing this my journal. On the 15th, before I took my walk, I eat some rice and then followed my usual employment, viz. the catching of those birds called boobies. I afterwards amused myself with reading and then endeavored to ease my tortured mind by a calm repose. On the 16th and 17th I caught several of the before-mentioned birds, one of which I kept alive for the space of eight days, and then it died. On the 18th two more. On the 19th and 20th nothing worth note.

On the 22nd I went to the other side of the island to try to make some discovery, but to no purpose. In the afternoon made a line and fished from a rock near four hours but had no success. Judge then what anxiety of mind, what midnight horrors I must undergo, whilst the night is an emblem of my crimes and each clear day renews my punishment. At my return my tent was filled with smoke, and remembering my tinder-box was left upon the quilt, I hastened to the sea-side for a bucket of salt water and soon quenched the flames. I immediately returned God thanks that all my wearing apparel was not consumed, having lost nothing but a Banjan, a shirt, the corner of the quilt and my Bible singed; and intreating the Almighty to give me patience to bear with these my present afflictions.

The 23rd I spent the whole day in admiring the infinite goodness of Almighty God, who had so miraculously preserved the small remainder of my worldly treasure; and sometime tortured myself with the melancholy reflection of the inexpressible punishment my crimes deserved, well knowing the wages of sin was inevitable death and that my crime was of the blackest dye; nor could I possibly form an idea in my mind of a punishment that could make the least atonement for so great an offence.

On the 24th I walked to my flag and returned again to my tent, having caught one bird only, which I broiled on the embers and eat. On the 25th after breakfast I went to catch sea fowls, then returned to my tent and dried them. On the 26th I repeated my usual endeavors in order to descry some ships sailing on the ocean, but to my great disappointment found my hopes frustrated; neither could I find any fowls or eggs that day. On the 27th met with the same ill success. On the 28th I ascended a hill so high that had my foot slipped I had inevitably been lost, but found nothing remarkable nor any food wherewith to satisfy my craving appetite. On the 29th and 30th I met the same disappointment. On the 31st I secured the provisions I had before salted and laid in the sun to dry. From the 1st to the 4th of June it would be useless to relate how often I strained my eyes, misled with distant objects, which the earnest desire of my delivery made me believe to be some ships approaching. The roaring torrent of the ocean, intermixed with the sun's bright rays, presented to my view a yellow gloom, not much unlike the moon when part obscured. The streaks of the element and every cloud seemed to me as a propitious sail. But reflect how dreadful was the shock when from my tired eyes the object flew and left behind sad scenes of black despair. When I was put on shore the captain told me it was the time for ships to pass that way, which made me more diligent in my search. From the 5th to the 7th I never failed to take my usual walks, although in vain.

On the 8th my water grew so scanty that I had but two quarts left, and so thick that I was obliged to strain it through my handkerchief. I then, too late, began to dig in the middle of the island, and after digging six or seven foot deep could find no moisture. I then returned to my tent and endeavored to make a new well, but found it impracticable. After having gone a fathom deep my grief was inexpressible to find no water to relieve me from this desolate island, where there is nothing left that can long subsist a human creature. On the 9th, finding no manner of food, I spent my time in meditating on my future state, and to appease the wrath of Him I had so highly offended. On the 10th I boiled some rice in the little water I had remaining, having little hopes of any relief but perishing. I recommended my soul to the Supreme Governor of all things. But recollecting that I had formerly heard there was a well of water on this island, whilst I was able to walk I travelled over hills and rocks to the other side, being determined to leave no place unsearched.

After four tedious hours' search I began to grow thirsty, and the intolerable heat of the sun made my life a burden to me, but was resolved to proceed, though very faint, and almost dead with heat and excessive fatigue. But God of his gracious goodness led me to a hollow place in a rock, from whence issued forth a stream of fresh water.

It is impossible for me to express my great joy and satisfaction at so agreeable a sight. I drank to that excess as to almost hurt myself, then sat down by the current for some time and drank again. After which refreshment I returned to my tent, having no vessel to carry any water away with me. On the 11th in the morning, after returning my sincere and humble thanks to the Maker of all things, I took my teakettle, together with some rice and wood, to the place where the spring was, and there boiled my rice and eat it. On the 12th I boiled some rice for my breakfast and afterwards with much trouble carried two buckets of water to my tent. My shoes being worn out, the rocks cut my feet in a terrible manner, insomuch that I was often in danger of falling and breaking my buckets, without which I could not possibly live. On the 13th I went out to look for food but found none, but chanced to meet with some small weeds like birch, which I brought to my tent and boiled some rice for my dinner. After which I walked to the seashore to look out as usual, but my flattered hopes created in me a deep melancholy.

On the 14th and 15th I took my teakettle and some rice to the place above mentioned and after having refreshed myself returned to my tent, mended my clothes and spent the remainder of the day in reading. On the 16th I took my walk on the beach as usual and with as little success as ever, then returned to my tent to repose myself, where in the solemn gloom and dead of night I was surprised by an uncommon noise that surrounded me, of bitter cursing and swearing mixed with the most blasphemous and libidinous expressions I ever heard. My hair stood on end with horror and cold sweat trickled down my pallid cheeks. Trembling I lay, fearful to speak, least some vile fiend more wicked than the rest should make a prey of me, food fit for devils after my revolt from the just laws of Heaven. For no man living but would have thought the Devil had forsook his dark abode and come attended by infernal spirits to keep his hell on earth, being very certain there was not a human creature on the island except myself, having never observed the footsteps of a man since my being there.

Their discourse and their actions was such that nothing but devils could be guilty of, and one more busy than the rest kept such a continual whisking of his tail about my face that I expected nothing less than to be instantly torn to picces by them. Among the rest I imagined to have heard the voice of a friend of mine, with whom in this lifetime I was very conversant. Sometimes I imagined myself to be agitated by an evil spirit, which made me apply to the Almighty for succor and forgiveness of my sin. I believe it was near three o'clock in the morning before this hellish tumult ceased; and then, being quite weary and spent, I fell asleep. About seven I arose and returned God thanks for my safe deliverance, but still heard bitter shrieks near my tent, yet could see nothing. Then, taking my prayer-book, read those prayers proper for a person in my condition; at the same time heard a voice saying, "Bugger, Bugger." I cannot afford paper sufficient to set down every particular of this unhappy day.

On the 17th I fetched two buckets of water but dreaded the ensuing night and interceded that God would not suffer me to be haunted any more with evil spirits. I believe my petition was heard, not being troubled with them that night. The day following, an apparition came to me in the likeness of a man that I perfectly knew. He conversed with me and touched so sensibly in exposing the dia-bolical life of Nature, for which I was then a sufferer and fiercely repented of, that I wished the shock would have ended my miserable life.

On the 18th, after my devotions, I went to look out as usual and took my hatchet with me; but, finding myself disappointed, made all possible haste to the other part of the island, where to my great satisfaction I found a tree, which I believe Providence had thrown on shore in some measure to alleviate my present misery. I divided it with my hatchet, the whole being more than I was capable of carry-ing at once. I took part of it on my shoulder, and having carried it halfway to my tent, laid it down and rested myself thereon. Alas! how wretched is that man whose bestial pleasures have rendered him odious to the rest of his fellow-creatures and turned him loose on a barren island, Nebuchadnezzar-like, to herd and graze with beasts, till, loathsome to himself and spurned by man, he prays to end his wretched days! His guilty conscience checks him, his crimes flare him full in the face, and his misspent life calls aloud for ven-geance from on high. Such was the case of me, unhappy wretch, which proves the justice of All-gracious Heaven; and whilst I was resting my wearied limbs and seriously reflecting with myself the apparition again appeared to me, which gave me horror inexpressible.

His name I am unwilling to mention, not knowing what the conse-quence may be. He haunted me so long that he began to be familiar with me. After I had rested some time I carried my burden to the tent and returned to fetch the other part. On the 19th I went in the morning to see my colors, where for some time I fed my longing eyes with the ocean in hopes to see some ship approaching, but being denied so agreeable a prospect, when night came on I laid me down to rest and found no interruption by those evil voices which had before disturbed me, nor heard anything of them the next day, which made me hope the damned had reassumed their dismal caves. But when night came on, to my great surprise the restless apparitions grew more enraged and doubled their fury, tumbling me up and down so in my tent that in the morning my flesh appeared like an Egyptian mummy. The person I had formerly been acquainted with spoke several times to me, nor could I think he meant any harm, for when he was living we were as friendly as brothers. He was a soldier in Batavia. The saucepan was thrown down, the light put out and all my things left in a strange disorder. I then began to hope that if just Heaven did not think fit to end my perfect torments these punishments would serve as an atonement for my heinous crimes, in making use of man to satisfy my hellish and ungovernable lust, despising woman, which his hand had made a far more worthy object. My death begins to draw near, my strength decays and life is now become an insupportable burden.

On the 21st I lifted up my voice to Heaven, imploring mercy, then went abroad to search for daily food, but found the hand of Providence withdrawn. Insuperable grief and care oppressed my anxious soul. My senses were overwhelmed in depth of thought and every moment threatened my destruction. What pangs, alas! do wretched mortals feel who headstrong tread the giddy maze of life and leave the beauteous paths of righteousness, pleased to increase the number of the damned.

On the 22nd I took my buckets to fetch more water to my tent, which I could not accomplish till the day was far spent, being forced to travel in great misery barefooted over the rocks. The 23rd I spent my time in prayer, viewed with eager eyes the raging main, and from the 24th to the 27th incessantly continued my prayers. On the 28th in the morning I went to see whether my flag was standing, and after having humbled myself before God and desired his mercy and forgiveness I returned to my tent, took my bedding and some other necessaries and went to the middle of the island, where I fixed a new habitation in the cavity of a rock, it being much nearer the rivulet of water before mentioned. But, to my great astonishment, when I went to get some there was not one drop. I fetched a few eggs and boiled them in my teakettle with some of the water I had left, then went to the south side of the island, where there is a large hill of sand and rocks, upon which I found more purslane, which I gathered and put into my sack, together with some eggs. I fried both and eat them with a good appetite but was obliged to return lest I should be belated and not be able to find my new abode. Before I arrived at the rock I was almost dead for want of drink and my skin blistered in a terrible manner with the scorching heat of the sun, so that it was ready to peel from my flesh.

On the 29th I went to the top of the hill to look out for shipping. Afterwards, walking on the seashore, I perceived a piece of wood sinking in the sand. At first I took it for a tree but, coming nearer, I found it to be a cross. I embraced it in my arms and prayed fervently to God to deliver me. I believe there had been a man buried there belonging to some ship. In my return to my cave my feet were miserably cut with the sharp stones, that I had liked to have perished in coming down the hill. When I had got to my tent I rested and then went out again and in my walk found a piece of glass bottle with which I descended into a deep pit and found some water of brackish taste, so that my search proved of no effect. As I was returning to my cave in a disconsolate manner, bemoaning my wretched fate, I found some scattered wood, which I made up into a bundle and carried with me. I was no sooner come to my cavern but I heard a dreadful noise, resembling many coppersmiths at work. I went again to get some greens and eggs, with which I eat and drank the last of the water I had left.

On the 30th I went in search of water but could find none, and now all hopes were lost, a ghastly skeleton appeared to me with his hand uplifted, pointed to his throat and seemed to tell me I should die with drought.

July the 1st. The water being dried up in every place where I was used to get it, I was ready to perish with thirst, therefore offered up my prayers to God to deliver and preserve me as he did Moses and the children of Israel, by causing the water to gush out of the rock; esteeming their sufferings not to equal mine, seeing that I was not only bereft of food and raiment but banished from all human society and left to be devoured by the birds of prey, who infest this desolate island. Whilst I was rambling up and down in quest, ascending the top of a hill, I espied a great number of goats a-grazing at a distance, which I chased with all the speed I was able, but to my sorrow found they were too swift for me. I still followed them at a distance, in hopes of finding the place where they watered, when, after a long pursuit, I came to a pit five or six fathom deep, which I descended, but found no water. I believe by the goats frequenting it there is sometimes water, chiefly occasioned by the fall of rain. It is a miracle to me how the goats keep themselves alive in a dry season, since water is so scarce throughout the whole island. I should long before this have perished had it not been for a gallon of water that I had before preserved, with a full resolution not to make use of it unless compelled by dire necessity.

I afterwards went to the strand but could discover nothing that would be of any service to me. I then proceeded farther up the island and, having ascended a lofty hill, espied a greater number of goats, with their kids accompanying them, which I pursued with the like ill success. As there are so many on the island it is surprising I had not discovered them sooner, but believe they give their young ones suck in the holes of the rocks, till the sun has drawn the moisture thence, then sally out abroad in search of more. Here I found about two gallons of water more in a rock.

July the 4th I moved my things from my cave and went to the other side of the island to settle my abode, being sure there was no water on this side. I prayed to God to send a plenteous rain but, waiting from the 5th to the 8th, found my prayers ineffectual.

On the 9th, as I was walking pensively on the sand, half dead with thirst, I heard a dismal noise of cursing and swearing in my own language, during which time a cloud of birds obscured the light of the sun. On the 10th I ascended another steep hill but found nothing but a piece of wood, which I took with me to prop my new habitation. From the 11th to the 18th nothing remarkable happened. On the 19th I went out in search of water but found none. I found some birds eggs and brought them home to eat, using my water very sparingly, which lasted me only the next day. From the 21st to the 31st tongue can't express nor thought devise the wretched torments I endured.

From the 1st to the 3rd of August I walked out with my bucket and found a little water which the goats had left in the hollow of a rock, which I carried to my tent. On the 4th I went to the sands and found a broken oar and three or four small pieces of wood, which was very acceptable. Proceeding a little further, I espied something which appeared to me at a distance like a house and, calling to mind that I had heard the Portuguese formerly inhabited this island, made all the haste possible thither, and to my great surprise found it to be a white hollow rock, in the cavity of which were some nails and broken glass bottles. These were but of little service to me; therefore I took my wood and went home.

On the 5th I went abroad again to seek for food but returned overwhelmed with grief and want. On the 6th I went to the beach and observed three or four of the calivances which I had before set were coming up, but upon a strict inquiry found the vermin had devoured all the rest, which damped my former joy. There has not been half an hour's rain for the space of three months, neither is there one drop of water to be found on the whole island except what I have preserved in my cask, and if God of his great goodness does not speedily refresh the earth with a plentiful rain I must inevitably perish.

From the 8th to the 10th could find no water, therefore endeavored to prepare myself for that great and terrible change which I was sufficiently convinced was near at hand, begging for salvation through the merits of my blessed Lord and Savior Jesus Christ, who shall change our vile bodies and make them like unto his.

On the 11th I went to my tent on the strand, where I again heard a terrible noise, but could not tell from whence it proceeded. I was resolved to go up the hill to endeavor to inform myself, but saw nothing there but a cloud of birds (of which mention has been made before) and am therefore fully persuaded the noise was made by them.

From the 12th to the 17th I could get no water, though I lost no time in search after it. I had not now above six gallons left in my cask, which made me boil nothing and drink but little. On the 18th and 19th the same; but, being near sunset, and I a great distance from my tent on the other side of the island, I lost my way; therefore was compelled to lie all night between two rocks; where I was disturbed with so great a number of rats that I was afraid of being devoured by them, heartily wishing myself on the strand again.

On the 20th I prayed incessantly to Almighty God to send rain, then took my spade and dug two fathoms, but found no moisture. I viewed the motions of the heaven, in hopes to see some friendly cloud o'ercharged with water, that might disgorge itself upon the barren rocks and grant relief to me in this distress, but my hopes were vain; then wildly wandered over the sterile hills and begged the rocks and sands might cover me, deeming the goats that browsed about the island far happier than that man whose boundless lust had been the occasion of his suffering.

On the 21st I went rambling about the island with my scoop in hand but found no refreshment. The small quantity of water I had left being almost exhausted, I was forced to make water in my scoop and drank my urine, thinking it wholesomer than salt water. I was so extremely thirsty that my lips stuck together.

On the 22nd I took a walk (after having offered up my sacrifice of prayer) on the strand, where I found a turtle, which I killed, and drank near a gallon of the blood instead of water, and took some of the fat and eggs and fried them together and eat them. But the blood did not agree with me, neither did it quench my raging thirst, so that I was forced to drink a large quantity of my urine.

On the 23rd, having no hopes of finding any more water, I took some of the turtle blood, which I had killed the day before, after letting it settle all night, which I mixed with my own urine and boiled some tea in it, and thought it far preferable to raw blood. About four in the afternoon I returned to my tent, having nothing to drink but turtle blood, but presently was taken so violently with the flux, occasioned by the drinking it, that I could hardly stand. This was rather a satisfaction to me than a shock, hoping the sooner to end my miserable days, desiring nothing more. I with great difficulty got to my tent.

From the 24th to the 27th I had no thought of anything but death, continuing very ill, but prayed earnestly that God would put an end to my misery. The fowl's eggs no way relieving my thirst, I was therefore forced to boil me some more tea in my urine and settled blood, there being plenty of the turtles on the island. On the 28th at three in the morning I went out and killed one turtle with my hatchet and put the blood in my bucket. There was a great quantity of water in the bladder which I drank, it being much better than the blood, but it did not continue long upon my stomach. I then cut off some of the flesh and carried it to my tent. And, being very dry, I boiled some more tea in the turtle blood, but my stomach, being weak, required greater nourishment; and the blood, being bitter, proved a strong emetic and I could no longer retain it. On the 29th I could not sleep, occasioned by a drought and dizziness in my head, which afflicted me to that degree that I thought I should have run mad. I once more went to search for water but found none.

On the 30th I prayed to be dissolved and be with Christ, for most part of the day thinking my sufferings exceeded that of Job, I being debarred the pleasure of human conversation, sick and had no clothing; my actions unjustifiable, my torments inexpressible and my destruction unavoidable. I tried to compose myself after I had prayed to the Almighty for rain or that I might die before morning. In the afternoon I endeavored to get out of my tent but could not walk, I was so weak; therefore dressed some turtle eggs. I had some turtle flesh in my tent but it was not sweet, but was in such agony for want of water that tongue can't express. I caught three boobies and drank the blood of them.

On the 31st as I was crawling on the sand, for I could not walk three steps, I espied a turtle and, being so weak that I could not carry my buckets, I cut off his head with my hatchet, then laid myself on my side and sucked the blood as it ran out; afterwards put my arm into the body and plucked his bladder out, which I crawled away with to my tent, and put the water into a teakettle; then returned back and cut it up, in order to get the eggs, in doing of which the helve of my hatchet broke. This was still an addition to my misfortunes; but I got out some of the eggs, carried them to my tent and fried them, then boiled me some tea in my own urine, which was very nauseous to me but revived me very much.

September the 1st I killed another turtle; but having broke my hatchet I crushed it to pieces and raking among the entrails broke the gall, which made the blood very bitter; but was forced to drink it or should instantly have died. My thoughts were bent upon another world, and the ardent desire to meet approaching death both cherished and tortured my departing soul. Drank a quart of salt water and expecting nothing but an immediate dissolution, I prostrate, begging to taste the bitter cup; till, oppressed and harassed out with care, obtained some interrupted slumbers. On the 3rd I awoke and, finding myself something better, employed my time in fitting a helve to my hatchet and eat some of the turtle which I had killed the night before.

From the 5th to the 8th I lived upon turtle blood and eggs, from the 8th to the 14th I lingered on with no other food to subsist me.

I am become a moving skeleton, my strength is entirely decayed, I cannot write much longer. I sincerely repent of the sins I committed and pray, henceforth, no man may ever merit the misery which I have undergone. For the sake of which, leaving this narrative behind me to deter mankind from following such diabolical inventions. I now resign my soul to him that gave it, hoping for mercy in. . . .

1756   *The Remarkable Shipwreck of the Sloop Betsy*

on the coast of Dutch Guiana, as related in his own
true words by Philip Aubin, Commander.

ON THE 1st of August 1756 I set sail for Suri-
nam from Carlisle Bay in the island of Barbadoes. My sloop, of about
eighty tons' burden, was built entirely of cedar and freighted by
Messrs. Roscoe and Nyles, merchants of Bridgetown. The cargo consisted of provisions of every kind, and horses. The Dutch colony
being in want of a supply of those animals passed a law that no
English vessel should be permitted to enter there if horses did not
constitute part of her cargo. The Dutch were so rigid in enforcing
this condition that if the horses chanced to die on their passage the
master of the vessel was obliged to preserve the ears and hoofs of the
animals and to swear upon entering the port of Surinam that when
he embarked they were alive and destined for that colony.

The coasts of Surinam, Berbice, Demerara, Oronoko and all the
adjacent parts are low lands and inundated by large rivers which
discharge themselves into the sea. The bottom all along this coast is
composed of a kind of mud or clay, in which the anchors sink to the
depth of three or four fathoms and upon which the keel sometimes
strikes without stopping the vessel. The sloop being at anchor three
leagues and a half from the shore in five fathoms water, the mouth
of the Demarara river bearing SSW, and it being the rainy season,
my crew drew up water from the sea for their use, which was just as
sweet as good river water. The current occasioned by the trade winds

and the numerous rivers which fall into the sea carried us at the rate of four miles an hour towards the west and northwest.

In the evening of the 4th of August I was tacking about, between the latitude of ten and twelve degrees north, with a fresh breeze, which obliged me to reef my sails. At midnight, finding that the wind increased in proportion as the moon, then on the wane, rose above the horizon, and that my bark, which was deeply laden, labored excessively, I would not retire to rest till the weather became more moderate. I told my mate, whose name was Williams, to bring me a bottle of beer, and both sitting down, I upon a hen coop and Williams upon the deck, we began to tell stories to pass the time, according to the custom of mariners of every country. The vessel suddenly turned with her broadside to windward. I called to one of the seamen to put the helm aweather but he replied it had been so for some time. I directed my mate to see if the cord were not entangled. He informed me that it was not. At this moment the vessel swung round with her head to the sea and plunged, her head filled in such a manner that she could not rise above the surf, which broke over us to the height of the anchor stocks, and we were presently up to our necks in water. Everything in the cabin was washed away. Some of the crew, which consisted of nine men, were drowned in their hammocks without a cry or groan. When the wave had passed I took the hatchet that was hanging up near the fireplace, to cut away the shrouds to prevent the ship from upsetting, but in vain. She upset and turned over again, with her masts and sails in the water. The horses rolled one over the other and were drowned, forming altogether a most melancholy spectacle.

I had but one small boat, about twelve or thirteen feet long. She was fixed, with a cable coiled inside of her, between the pump and the side of the ship. Providentially for our perservation there was no occasion to lash her fast; but we at this time entertained no hope of seeing her again, as the large cable within her, together with the weight of the horses and their stalls entangled one among another, prevented her from rising to the surface of the water.

In this dreadful situation, holding by the shrouds and stripping off my clothes, I looked round me for some plank or empty box to preserve my life as long as it should please the Almighty, when I perceived my mate and two seamen hanging by a rope and imploring God to receive their souls. I told them that the man who was not resigned to die when it pleased his Creator to call him out of the world was not fit to live. I advised them to undress as I had done and to endeavor to seize the first object that could assist them in preserving their lives. Williams followed my advice, stripped himself quite naked and betook himself to swimming, looking out for whatever he could find. A moment afterwards he cried out, "Here is the boat, keel uppermost!" I immediately swam to him and found him holding the boat by the keel. We then set to work to turn her, but in vain. At length, however, Williams, who was the heaviest and strongest of the two, contrived to set his feet against the gunwale of the boat, laying hold of the keel with his hands, and with a violent effort nearly succeeded in overturning her. I, being to windward, pushed and lifted her up with my shoulders on the opposite side. At length, with the assistance of the surf, we turned her over, but she was full of water. I got into her and endeavored by the means of a rope belonging to the rigging to draw her to the mast of the vessel. In the intervals between the waves the mast always rose to the height of fifteen or twenty feet above the water. I passed the end of the rope fastened to the boat once round the head of the mast, keeping hold of the end. Each time that the mast rose out of water it lifted up both the boat and me. I then let go the rope and by this expedient the boat was three-fourths emptied; but having nothing to enable me to disengage her from the mast and shrouds, they fell down upon me, driving the boat and me again under water.

After repeated attempts to empty her, in which I was cruelly wounded and bruised, I began to haul the boat, filled with water, towards the vessel, by the shrouds; but the bark had sunk by this time to such a depth that only a small part of her stern was to be seen, upon which my mate and two other seamen were holding fast by a rope. I threw myself into the water with the rope of the boat in the mouth and swam towards them to give them the end to lay hold of, hoping, by our united strength, that we should be able to haul the boat over the stern of the vessel. We exerted our utmost efforts and at this moment I nearly had my thigh broken by a shock of the boat, being between her and the ship. At length we succeeded in hauling her over the stern but had the misfortune to break a hole in her bottom in this maneuver. As soon as my thigh was a little recovered from the blow, I jumped into her with one of the men and stopped the leak with a piece of his coarse shirt. It was extremely fortunate for us that this man did not know how to swim. Being unable to swim, he had not stripped, and had thus preserved his coarse shirt, a knife that was in his pocket, and an enormous hat, in the Dutch fashion. The boat, being fastened to the rigging, was no sooner cleared of the greatest part of the water than a dog of mine came to me, running along the gunwale. I took him in, thanking God for having thus sent provision for a time of necessity. A moment after the dog had entered, the rope broke with a jerk of the vessel, and I found myself drifting away. I called my mate and the other man, who swam to me. The former had fortunately found a small spare topmast, which served us for a rudder. We assisted the two others to get into the boat and soon lost sight of our ill-fated bark.

It was then four o'clock in the morning, as I judged by the dawn of day, which began to appear, so that about two hours had elapsed since we were obliged to abandon her. What prevented her from foundering sooner was my having taken on board about 150 barrels of biscuit, as many or more casks of flour, and 300 firkins of butter, all which substances float upon the water and are soaked through but slowly and by degrees. As soon as we were clear of the wreck we kept the boat before the wind as well as we could, and when it grew light I perceived several articles that had floated from the vessel. I perceived my box of clothes and linen, which had been carried out of the cabin by the violence of the waves. I felt an emotion of joy. The box contained some bottles of orange and lime water, a few pounds of chocolate, sugar, etc. Reaching over the gunwale of our boat, we laid hold of the box and used every effort to open it on the water, for we could not think of getting it into the boat, being of a size and weight sufficient to sink her. In spite of all our endeavors we could not force open the lid. We were obliged to leave it behind, with all the good things it contained, and to increase our distress we had by this effort almost filled our boat with water and had more than once nearly sunk her.

We, however, had the good fortune to pick up thirteen onions. We saw many more but were unable to reach them. These thirteen onions and my dog, without a single drop of fresh water or any liquor whatever, were all that we had to subsist upon. We were, according to my computation, above fifty leagues from land, having neither mast, sails, nor oars to direct us, nor any kind of articles besides the knife of the sailor who could not swim, his shirt, a piece of which we had already used to stop the leak in our boat, and his wide trousers. We this day cut the remainder of his shirt into strips, which we twisted for rigging, and then fell to work alternately to loosen the planks with which the boat was lined, cutting, by dint of time and patience, all round the heads of the nails that fastened them. Of these planks we made a kind of mast, which we tied to the foremast bench. A piece of board was substituted for a yard, to which we fastened the two parts of the trousers, which served for sails and assisted us in keeping the boat before the wind, steering with the topmast as mentioned before.

As the pieces of plank which we had detached from the inside of the boat were too short and were not sufficient to go quite round the edge, when the sea ran very high we were obliged, in order to prevent the waves from entering the boat, to lie down several times along the gunwale on each side, with our backs to the water and thus with our bodies to repel the surf, while the other, with the Dutch hat, was incessantly employed in bailing out the water; besides which the boat continued to make water at the leak, which we were unable entirely to stop.

It was in this melancholy situation, and stark naked, that we kept the boat before the wind as well as we could. The night of the first day after our shipwreck arrived before we had well completed our sail. It grew dark and we contrived to keep our boat running before the wind at the rate of about a league an hour. The second day was more calm. We each ate an onion, at different times, and began to feel thirst. In the night of the second day the wind became violent and variable and sometimes blowing from the north, which caused me great uneasiness, being obliged to steer south in order to keep the boat before the wind, whereas we could only hope to be saved by proceeding from east to west.

The third day we began to suffer exceedingly, not only from hunger and thirst but likewise from the heat of the sun, which scorched us in such a manner that from the neck to the feet our skin was as red and as full of blisters as if we had been burned by a fire. I then seized my dog and plunged the knife in his throat. I cannot even now refrain from weeping at the thought of it; but at the moment I felt not the least compassion for him. We caught his blood in the hat, receiving in our hands and drinking what ran over. We afterwards drank in turn out of the hat and felt ourselves refreshed. The fourth day the wind was extremely violent and the sea ran very high, so that we were more than once on the point of perishing. It was on this day in particular that we were obliged to make a rampart of our bodies in order to repel the waves. About noon a ray of hope dawned upon us but soon vanished.

We perceived a sloop, commanded by Captain Southey, which, like my vessel, belonged to the island of Barbadoes and was bound to Demerara. We could see the crew walking upon the deck, and shouted to them, but were neither seen nor heard. Being obliged by the violence of the gale, to keep our boat before the wind for fear of foundering, we had passed her a great distance before she crossed us— she steering direct south, and we bearing away to the west. Captain Southey was one of my particular friends. This disappointment so discouraged my two seamen that they refused to endeavor any longer to save their lives. In spite of all I could say one of them would do nothing, not even bail out the water which gained upon us. I had recourse to entreaties, fell at his knees, but he remained unmoved. My mate and I at length prevailed upon him by threatening to kill him instantly with the top mast, which we used to steer by, and to kill ourselves afterwards, to put a period to our misery. This menace made some impression on him and he resumed his employment of bailing as before.

On this day I set the others the example of eating a piece of the dog with some onions. It was with difficulty that I swallowed a few mouthfuls. But in an hour I felt that this morsel of food had given me vigor. My mate, who was of a much stronger constitution, eat more, which gave me much pleasure. One of the two men likewise tasted it, but the other, whose name was Cummings, either would not or could not swallow a morsel.

The fifth day was more calm and the sea much smoother. At daybreak we perceived an enormous shark, as large as our boat, which followed us several hours, as a prey that was destined for him. We also found in our boat a flying fish, which had dropped there during the night. We divided it into four parts, which we chewed to moisten our mouths. It was on this day that, when pressed with hunger and despair, my mate, Williams, had the generosity to exhort us to cut off a piece of his thigh to refresh ourselves with the blood and to support life. In the night we had several showers, with some wind. We tried to get some rain water by wringing the trousers which served us for a sail, but when we caught it in our mouths it proved to be as salt as that of the sea, the trousers having been so often soaked with sea water that they as well as the hat were quite impregnated with salt. Thus we had no other resource but to open our mouths and catch the drops of rain upon our tongues, in order to cool them. After the shower was over we again fastened the trousers to the mast.

On the sixth day the two seamen, notwithstanding all my remonstrances, drank sea water, which purged them so excessively that they fell into a kind of delirium and were of no more service to Williams and me. Both he and I kept a nail in our mouths and often sprinkled our heads with water to cool them. I perceived myself the better for these ablutions and that my head was more easy. We tried several times to eat of the dog's flesh, with a morsel of onion; but I thought myself fortunate if I could get down three or four mouthfuls. My mate always eat rather more than I could.

The seventh day was fine, with a moderate breeze and the sea perfectly calm. About noon the two men who had drank the sea water grew so weak that they began to talk wildly, like people who are lightheaded, not knowing any longer whether they were at sea or on shore. My mate and I were so weak too that we could scarcely stand on our legs or steer the boat in our turns, or bail the water from the boat, which made a great deal at the leak.

In the morning of the eighth day John Cummings died, and three hours afterwards George Simpson likewise expired. The same evening, at sunset, we had the inexpressible satisfaction of discovering the highlands on the west point of the island of Tobago. Hope gave us strength. We kept the head of the boat towards the land all night, with a light breeze and a current, which was in our favor. Williams and I were that night in an extraordinary situation, our two comrades lying dead before us, with the land in sight, having very little wind to approach it, and being assisted only by the current, which drove strongly to the westward. In the morning we were not, according to my computation, more than five or six leagues from the land. That happy day was the last of our sufferings at sea. We kept steering the boat the whole day towards the shore, though we were no longer able to stand. In the evening the wind lulled and it fell calm; but about two o'clock in the morning the current cast us on the beach of the island of Tobago, at the foot of a high shore, between little Tobago and Man-of-War Bay, which is the easternmost part of the island. The boat soon bulged with the shock. My unfortunate companion and I crawled to the shore, leaving the bodies of our two comrades in the boat, and the remainder of the dog, which was quite putrid.

We clambered as well as we could on all fours along the high coast, which rose almost perpendicularly to the height of three or four hundred feet. A great quantity of leaves had dropped down to the place where we were, from the numerous trees over our heads. These we collected and lay down upon them to wait for daylight. When it began to dawn we sought about for water and found some in the holes of the rocks, but it was brackish and not fit to drink. We perceived on the rocks around us several kinds of shellfish, some of which we broke open with a stone and chewed them to moisten our mouths.

Between eight and nine o'clock we were perceived by a young Carib, who was sometimes walking and at others swimming towards the boat. As soon as he had reached it he called his companions with loud shouts, making signs of the greatest compassion. His comrades instantly followed him and swam towards us, having perceived us almost at the same time.

The oldest, who was about sixty, approached us with the two youngest, whom we afterwards found to be his son and son-in-law. At the sight of us the tears flowed from their eyes. I endeavored by words and signs to make them comprehend that we had been nine days at sea, in want of everything. They understood a few French words and signified that they would fetch a boat to convey us to their hut. The old man took a handkerchief from his head and tied it round mine, and one of the young Caribs gave Williams his straw hat. The other swam round the projecting rock and brought us a calabash of fresh water, some cakes of cassava and a piece of broiled fish, but we could not eat. The two others took the two corpses out of the boat and laid them upon the rock, after which all three of them hauled the boat out of the water. They then left us, with marks of the utmost compassion, and went to fetch their canoes.

About noon they returned in their canoe, to the number of six, and brought with them, in an earthen pot, some soup which we thought delicious. We took a little, but my stomach was so weak that I immediately cast it up again. Williams did not vomit at all. In less than two hours we arrived at Man-of-War Bay, where the huts of the Caribs were situated. They had only one hammock, in which they laid me, and the woman made us a very agreeable mess of herbs and broth of *quatracas* and pigeons. They bathed my wounds, which were full of worms, with a decoction of tobacco and other plants. Every morning the man lifted me out of the hammock and carried me in his arms beneath a lemon tree, where he covered me with plantain leaves to screen me from the sun. There they anointed our bodies with a kind of oil to cure the blisters raised by the sun. Our compassionate hosts even had the generosity to give each of us a shirt and a pair of trousers, which they had procured from the ships that came from time to time to trade with them for turtles and tortoise shell.

After they had cleansed my wounds of the vermin they kept me with my legs suspended in the air and anointed them morning and evening with an oil extracted from the tail of a small crab, resembling what the English call the soldier crab, because its shell is red. They take a certain quantity of these crabs, bruise the ends of their tails and put them to digest in a large shell upon the fire. It was with this ointment that they healed my wounds, covering them with nothing but plantain leaves.

Thanks to the nourishing food procured us by the Caribs and their humane attention, I was able, in about three weeks, to support myself upon crutches, like a person recovering from a severe illness. The natives flocked from all parts of the island to see us and never came empty-handed, sometimes bringing eggs and at others fowls, which were given with pleasure and accepted with gratitude. We even had visitors from the island of Trinidad. I cut my name with a knife upon several boards and gave them to different Caribs to show them to any ships which chance might conduct to the coast. We almost despaired of seeing any arrive, when a sloop from Oronoko, laden with mules and bound to St. Pierre in the island of Martinique, touched at the sandy point on the west side of Tobago. The Indians showed the crew a plank upon· which my name was carved, and acquainted them with our situation. Upon the arrival of this vessel at St. Pierre, those on board related the circumstance. Several merchants of my acquaintance, who traded under Dutch colors, happened to be there; they transmitted the information to my owners, Messrs. Roscoe and Nyles, who instantly despatched a small vessel in quest of us. After living about nine weeks with this benevolent and charitable tribe of savages I embarked and left them, when my regret was equal to the joy and surprise I had experienced at meeting with them.

When we were ready to depart they furnished us with an abundant supply of bananas, figs, yams, fowls, fish and fruits; particularly oranges and lemons. I had nothing to give them as an acknowledgement of their generous treatment but my boat, which they had repaired, and used for occasionally visiting their nests of turtles. Being larger than their canoes, it was much more fit for that purpose. Of this I made them a present and would have given them my blood. My friend, Captain Young, assisted me to remunerate my benefactors. He gave me all the rum he had with him, being about seven or eight bottles, which I likewise presented to them. He also gave them several shirts and trousers, some knives, fishhooks, sailcloth for the boat, with needles and ropes.

At length after two days spent in preparations for our departure, we were obliged to separate. They came down to the beach to the number of about thirty men, women and children, and all appeared to feel the sincerest sorrow, especially the old man, who had acted like a father to me. When the vessel left the bay the tears flowed from our eyes, which still continued fixed upon them. They remained standing in a line upon the shore till they lost sight of us. As we set sail about nine o'clock in the morning, steering northeast, and as Man-of-War Bay is situated to the northeast point of the island, we were a long time in sight of each other. I still recollect the moment when they disappeared from my sight, and the profound regret which filled my heart. I feared that I should never again be so happy as I had been among them. I love them and will continue to love my dear Caribs as long as I live. I would shed my blood for the first of those benevolent savages that might stand in need of my assistance, if chance should ever bring one of them to Europe or my destiny should again conduct me to their island.

In three days we arrived at Barbadoes. I continued to have a violent oppression on my breast, which checked respiration, and was not yet able to go without crutches. We received from the whole island marks of the most tender interest and the most generous compassion. The benevolence of the inhabitants was unbounded. The celebrated Dr. Hilery, the author of a treatise on the diseases peculiar to that island, came to see me, with Dr. Lilihorn. They prescribed various remedies but without effect. Both Williams and myself were unable to speak without the greatest difficulty. Williams remained at Barbadoes but I, being more affected and less robust, was advised to return to Europe. In compliance with their advice I went to London, where I was attended by Doctors Reeves, Akenside, Schomberg and the most celebrated physicians in that metropolis, but I received scarcely any relief. At length, after I had been about a week in London, Dr. Alexander Russell, on his return from Bath, heard my case mentioned. He came to see me, and with his accustomed humanity promised to undertake my cure without any fee; but he candidly acknowledged that it would be both tedious and expensive. I replied that the generosity of the inhabitants of Barbadoes had rendered me easy on that head, entreating him to prescribe for me and thanking him for his obliging offers.

As he had practiced for a long time at Aleppo, he had there seen great numbers afflicted with the same malady as myself, produced by long thirst in traversing the deserts of Africa. He ordered me to leave town to enjoy a more wholesome air. I took a lodging at Homerton, near Hackney. There he ordered me to be bathed every morning, confining me to asses' milk as my only food, excepting a few new-laid eggs, together with moderate exercise and a ride on horseback every day. After about a month of this regimen he ordered a goat to be brought every morning to my bedside. About five o'clock I drank a glass of her milk, quite hot, and slept upon it. He then allowed me to take some light chicken broth, with a morsel of the wing. By means of this diet my malady was in great degree removed in the space of about five months, and I was in a state to resume any occupation I pleased. But my constitution has ever since been extremely delicate, and my stomach in particular very weak.

1765   The Melancholy Narrative

of the distressful voyage and miraculous deliverance
of Captain David Harrison, of the sloop Peggy of
New York, on his voyage from Fyal, one of the
western islands, to New York. Written by himself.

I WEIGHED anchor at New York on the
25th of August, 1765, and came to sail from Sandy Hook on the
27th with a cargo consisting of lumber, staves, beeswax and
fish. I proceeded on my intended voyage with a small breeze of
wind at SSW. Nothing remarkable occurred on the outward-bound
part of my passage, and I arrived safe at Fyal on the 5th of October
following, where I immediately addressed myself to the British consul
at that place and to his partner, pursuant to my instructions. After
clearing my ship in the customary mercantile course I got a cargo
of wine brandy for New York by the 22nd of October, which
I had no sooner completed than I went immediately on shore
for my letters and dispatches, apprehensive of the consequences of
coming on the coast of America in a single deck vessel in the winter
season, a time in which these seas are uncommonly dangerous.

Everything being ready by the 24th, I set sail about half
after eleven in the morning from Fyal, with a fine breeze of wind
at SE. At six o'clock in the evening the body of the island bearing
from me north, three leagues, I lost sight of land and began to flatter
myself with the hopes of a very expeditious voyage. On the
29th, however, matters put on quite a different aspect. The wind
blowing pretty fresh, my standing jib, a very old one indeed, was
split, and as we had no other on board we unbent and put it into as

good a condition as the nature of our circumstances would admit. The violence of the weather still continuing, we went under an easy sail, a double-reefed mainsail and jib. Nevertheless on Wednesday, the 6th of November, two pair of my foremost main shrouds on the larboard side were carried away, being old and unable to resist the severity of the weather. On this we immediately set up stoppers and got a runner and tackle as a support to the mast, lying to under a balanced mainsail as it blew extremely hard.

The next day the wind shifting to the WNW and blowing more violently, we wore ship and laid her head to the southward, but about eight o'clock in the morning my two fore main shrouds on the starboard side were carried away, which obliged us to get up another runner and tackle for the additional security of the mast. Till the 12th of November the weather was intolerably bad, the seas excessively heavy. The continued peals of thunder, joined to our incapacity of carrying any sail unless for a few hours, threw a horror over our situation which is not to be conceived by any but those who have unhappily experienced something like our circumstances.

On Tuesday, the 12th of November, the weather seemed more moderate, though the change did not carry the appearance of any great duration. And, indeed, next day, to our unspeakable mortification, it came on to blow as hard as ever at WNW, so that my forestay and foresheets were not only torn away but the foresail itself rent in pieces. And what added considerably to the loss was my not having any other to put in its place. In this situation we lay to as before under a balanced reefed mainsail, the impetuosity of the storm still continuing and the seas rolling mountains high, all of us expecting that the vessel would prove leaky as she strained inconceivably hard.

Scudding away, however, on the 16th or 17th under the square sail head about two in the morning, the tack unfortunately happening to give way, this sail was torn all to tatters, so that we were obliged to cut it from the yard and to heave to immediately under bare poles till the mainsail was balanced reefed. One misfortune is generally the forerunner of another. At least we found it so. For while we lay to in the same gale of wind which destroyed our square sail, the flying jib blew overboard from a new set of points although it was a new sail and made of topgallant duck. Notwithstanding all these accidents we made some little way at intervals under an easy sail till the 1st of December, when, being attacked by another violent gale in the latitude of 40 degrees 1 minute north, and longitude 58 degrees 37 minutes west from London, a dreadful sea broke two of my main chain-plates and shattered my foresail to such a degree as rendered it utterly unserviceable.

The only bit of canvas now left was the mainsail, which we backed and lay to, having no prospect whatever before us but what was pregnant with the bitterest distress. For the conflict which our vessel had so long maintained against waves and winds had by this time occasioned her to leak excessively; and our provisions were so much exhausted that we found it absolutely necessary to come to an immediate allowance of two pounds of bread a week for each person, besides a quart of water and a pint of wine a day. The alternative was really deplorable, between the shortness of our provisions and the wreck of our ship. If we contrived to keep the latter from sinking we were in danger of perishing with hunger, and if we contrived to spin out the former with a rigid perseverance of economy for any time, there was but little probability of being able to preserve our ship. Thus on either hand little less than a miracle could save us from inevitable destruction. If we had an accidental gleam of comfort on one hand, the fate with which the other so visibly teemed gave an instant check to our satisfaction and obscured every rising ray of hope with an instant cloud of horror and despair.

We met, indeed, a couple of vessels, one from Jamaica for London and another to Dublin from New York, who would have probably relieved us had there been a possibility in so severe a gale to open any communication from ship to ship. All they could do was to speak to us, a circumstance which the reader's own imagination must naturally suppose did not a little add to the misery of our situation. Disappointed of succor in this quarter, I was under a necessity of contracting the little allowance which had been lately settled for each man; and continued gradually lessening the quantity of provisions till every morsel was entirely exhausted and not above two gallons of dirty water remaining in the bottom of a cask. My poor fellows, who from incessant fatigue and a long want of necessaries were now reduced to a very weakly condition, began at last to grow impatient and seized on the cargo, naturally enough observing that the wine and brandy were the only things they had now remaining in the world. What gave me concern was the continual excess to which they drank and the continual course of execration and blasphemy which was occasioned by that excess. For my own part I abstained as much as possible from wine and very gladly husbanded the dregs of the water cask, which afterwards proved of infinite service to me and may be not improperly reckoned an essential means of my surviving a complication of the most affecting calamities.

Our vessel had been for some time tossed about at the mercy of the winds and waves when in the midst of our despair we were suddenly transported with the most extravagant sensations of joy by the discovery of a sail to the leeward the 25th of December, in the morning. Distress generally inspires the human mind with lively sentiments of devotion, and those who perhaps dispute or disregard the existence of a Deity at other times are ready enough in the day of adversity to think every advantageous turn in their affairs a particular exertion of the Divine benignity. It was, therefore, but natural for some of the people to think that the 25th of December was appointed for their preservation. Our thanksgivings, however, to Providence, though profoundly sincere, were not offered in any great form. We all crowded upon deck and hung out with our utmost expedition a proper signal of distress and about eleven o'clock had the unspeakable satisfaction to come near enough to the ship to engage her in conversation, to inform her of our distresses and to obtain from the captain an assurance of relief. Indeed the promised relief was but small; nevertheless the smallest to people in our circumstances was inestimable. It was to be nothing more than a little bread, which was all, as the captain assured me, that he could spare, as he himself was contracted in every other article. This, however, he said we should have as soon as he had finished an observation which he was taking, for it was now near twelve o'clock. Having no doubt but the captain would punctually perform his promise, I retired to rest myself in the cabin, being much emaciated with fasting and fatigue and laboring at the same time not only under a very dreadful flux but a severe rheumatism in my right knee. My sight also was considerably impaired, so that upon the whole I exhibited as striking a picture of misery as could possibly be painted to the eye of imagination.

I had not been many minutes in the cabin when my people came running down with looks of unutterable despair and informed me, in accents scarce intelligible, that the vessel was making from us as fast as she could and that there was nothing now left for us but inevitable destruction. I crawled up to the deck at this terrible intimation with the expedition I was master of and found, to my inexpressible affliction, that their account was but too true. The captain had taken the reefs out of his topsails and mainsail and, in less than five hours, having a fine breeze in his favor, was entirely out of sight. As long as my poor fellows could retain the least trace of him they hung about the shrouds or ran in a state of absolute frenzy from one part of the ship to the other. They pierced the air with their cries, increasing in their lamentations as he lessened upon their view and straining their very eyeballs to preserve him in sight, through a despairing hope that some dawning impulse of pity would yet induce him to commiserate our situation and lead him to stretch out the blessed hand of relief.

But alas! to what purpose did we exhaust our little strength in supplicating for compassion, or aggravate our own misfortunes with a fruitless expectation of such a change? The inexorable captain pursued his course without regarding us and steeled, as he undoubtedly must be, to every sentiment of nature and humanity, possibly valued himself not a little upon his dexterity in casting us off. Notwithstanding I must feel an everlasting indignation against this barbarous man for flattering people in our circumstances with promises which he never meant to fulfil, I shall not hang him up to universal detestation or infamy by communicating his name to the reader. If he is capable of reflection his own conscience must sufficiently avenge my cause and God grant that the pungency of that conscience may be my only avenger.

One instance of his cruelty I must not forbear to mention. At our first meeting I told him that neither I nor any of my men would desire a single morsel of his provisions provided he only took us out of our own wreck, in which we were every moment exposed to the mercy of the waves, as our leaks were continually increasing and the men declining in their strength in proportion as the necessity grew urgent to employ them at the pumps. This request he absolutely refused though the indulgence of it might, in any succeeding distress, have done him an essential service and could not possibly expose him to the least inconvenience.

My people, being thus unhappily cut off from all assistance where they were so fully persuaded of meeting with an instant relief, became now as much dejected with their disappointment as they grew formerly transported with their joy. A desperate kind of gloom sat upon every face. Accentuated by a resolution of holding out as long as we were able, we turned our thoughts upon a pair of pigeons and a cat, which we had not yet destroyed, and which were the only living animals on board besides ourselves. The pigeons we killed for our Christmas dinner and the day following made away with our cat, casting lots for the several parts of the poor creature, as there were no less than nine of us to partake of the repast. The head fell to my share; and, in all my days I never feasted on anything which appeared so delicious to my appetite. The piercing sharpness of necessity had entirely conquered my aversion to such food, and the rage of an incredible hunger rendered that an exquisite regale which on any other occasion I must have loathed with the most insuperable disgust. After the cat was entirely consumed my people began to scrape the barnacles from the ship's bottom; but the relief afforded from this expedient was extremely trivial, as the waves had beaten off the greatest number that were above water, and the men were infinitely too weak to hang over the ship's side to gather them. Their continued intoxication, however, seemed in some measure to keep up their spirits, though it hastened the destruction of their health, and every dawn of reflection was carried off in a storm of blasphemy and execration.

For my own part I imbibed the strongest aversion imaginable to wine. The complicated disorders under which I labored induced me to abstain from it at first and, as the men were perpetually heating it in the steerage, the smell of it became offensive to the last degree, so that I subsisted entirely on the dirty water which they had forsaken, half a pint of which, together with a few drops of Turlington's balsam, being my whole allowance for four and twenty hours. In this situation I patiently expected that destiny which I thought it utterly impossible to avoid. And had it not been for the pangs which I felt on account of my wife and family I should have longed for the moment of dissolution and rejoiced at the approach of that awful period which was to put an end to all my misfortunes.

When the reader comes to consider our total want of necessaries, that my vessel had been for some time leaky, that I myself was emaciated with sickness and had but one sail in the world to direct her; when he considers that the men were either too weak or too much intoxicated to pay a necessary attention to the pump; when he likewise considers the severity of the season, that it blew "black December," as Shakespeare phrases it; and is told that we had not an inch of candle nor a morsel of slush to make any, having long since eaten up every appearance of either which could be found; when the reader comes to consider all these things and is moreover informed that the general distress had deprived me of all command on board my own ship, he will scarcely suppose that I could sustain any new misfortune. Yet, such was the severity of my destiny that on the 28th of December (being then driven as far to the northward by a series of southerly winds as 41 or 42 north latitude) I was overtaken by a most dreadful storm at NW by N and NW and had my only remaining bit of canvas, the mainsail, torn entirely away, so that I was now become a wreck in the fullest sense of the expression. Death became so seemingly unavoidable that I even gave up hope, that last consolation of all the wretched, and prepared for an immediate launch into the dreadful gulf of eternity. Providence, however, thought proper to dispose of me otherwise; and, everlasting thanks to its infinite mercy, I am still alive to labor for the advancement of my little family.

To this period of my relation I have been able to proceed circumstantially from a reference to my journal. The remainder, as I grew from this time utterly unable to hold a pen, must be collected from my memory and from memorandums which I made at intervals with chalk, of the most remarkable occurrences. The reader will recollect that the last morsel of meat that we tasted was our cat on the 26th of December. On the 13th of January following, being still tossed about at the discretion of the sea and wind, my mate, at the head of all the people, came to me in the cabin, half drunk indeed but with looks so full of horror as partly indicated the nature of their dreadful purpose, and informed me that they could hold out no longer, that their tobacco was entirely exhausted, that they had eaten up all the leather belonging to the pump and even the buttons off their jackets, that now they had no chance in nature but to cast lots and to sacrifice one of themselves for the preservation of the rest. They therefore expected my concurrence to the measure and desired me to favor them with an immediate determination.

Perceiving them in liquor, I endeavored to soothe them from their purpose as well as I could, begged they would retire to rest and that in case Providence did not interpose in their favor by the next morning we would consult farther on the subject. Instead of regarding my request, however, they swore with a determined horror of execration that what was to be done must be done immediately and that it was indifferent to them whether I acquiesced or not, for although they had been so kind as to acquaint me with their resolution they would oblige me to take my chance as well as another man, since the general misfortune had leveled all distinction of persons.

As I had long expected some violence to myself from the excesses of their intoxication I had for some time taken to my arms to prevent a surprise. But alas! this was an idle precaution, as I was by no means able to repel force by force. Finding them, therefore, still deaf to my remonstrances, I told them they might pursue their own course but that I would on no account either give orders for the death of the person on whom the lot might fall nor partake by any means of so shocking a repast. To this they answered that they would not ask my consent to slaughter the victim; and as to eating or not eating, I might just follow the bias of my own inclination. So saying, they left me and went into the steerage but in a few minutes came back, informing me that they had each taken a chance for their lives and that the lot had fallen on a Negro who was part of my cargo. The little time taken to cast the lot and the private manner of conducting the decision gave me some strong suspicions that the poor Ethiopian was not altogether treated fairly. But on recollection I almost wondered that they had given him even the appearance of an equal chance with themselves. The miserable black, however, well knowing his fate was at hand, and seeing one of the fellows loading a pistol to dispatch him, ran to me begging I would endeavor to save his life. Unfortunately for him I was totally without power.

They therefore dragged him into the steerage, where, in less than two minutes, they shot him through the head. They suffered him to lie but a very little time before they ripped him open, intending to fry his entrails for supper, there being a large fire made ready for the purpose. But one of the foremast men, whose name was James Campbell, being ravenously impatient for food, tore the liver from the body and devoured it raw as it was, notwithstanding the fire at his hand where it could be immediately dressed. The unhappy man paid dear for such an extravagant impatience, for in three days after he died raving mad and was, the morning of his death, thrown overboard, the survivors, greatly as they wished to preserve his body, being fearful of sharing his fate if they ventured to make as free with him as with the unfortunate Negro.

The black affording my people a luxurious banquet, they were busy the principal part of the night in feasting on him and did not retire to rest till two in the morning. About eight o'clock next day the mate came to ask my orders relative to pickling the body, an instance of brutality which shocked me so much that I grasped a pistol and, mustering all the strength I was master of, I swore unless he instantly quitted the cabin I would send him after the Negro. Seeing me determined, he withdrew but muttered as he went out that the provision should be taken care of without my advice and that he was sorry he had applied to me, since I was no longer considered as master of the ship. Accordingly he called a council, where it was unanimously agreed to cut the body into small pieces and to pickle it after chopping off the head and fingers, which they threw overboard by common consent.

Three or four days after, as they were stewing and frying some steaks, as they called the slices which they cut from the poor Negro (for they stewed these slices first in wine and afterward either fried or broiled them), I could hear them say, "Damn him, though he would not consent to our having any meat let us give him some." And immediately one of them came into the cabin and offered me a steak. I refused the tender with indignation and desired the person who brought it, at his peril to make the offer a second time. In fact the constant expectation of death, joined to the miserable state to which I was reduced through sickness and fatigue, to say nothing of my horror at the food with which I was presented, entirely took away my desire of eating. Add also to this that the stench of their stewing and frying threw me into an absolute fever and that this fever was aggravated by a strong scurvy and a violent swelling in my legs. Sinking under such an accumulated load of afflictions and being, moreover, fearful, if I closed my eyes, that they would surprise and murder me for their next supply, it is no wonder that I lost all relish for sustenance. In reality, it would have been wonderful had I preserved the least; and therefore my abstinence is not altogether so meritorious a circumstance.

Notwithstanding the excesses into which my people ran, they nevertheless husbanded the Negro's carcass with the severest economy and stinted themselves to an allowance which made it last for many days. But when it was nearly expended I could hear them frequently consulting among one another on the most expedient course to provide another supply. The result of all these determinations was to destroy me before they ran any risk of destroying themselves. The reader will naturally suppose that if I slept little before I received any positive knowledge of their intention I slept still less when I became acquainted with their designs. In proportion as the Negro grew less, so in proportion my apprehensions were increased, and every meal which they sat down to I considered as a fresh approach to destruction.

In this manner matters went on till the 28th or 29th of January, when the mate, with more generosity than I could well expect from the nature of their late private consultations, came to me again at the head of the people, saying that the Negro had for some days been entirely eaten up and as no vessel had yet appeared to give us the most distant glimmer of relief there was a necessity for casting lots again, since it was better to die separately than all at once. They also told me that they did not doubt but what I was now hungry and would of course take my chance with them, as I had before done, when my situation was infinitely less desperate. I again attempted to argue with them and observed that the poor Negro's death had done them no service, as they were as greedy and as emaciated as ever. I therefore advised them to submit to the dispensations of Providence with temper and offered to pray with them for an immediate relief or an immediate eternity. The answer which they gave to this was that they were now hungry and must have something to eat and therefore it was no time to pray and if I did not instantly consent to cast lots they would instantly proceed without me.

Finding them thus inflexible and having but too much reason to suspect some foul proceedings unless I became a principal agent in the affair, I made a shift to rise up in my bed, ordered pen, ink and paper and called them all into the cabin. There were seven of us now left, and the lots were drawn in the same manner as the tickets are drawn for a lottery at Guildhall. The lot indeed did not fall on me but on one David Flatt, a foremastman, the only man in the ship on whom I could place any certain dependence. The shock of the decision was great and the preparations for execution were dreadful. The fire already blazed in the steerage and everything was prepared for sacrificing the wretched victim immediately. A profound silence for some time took possession of the whole company and would possibly have continued longer had not the unhappy victim himself, who appeared quite resigned, delivered himself to the following effect:

"My dear friends, messmates and fellow sufferers, all I have to beg of you is to dispatch me as soon as you did the Negro and to put me to as little torture as you can."

Then, turning to one James Doud (the man who shot the Negro), he said, "It is my desire that you should shoot me."

Doud readily, yet reluctantly, assented. The unhappy victim then begged a small time to prepare himself for death, to which his companions very cheerfully agreed, and even seemed at first unwilling to insist upon his forfeit of life, as he was greatly respected by the whole ship's company. A few draughts of wine, however, soon suppressed these dawnings of humanity. Nevertheless, to show their regard they consented to let him live till eleven the next morning, in hopes that the Divine goodness would, in the meantime, raise up some other source of relief. At the same time they begged of me to read prayers, promising to join me with the utmost fervency. I was greatly pleased with this motion and though but little able to go through a task of that kind I exerted all my strength and had the satisfaction to observe that they behaved with tolerable decency.

Fatigued with reading so much, I lay down almost ready to faint, yet could hear the whole ship's company talking to the wretched Flatt, hoping that the Deity would interpose for his preservation and assuring him though they never yet could catch or even see fish, they would at daybreak put out all their hooks again to try if anything could be caught to mitigate their distresses or to avert the severity of his sentence. Unhappily, however, the poor fellow, unable to stand the shock of his destiny, grew astonishingly deaf by midnight and was quite delirious by four in the morning. His messmates, discovering this alteration, debated whether it would not be an act of humanity to dispatch him immediately. But the first resolution to spare him till eleven visibly preponderating, they all retired to rest, except the person who was to take care of the fire. On all their excesses they were sensible of what importance it was to preserve the fire, and therefore never went to bed without leaving a sentinel to keep it up.

About eight o'clock the next morning, as I was ruminating in my cabin on the approaching fate of the poor fellow, who had now but three hours to live, two of my people came hastily down with looks full of the strongest expectation and, seizing my hands without saying a syllable, gave me no little apprehension that they intended to postpone his fate for some time and to sacrifice me in his stead. I was the more confirmed in this opinion as the unhappy man still continued out of his senses and on that account might be judged improper sustenance; especially as notwithstanding all their necessities they threw Campbell overboard through a fear of catching his infection. Fraught with a notion of this nature, I disengaged myself as well as I was able and, snatching up one of my pistols, resolved to sell my life as dearly as I could. The poor men, guessing at my mistake, with some difficulty told me that their behavior was not the effect of any ill intention but the actual consequence of their joy, that they had descried a sail to the leeward which appeared to be a large vessel and that she seemed to stand for us in as fair a direction as we could possibly wish. The rest of the crew came down immediately after their companions and confirmed the report of a sail, but with this material difference, that she seemed to bear off upon quite a contrary course.

It is impossible to describe the excess of my transport upon hearing that there was a sail at any rate in sight. My joy in a manner overpowered me and it was not without the utmost exertion of my strength that I desired them to use every expedition in making a signal of distress. Our vessel, indeed, itself was a most striking signal; but as there was a possibility for the ship in view to suppose that there was not a living creature on board I judged it absolutely expedient to prevent the likelihood of so dreadful a mistake. My poor men found my orders now so essential to their own preservation that I was obeyed with all imaginable alacrity and had frequently the inexpressible happiness to hear them jumping on the deck and crying out, "She nighs us, she nighs us, she is standing this way." The ship coming visibly nearer and nearer, my people now began to think of their unfortunate messmate Flatt, who was, however, utterly unable to receive any account of the deliverance which was so happily at hand. Nevertheless, in the midst of all their sympathy for his situation they proposed a can of joy and it was with the greatest difficulty that I could prevail on them to acknowledge the strong impropriety of such a motion in their present circumstances. I observed that if they appeared any way disguised with liquor the ship might probably decline to take us on board, and endeavored to convince them that their deliverance in a very great measure depended upon the regularity of this moment's behavior. My remonstrances had some effect and all but my mate, who had for a considerable time abandoned himself to a brutality of intoxication, very prudently postponed so untimely an instance of indulgence.

After continuing for a considerable time, eagerly observing the progress of the vessel and undergoing the most tumultuous agitation that could be created by so trying a suspense, we had at last the happiness to see a boat drop astern and row towards us full manned, with a very vigorous dispatch. It was now quite calm, yet the impatience with which we expected the arrival of the boat was incredible. The numberless disappointments we had met in the course of our unfortunate voyage filled us with an apprehension of some new accident that might frustrate all our hopes and plunge us again into an aggravated distress. Life and death seemed, in short, to sit upon every stroke of the oar; and as we still considered ourselves tottering on the very verge of eternity, the conflict between our wishes and our fears may be easily supposed by a reader of imagination. The boat at length came alongside; but our appearance was so ghastly that the men rested upon their oars and, with looks of inconceivable astonishment, demanded what we were. Having satisfied them in this point, they immediately came on board and begged we would use the utmost expedition in quitting our miserable wreck, lest they should be overtaken by any gale before they were able to recover their ship; at the same time, seeing me totally incapable of getting into the boat without assistance, they provided ropes by which I was quickly let down, and my people followed me with all the alacrity they possessed.

We were now just preparing to set off when one of my people cried out that the mate was still on board. In the general hurry every man's attention was engaged by the thought of his own preservation and it was almost a matter of wonder that anybody remembered the absence of the mate. He was, however, immediately called to, and, after some time, came to the gunnel in a seeming astonishment at such a number of people, the can of joy with which he had been busy having completely erased every idea of the preceding occurrences from his recollection. Having got him into the boat, we instantly put off and in about an hour came up to the ship, which was rather better than two miles from our wreck. We were received with a humanity on board that did the highest honor imaginable to the character of the captain. When we came alongside, he, together with his passengers and people, were upon deck from an equal mixture of compassion and curiosity. But our hollow eyes, shriveled cheeks, long beards and squalid complexions had such an effect upon them that the captain himself absolutely shook with horror as he was politely leading me to his cabin and generously thanking God for being made the instrument of my deliverance.

Before I proceed farther it is necessary to inform the reader of the person to whose benignity my people and I were indebted for our preservation. His name is Thomas Evers, he commands the ship Susanna in the Virginia trade and was now returning from Virginia to London, to the latter of which places his vessel belongs.

I had no sooner got on board the Susanna than, dropping on my knees against a hen coop on the deck, I poured out my soul in a strain of the sincerest gratitude to the great Author of all things for the abundance of his mercy, and in the fulness of my heart began also to express my sensibility to the captain for his readiness to assist the distressed; but it was much easier for the generous Evers to perform fifty good actions than to hear the just applause of one. He begged I would be silent on the subject, at least for that time, advised me to take a little rest and promised, if the weather proved any way moderate, he would lie by my wreck the whole night and try if there was not a possibility to save some of my clothes, assuring me at the same time that my people should be treated with every necessary attention.

I was now on board for three or four days when I found some little inclination to eat, the rest which I had taken during that interval giving me some distant dawnings of an appetite. I therefore hinted my desire to the captain, who had repeatedly applied to me from my first arrival to take a little food, and he immediately ordered some sego to be dressed, of which I ate without finding any relish whatever, my taste being rendered insensible, as I apprehend, from so long a discontinuance of sustenance. Next day I had a little chicken broth, which agreed tolerably well with the weakness of my stomach; but, having an occasion for a particular indulgence of nature, I thought I should have expired in performing it. The pain it gave me was excruciating to the last degree and the parts were so contracted, having never been once employed for a space of thirty-six or thirty-seven days, that I almost began to despair restoring them to their necessary operations. I was, however, at last relieved by the discharge of a callous lump about the size of a hen's egg, and enjoyed a tranquility of body, notwithstanding all my disorders, with which I was utterly unacquainted for some preceding weeks.

The undeviating tenderness which my worthy friend, the captain, showed to everything which concerned my case or tended to the recovery of my health in a short time made me able to crawl upon deck by myself, though at first I could by no means face the wind. The air, however, did me incredible service and I continued daily increasing my strength—when a fresh calamity seemed ready to involve us and threatened not only to fall upon my people and myself but in some measure through our means upon the worthy Captain Evers, his passengers and ship's company. The Susanna, it seems, a few days before she took me up had been attacked by a hard gale of wind in which, shipping a heavy sea, they lost four hogs, four or five hogsheads of fresh water, forty or fifty head of fowl, and twenty or thirty geese and turkeys. She had also lost her caboose and copper and, in short, had suffered not a little, although, to the infinite credit of her commander, these misfortunes did not occasion the least diminution of his humanity when he was called to by the voice of distress.

These losses, together with the unexpected addition of seven persons and a long series of very bad weather, obliged the captain to set all hands to an allowance, which was established at two pounds and a half of bread per week, a quart of water and half a pound of salt provisions a day for each man on board. In this situation, with a head wind, and the pumps continually at work, his ship being very leaky, we began to keep as good a lookout as possible in hopes of meeting with some vessel which might oblige us with a salutary supply of provisions. No vessel, however, encountered us but a Frenchman from Cape François, who stood as much in want of necessaries as ourselves.

Nevertheless, about the first or second of March we happily reached the Land's End and took in a pilot, who hailed us off Dartmouth, came on board and carried the ship into that harbor. There the captain and the passengers went on shore and gave me a most cordial congratulation on my arrival.

One circumstance I had almost forgot, though it was to me a very material one. After I had gained a little strength on board the Susanna I thought I might mess in common with the captain and passengers; but, indulging myself rather too freely on a roasted turkey, it threw me into a fever, at which the good-natured captain was so much affected that he took upon himself the office both of physician and nurse and kept me under a proper restraint in my food during the remainder of our voyage.

The next day my inconsiderate mate, Mr. Archibald Nicolson, who had so long wallowed, as I may say, in every mire of excess, having reduced himself by a continued intoxication to such a state that no proper sustenance would stay on his stomach, fell a martyr to his inebriety. Having a watch and some trinkets about him, which defrayed the expense of his funeral, he was decently interred. As to the rest of my people, the unhappy Flatt still continued out of his senses and there were but two of the whole six in a condition to do any duty from the time of our being taken up by Captain Evers till our arrival at Dartmouth.

1780   The Loss of H.M.S. Phoenix,

a true and lively account found in a letter of Lieutenant Archer, of the aforementioned ill-fated ship, written to his mother.

At sea, June 30, 1780

My dearest Madam,

I am now going to give you an account of our last cruise in the Phoenix; and must premise that, should any one see it beside yourself, they must put this construction on it—that it was originally intended for the eyes of a mother, and a mother only—as upon that supposition my feelings may be tolerated. You will also meet with a number of sea terms which if you do not understand, why, I cannot help you, as I am unable to give a sea description in any other words.

To begin then. On the 2nd of April, 1780 we weighed and sailed from Port Royal, bound for Pensacola, having two store-ships under convoy and to see safe in; then cruised off the Havana and the gulf of Mexico for six weeks. In a few days we made the two sandy islands that look as if they had just risen out of the sea or fallen from the sky; inhabited nevertheless by upward of three hundred Englishmen, who get their bread by catching turtles and parrots and raising vegetables, which they exchange, with ships that pass, for clothing and a few of the luxuries of life.

About the 12th we arrived at Pensacola without anything remarkable happening except our catching a vast quantity of fish, sharks, dolphins and bonettos. On the 13th sailed singly and on the 14th had a very heavy gale of wind at north, right off the land, so that we soon left the sweet place, Pensacola, a distance astern. We then looked into the Havana, saw a number of ships there and, knowing that some of them were bound round the bay, we cruised in the track. A fortnight, however, passed and not a single ship hove in sight to cheer our spirits. We then took a turn or two round the gulf but not near enough to be seen from the shore. Vera Cruz we expected would have made up happy but the same luck still continued; day followed day, and no sail. The dollar bag began to grow a little bulky, for everyone had lost two or three times and no one had won. This was a small gambling party entered into by Sir Hyde and ourselves. Everyone put a dollar into a bag and fixed on a day when we should see a sail, but no two persons were to name the same day and whoever guessed right first was to have the bag.

Being now tired of our situation and glad the cruise was almost out, for we found the navigation very dangerous owing to unaccountable currents, we shaped our course for Cape Antonio. The next day the man at the masthead, at about one o'clock in the afternoon, called out, "A sail upon the weather bow! Ha! Ha! Mr. Spaniard, I think we have you at last! Turn out all hands! Make sail! All hands give chase!" There was scarcely any occasion for this order, for the sound of a sail being in sight flew like wildfire through the ship and every sail was set in an instant, almost before the orders were given.

A lieutenant at the masthead, with a spyglass, called, "What is she?"

"A large ship studding athwart right before the wind. P-o-r-t! Keep her away! Set the studding sails ready!"

Up comes the little doctor, rubbing his hands. "Ha! Ha! I have won the bag."

"The devil take you and the bag. Look, what's ahead will fill all our bags."

Masthead again: "Two more sail on the larboard beam!"

"Archer, go up and see what you can make of them."

"Upon deck here. I see a whole fleet of twenty sail coming right before the wind."

"Confound the luck of it, this is some convoy or other. But we must try if we can pick some of them out."

"Haul down the studding sails! Luff! Bring her in the wind! Let us see what we can make of them."

About five we got pretty near them and found them to be twenty-six sail of Spanish merchantmen, under convoy of three line-of-battle ships, one of which chased us. But when she found we were playing with her (for the old Phoenix had heels) she left chase and joined the convoy which they drew up into a lump, and placed themselves at the outside. But we still kept smelling about till after dark. O for the Hector, the Albion and a frigate, and we should take the whole fleet and convoy, worth some millions! About eight o'clock perceived three sail at some distance from the fleet; dashed in between them and gave chase and were happy to find they steered from the fleet. About twelve, came up with a large ship of twenty-six guns.

"Archer, every man to his quarters! Run the lower deck guns out and light the ship up. Show this fellow our force. It may prevent his firing into us and killing a man or two."

No sooner said than done. "Hoa, the ship ahoy! Lower your sails and bring to instantly or I'll sink you." Clatter clatter went the blocks, and away flew all their sails in proper confusion.

"What ship is that?"

"The Polly."

"Whence came you?"

"From Jamaica."

"Where are you bound?"

"To New York."

"What ship is that?"

"The Phoenix."

Huzza, three times by the whole ship's company. An old grum fellow of a sailor standing close by me: "O damn your three cheers, we took you to be something else." Upon examination we found it to be as he reported and that they had fallen in with the Spanish fleet that morning and were chased the whole day and that nothing saved them but our stepping in between, for the Spaniards took us for three consorts and the Polly took the Phoenix for a Spanish frigate till we hailed them. The other vessels in company were likewise bound to New York.

Thus was I, from being worth thousands in idea, reduced to the old 4s. 6d. per day again; for the little doctor made the most prize money of us all that day by winning the bag, which contained between thirty and forty dollars, but this is nothing to what we sailors undergo.

After parting company we steered SSE to go round Antonio and so to Jamaica (our cruise being out) with our fingers in our mouths and all of us as green as you please. It happened to be my middle watch, and about three o'clock the man upon the forecastle bawls out, "Breakers ahead, and land upon the lee bow!" I looked out and it was so, sure enough. "Ready about! Put the helm down! Helm a lee!" Sir Hyde, hearing me put the ship about, jumped upon deck.

"Archer, what's the matter? You are putting the ship about without my orders!"

"Sir, 'tis time to go about. The ship is almost ashore. There is the land."

"Good God, so it is! Will the ship stay?"

"Yes, sir. I believe she will, if we don't make any confusion. She is all aback—forward now?"

"Well," says he, "work the ship. I will not speak a single word." The ship stayed very well.

"Then heave the lead! See what water we have!"

"Three fathom."

"Keep the ship away, WNW."

"By the mark three."

"This won't do, Archer."

"No sir, we had better haul more to the northward. We came SSE and had better steer NNW."

"Steady, and a quarter three."

"This may do, as we deepen a little."

"By the deep four."

"Very well, my lad, heave quick."

"Five fathom."

"That's a fine fellow! Another cast nimbly."

"Quarter less eight."

"That will do. Come, we shall get clear by and by."

"Mark under water five."

"What's that?"

"Only five fathom, sir."

"Turn all hands up. Bring the ship to an anchor, boy! Are the anchors clear?"

"In a moment, sir—all clear."

"What water have you in the chains now?"

"Eight, half nine."

"Keep fast the anchors till I call you."

"Ay, ay, sir, all fast."

"I have no ground with this line."

"How many fathoms have you out? Pass along the deep-sea line!"

"Ay, ay, sir."

"Heave away—watch! Bear away, veer away."

"No ground, sir, with a hundred fathom."

"That's clever! Come, Madam Phoenix, there is another squeak in you yet. All down but the watch! Secure the anchors again! Heave the maintopsail to the mast! Luff, and bring her to the wind!"

I told you, Madam, you should have a little sea jargon. If you can understand half of what is already said I wonder at it, though it is nothing to what is to come yet, when the old hurricane begins. As soon as the ship was a little to rights and all quiet again Sir Hyde came to me in the most friendly manner, the tears almost starting from his eyes. "Archer, we ought all to be much obliged to you for the safety of the ship, and perhaps of ourselves. I am particularly so; nothing but that instantaneous presence of mind and calmness saved her. Another ship's length and we should have been fast on shore. Had you been the least diffident or made the least confusion, so as to make the ship haulk in her stays, she must have been inevitably lost."

"Sir, you are very good but I have done nothing that I suppose anybody else would not have done in the same situation. I did not turn all the hands up, knowing the watch able to work the ship. Besides, had it spread immediately about the ship that she was almost ashore it might have created a confusion that was better avoided."

"Well," says he, " 'tis well indeed."

At daylight we found that the current had set us between the Colladora rocks and Cape Antonio and that we could not have got out any other way than we did; there was a chance, but Providence is the best pilot. We had sunset that day twenty leagues to the SE of our reckoning by the current.

After getting clear of this scrape we thought ourselves fortunate and made sail for Jamaica but misfortune seemed to follow misfortune. The next night, my watch upon deck too, we were overtaken by a squall, like a hurricane while it lasted; for though I saw it coming and prepared for it, yet when it took the ship it roared and laid her down so that I thought she would never get up again. However, by keeping her away, and clewing up everything, she righted. The remainder of the night we had very heavy squalls and in the morning found the mainmast sprung half the way through: one hundred and twenty-three leagues to the leeward of Jamaica, the hurricane months coming on, the head of the mainmast almost off, and at a short allowance; well, we must make the best of it. The mainmast was well finished but we were obliged to be very tender of carrying the sail.

Nothing remarkable happened for ten days afterward, when we chased a Yankee man of war for six hours, but could not get near enough to her before it was dark to keep sight of her; so that we lost her because unable to carry any sail on the mainmast. In about twelve days more made the island of Jamaica, having weathered all the squalls, and put into Montego Bay for water; so that we had a strong party for kicking up a dust on shore, having found three men of war lying there. We danced till two o'clock every morning, little thinking what was to happen in four days' time. For out of the four men of war that were there not one was in being at the end of that time and not a soul alive but those left of our crew. Many of the houses where we had been so merry were so completely destroyed that scarcely a vestige remained to mark where they stood. Thy works are wonderful, O God! Praised be thy holy name!

September the 30th, weighed; bound for Port Royal, round the eastward of the island. The Barbadoes and Victor had sailed the day before, and the Scarborough was to sail the next. Moderate weather until October the 2nd. Spoke to the Barbadoes, off Port Antonio, in the evening. At eleven at night it began to snuffle, with a monstrous heavy bill from the eastward. Close-reefed the topsails. Sir Hyde sent for me: "What sort of weather have we, Archer?"

"It blows a little and has a very ugly look. If any other quarter but this I should say we were going to have a gale of wind."

"Ay, it looks so very often here when there is no wind at all. However, don't hoist the topsails till it clears a little, there is no trusting any country."

At twelve I was relieved. The weather had the same rough look. However, they made sail upon her but had a very dirty night. At eight in the morning I came up again, found it blowing hard from the ENE with close-reefed topsails upon the ship and heavy squalls at times. Sir Hyde came upon deck. "Well, Archer, what do you think of it?"

"O, sir, 'tis only a touch of the times. We shall have an observation at twelve o'clock. The clouds are beginning to break. It will clear up at noon or else blow very hard afterward."

"I wish it would clear up, but I doubt it much. I was once in a hurricane in the East Indies, and the beginning of it had much the same appearance as this. So take in the topsails, we have plenty of searoom."

At twelve the gale still increasing, we wore ship, to keep as near midchannel between Jamaica and Cuba as possible. At one the gale increasing still. At two harder! Reefed the courses and furled them. Brought to under a foul mizzen staysail, head to the northward. In the evening no sign of the weather taking off, but every appearance of the storm increasing. Prepared for a proper gale of wind. Secured all the sails with spare gaskets. Good rolling tackles upon the yards. Squared the booms. Saw the boats all made fast. New lashed the guns. Double-breeched the lower deckers. Saw that the carpenters had the tarpaulins and battens all ready for hatchways. Got the topgallant mast down upon the deck. Jibboom and spritsail yard fore and aft. In fact everything we could think of to make a snug ship.

The poor devils of birds now began to find the uproar in the elements, for numbers both of sea and land kinds came on board of us. I took notice of some, which happening to be leeward, turned to windward like a ship, back and tack, for they could not fly against it. When they came over the ship they dashed themselves down upon the deck, without attempting to stir till picked up; and when let go again they would not leave the ship but endeavored to hide themselves from the wind.

At eight o'clock a hurricane. The sea roaring, but the wind still steady to a point. Did not ship a spoonful of water. However, got the hatchways all secured, expecting what would be the consequence should the wind shift. Placed the carpenters by the mainmast with broadaxes, knowing from experience that at the moment you may want to cut it away to save the ship an ax may not be found. Went to supper. Bread, cheese and porter. The purser frightened out of his wits about his bread-bags. The two marine officers as white as sheets, not understanding the ship's working so much; and the noise of the lower-deck guns, which by this time made a pretty screeching to the people not used to it. It seemed as if the whole ship's side was going at each roll. Wooden, our carpenter, was all this time smoking his pipe and laughing at the doctor. The second lieutenant upon deck and the third in his hammock.

At ten o'clock I thought to get a little sleep. Came to look into my cot. It was full of water, for every seam, by the straining of the ship, had begun to leak. Stretched myself, therefore, upon deck between two chests, and left orders to be called should the least thing happen. At twelve a midshipman came to me. "Mr. Archer, we are just going to wear ship, sir."

"O, very well, I'll be up directly. What sort of weather have you got?"

"It blows a hurricane."

Went upon deck, found Sir Hyde there. "It blows hard, Archer."

"It does indeed, sir."

"I don't know that I ever remember its blowing so hard before. But the ship makes a very good weather of it upon this tack, as she bows the sea; but we must wear her, as the wind has shifted to the SE and we were drawing right upon Cuba. So do you go forward and have some hands stand by. Loose the lee yardarm of the foresail, and when she is right before the wind, whip the clew garnet close up and roll up the sail."

"Sir, there is no canvas can stand against this a moment. If we attempt to loose him he will fly into ribbons in an instant and we may lose three or four of our people. She'll wear by manning the foreshrouds."

"O, I don't think she will."

"I'll answer for it, sir. I have seen it tried several times on the coast of America with success."

"Well, try it. If she does not wear we can only loose the foresail afterward."

This was a great condescension from such a man as Sir Hyde. However, by sending about two hundred people into the forerigging, after a hard struggle she wore. Found she did not make so good weather on this tack as on the other, for as the sea began to run across she had not time to rise from one sea before another dashed against her. Began to think we should lose our masts, as the ship lay very much along by the pressure of the wind constantly upon the yards and masts alone. For the poor mizzenstaysail had gone in shreds long before and the sails began to fly from the yards through the gaskets into coach whips. My God! To think that the wind could have such force!

Sir Hyde now sent me to see what was the matter between decks, as there was a good deal of noise. As soon as I was below, one of the marine officers calls out, "Good God, Mr. Archer, we are sinking! The water is up to the bottom of my cot."

"Pooh, pooh! As long as it is not over your mouth you are well off. What the devil do you make so much noise for?"

I found there was some water between decks but nothing to be alarmed at. We scuttled the deck and run it into the well. Found she made a good deal of water through the sides and decks. Turned the watch below to the pumps, though only two feet of water in the well; but expected to be kept constantly at work now, as the ship labored much, with scarcely a part of her above water but the quarterdeck, and that but seldom. "Come, pump away, my boys. Carpenters, get the weather chainpump rigged."

"All ready, sir."

"Then man it, and keep both pumps going."

At two o'clock the chainpump being choked, we set the carpenters at work to clear it, the two head pumps at work upon deck. The water gained upon us while our chainpumps were idle. In a quarter of an hour they were at work again and we began to gain upon it. While I was standing at the pumps cheering the people the carpenter's mate came running to me with a face as long as my arm. "O, sir! The ship has sprung a leak in the gunner's room."

"Go, then, and tell the carpenter to come to me, but do not speak a word to any one else. . . . Mr. Goodinoh, I am told there is a leak in the gunner's room. Go and see what is the matter but do not alarm anybody, and come and make your report privately to me."

In a short time he returned. "Sir, there is nothing there. It is only the water washing up between the timbers that this booby has taken for a leak."

"O, very well. Go upon deck and see if you can keep any of the water from washing down below."

"Sir, I have had four people constantly keeping the hatchways secure, but there is such a weight of water upon the deck that nobody can stand when the ship rolls."

The gunner soon afterward came to me, saying, "Mr. Archer, I should be glad to have you step this way into the magazine for a moment." I thought some damned thing was the matter, and ran directly. "Well, what is the matter here?" He answered, "The ground tier of the powder is spoiled and I want to show you that it is not out of carelessness in me in stowing it, for no powder in the world could be better stowed. Now, sir, what am I to do? If you do not speak to Sir Hyde he will be angry with me." I could not forbear smiling to see how easy he took the danger of the ship, and said to him, "Let us shake off this gale of wind first and talk of the damaged powder afterward."

At four we had gained upon the ship a little and I went upon deck, it being my watch. The second lieutenant relieved me at the pumps. Who can attempt to describe the appearance of things upon deck? If I was to write forever I could not give you an idea of it—a total darkness all above; the sea on fire, running as if it were in the Alps, or Peaks of Teneriffe (mountains are too common an idea); the wind roaring louder than thunder (absolutely no flight of imagination); the whole made more terrible, if possible, by a very uncommon kind of blue lightning; the poor ship very much pressed, yet doing what she could, shaking her sides and groaning at every stroke. Sir Hyde upon deck lashed to windward! I soon lashed myself alongside of him and told him the situation of things below, saying the ship did not make more water than might be expected in such weather and that I was only afraid of a gun breaking loose. "I am not in the least afraid of that," he said. "I have commanded her six years and have many a gale of wind in her. So that her ironwork, which always gives way first, is pretty well tried. Hold fast! That was an ugly sea. We must lower the yards, I believe, Archer. The ship is much pressed."

"If we attempt it, sir, we shall lose them, for a man can do nothing. Besides, their being down would ease the ship very little. The mainmast is a sprung mast. I wish it was overboard without carrying anything else along with it but that can soon be done, the gale cannot last for ever, 'twill soon be daylight now."

Found by the master's watch that it was five o'clock, though but a little after four by ours. I was glad it was so near daylight and looked for it with much anxiety. Cuba, thou art much in our way! Another ugly sea. Sent a midshipman to bring news from the pumps. The ship was gaining on them very much, for they had broken one of their chains, but it was almost mended again. News from the pump again. "She still gains! A heavy lee!" Backwater from leeward, halfway up the quarterback. Filled one of the cutters upon the booms and tore her all to pieces, the ship lying almost on her beam ends and not attempting to right again. Word from below that the ship still gained on them, as they could not stand to the pumps, she lay so much along. I said to Sir Hyde: "This is no time, sir, to think of saving the masts. Shall we cut the mainmast away?"

"Ay! As fast as you can."

I accordingly went into the weather-chains with a pole-ax, to cut away the lanyards. The boatswain went to leeward and the carpenters stood by the masts. We were all ready, when a very violent sea broke right on board of us, carried everything upon deck away, filled the ship with water, the main mizzenmasts went, the ship righted, but was in the last struggle of sinking under us.

As soon as we could shake our heads above water, Sir Hyde exclaimed: "We are gone at last, Archer! Foundered at sea!"

"Yes, sir, farewell, and the Lord have mercy upon us!"

I then turned about to look at the ship and thought she was struggling to get rid of some of the water but all in vain, she was almost full below. "Almighty God! I thank thee, that now I am leaving this world, which I have always considered as only a passage to a better. I die with a full hope of thy mercies through the merits of Jesus Christ, thy Son, our Savior!"

I then felt sorry that I could swim, as by that means I might be a quarter of an hour longer dying than a man who could not, and it is impossible to divest ourselves of a wish to preserve life. At the end of these reflections I thought I heard the ship thump and grind under our feet. It was so. "Sir, the ship is ashore!"

"What do you say?"

"The ship is ashore, and we may save ourselves yet!"

By this time the quarterdeck was full of men who had come up from below; and the "Lord have mercy upon us" flying about from all quarters. The ship now made everybody sensible that she was ashore, for every stroke threatened a total dissolution of her whole frame. We found she was stern ashore, and the bow broke the sea a good deal, though it was washing clean over at every stroke. Sir Hyde cried out, "Keep to the quarterdeck, my lads! When she goes to pieces it is your best chance!" Providentially got the foremast cut away, that she might not pay round broadside. Lost five in cutting away the foremast, by the breaking of a sea on board just as the mast went. That was nothing. Everyone expected it would be his own fate next. Looked for daybreak with the greatest impatience. At last it came, but what a scene did it show us! The ship upon a bed of rocks, mountains of them on one side, and Cordilleras of water on the other. Our poor ship grinding and crying out at every stroke between them, going away by piecemeal. However, to show the unaccountable workings of Providence, that which often appears to be the greatest evil proves to be the greatest good. That unmerciful sea lifted and beat us up so high among the rocks that at last the ship scarcely moved. She was very strong and did not go to pieces at the first thumping, though her decks tumbled in. We found afterward that she had beat over a ledge of rocks almost a quarter of a mile in extent beyond us, where, if she had struck, every soul of us must have perished.

I now began to think of getting on shore, so I stripped off my coat and shoes for a swim, and looked for a line to carry the end with me. Luckily I could not find one, which gave me time for recollection. "This won't do for me, to be the first man out of the ship, and first lieutenant. We may get to England again and people may think I paid a great deal of attention to myself and did not care for anybody else. No, that won't do. Instead of being the first I'll see every man, sick and well, out of her before me."

I now thought there was no probability of the ship's soon going to pieces, therefore had not a thought of instant death. Took a look round with a kind of philosophic eye, to see how the same situation affected my companions and was surprised to find the most swaggering, swearing bullies in fine weather now the most pitiful wretches on earth, when death appeared before them. However, two got safe; by which means, with a line, we got a hawser on shore and made fast to the rocks, upon which many ventured and arrived safe. There were some sick and wounded on board, who could not avail themselves of this method. We therefore got a spare topsail yard from the chains and placed one end ashore and the other on the cabin window, so that most of the sick got ashore this way.

As I had determined, so I was the last man out of the ship. This was about ten o'clock. The gale now began to break. Sir Hyde came to me and, taking me by the hand, was so affected that he scarcely able to speak. "Archer, I am happy beyond expression to see you on the shore, but look at our poor Phoenix!" I turned about, but could not say a single word, being too full. My mind had been too intensely occupied before. But everything now rushed upon me at once, so that I could not contain myself, and I indulged for a full quarter of an hour.

By twelve it was pretty moderate. Got some nails on shore and made tents. We found great quantities of fish driven up by the sea into holes of the rocks. Knocked up a fire and had a most comfortable dinner. In the afternoon we made a stage from the cabin windows to the rocks and got out some provisions and water, lest the ship should go to pieces, in which case we must all have perished of hunger and thirst. For we were upon a desolate part of the coast and under a rocky mountain that could not supply us with a single drop of water.

Slept comfortably this night, and the next day the idea of death vanishing by degrees, the prospect of being prisoners during the war, at the Havana, and walking three hundred miles to it through the woods, was rather unpleasant. However, to save life for the present we employed this day in getting more provisions and water on shore, which was not an easy matter, on account of decks, guns and rubbish and ten feet of water that lay over them. In the evening I proposed to Sir Hyde to repair the remains of the only boat left and to venture in her to Jamaica myself. And, in case I arrived safe, to bring vessels to take them all off. A proposal worthy of consideration. It was next day agreed to. Therefore we got the cutter on shore and set the carpenters to work on her. In two days she was ready and at four o'clock in the afternoon I embarked with four volunteers and a fortnight's provisions. Hoisted English colors as we put off from shore, and received three cheers from the lads left behind, and set sail with a light heart, having not the least doubt that, with God's assistance, we should come and bring them all off. Had a very squally night and a very leaky boat, so as to keep two buckets constantly bailing. Steered her myself the whole night by the stars and in the morning saw the coast of Jamaica, distant twelve leagues. At eight in the evening arrived at Montego Bay.

I must now begin to leave off, particularly as I have but half an hour to conclude. Else my pretty little short letter will lose its passage, which I should not like, after being ten days, at different times, writing it, beating up with the convoy to the northward, which is a reason that this epistle will never read well. For I never sat down with a proper disposition to go on with it. But as I knew something of the kind would please you, I was resolved to finish it. Yet it will not bear an overhaul, so do not expose your son's nonsense.

But to proceed—I instantly sent off an express to the Admiral, another to the Porcupine man of war, and went myself to Martin Bray to get vessels. For all their vessels here, as well as many of their houses, were gone to Moco. Got three small vessels and set out back again to Cuba, where I arrived the fourth day after leaving my companions. I thought the ship's crew would have devoured me on my landing. They presently whisked me up on their shoulders and carried me to the tent where Sir Hyde was.

I must omit many little occurrences that happened on shore, for want of time; but I shall have a number of stories to tell when I get alongside of you; and the next time I visit you I shall not be in such a hurry to quit you as I was the last, for then I hoped my nest would have been pretty well feathered. But my tale is forgotten.

I found the Porcupine had arrived that day and the lads had built a boat almost ready for launching that would hold fifty of them, which was intended for another trial, in case I had foundered. Next day embarked all our people that were left, amounting to two hundred and fifty. For some had died of the wounds they received in getting on shore, others of drinking rum, and others had straggled into the country. All our vessels were so full of people that we could not take away the few clothes that were saved from the wreck, but that was a trifle, since we had preserved our lives and liberty. To make short my story, we all arrived safe at Montego Bay and shortly after at Port Royal—in the Janus, which was sent on purpose for us, and were all honorably acquitted for the loss of the ship. I was made admiral's aid-de-camp, and a little time afterward sent down to St. Juan as captain of the Resource, to bring what were left of the poor devils to Blue Fields, on the Mosquito shore, and then to Jamaica, where they arrived after three months' absence, without a prize, though I looked out hard off Porto Bello and Cartha-gena. Found that in my absence I had been appointed captain of the Tobago, where I remain His Majesty's most true and faithful servant, and my dear mother's most dutiful son,

ARCHER

1809 Daniel Foss, of Elkton, Maryland:

being the journal of his shipwreck and sufferings, who was the only person saved from on board the brig Negociator, of Philadelphia, which foundered in the Pacific Ocean, and who lived five years on a small barren island, during which time he subsisted on seals and never saw the face of any human creature.

ON THE 3rd September, 1809, I sailed from Philadelphia in the capacity of a Mariner on board the brig Negociator, James Nicoll, master, bound to the northwest coast on a sealing voyage. On the 20th October we touched at the Cape of Good Hope, from which we shaped our course for the Friendly Islands. As we proceeded north the weather became extremely cold, so that we were obliged to exchange our clothing for such as were better calculated for the climate. On the 29th we passed several islands of ice, some of them nearly three miles in circuit and sixty or seventy feet in height. This exhibited a view which for a few moments was pleasing to the eye; but when we reflected on the danger, the mind was filled with horror, for were a ship to get against the weather side of one of these islands when the sea runs high she would be dashed to pieces in a moment.

On the 25th November we experienced a severe snowstorm; the brig's sails and rigging were all hung with icicles. At twelve at night it blew a gale of wind and at half past two we struck an island of ice. The consternation we were thrown into by this unexpected shock . . . created a scene of horror past description. As we found the brig in a sinking condition we hastily threw into the longboat such articles of provision as could easily be got at and embarked, twenty-one of us, in a small open boat many hundred leagues from land, in a cold climate, and some without jackets, hats or shoes, myself having on only one thin jacket and a pair of trousers. Five minutes after we left the brig she went down.

At daylight the storm having somewhat abated, we had a chance to examine our little stock of provision, which was found small indeed for so great a number of us—it consisted of about 50 wt. of beef, half a barrel of pork, a barrel of water and a small keg of beer. We made such arrangement for the preservation of our lives as our miserable situation would admit of. Every man was put on an allowance of provision and water and an equal proportion of time allotted each to labor at the oars and to bail the boat, each being eager to claim his turn, as it was considered the only means to preserve our lives from the inclemency of the weather. But these precautionary means did not avail, for in nine days from that of our leaving the brig our number was reduced to eight, and four of these so severely frostbitten as to be unable to stand on their feet. To add to our misfortune, our water froze to a solid cake of ice, which we were obliged to cut off in small pieces and dissolve in our mouths.

As we had more to fear from the intense cold than from the want of provision and water our great object from the time of our leaving the brig was to reach a warmer latitude, which on the 10th January we succeeded in doing. But alas! there were but three of us now remaining to experience a change of air, so eagerly wished for by my poor unfortunate companions. We continued to steer a southwest course, but without the most distant prospect of discovering land, although five weeks had now passed since we left the brig. Of our provisions we had eaten sparingly but we on the 20th consumed our last pound of pork. Death by starvation appeared now inevitable. Five days passed without being enabled to obtain anything to satisfy the cravings of nature. We cut even our shoes in small pieces, which, after soaking in fresh water, we devoured with the keenest appetite.

We were now driven to the awful alternative of casting lots between us to determine who should die for the sustenance of the remaining two. Famine frequently leads men to the commission of the most horrible excesses. Insensible on such occasions to the appeals of nature and reason, man assumes the character of a beast of prey. He is deaf to every representation and coolly meditates the death of his fellow creature. Fate had decreed that I should now myself take an active part in one of those shocking instances. Having cut a small piece of my jacket into three small detached pieces, one of which was marked with a brown thread, they were deposited in a hat, from which each with a trembling hand drew a piece. The unfortunate man on whom the lot fell had acted as surgeon on board of the brig. He appeared perfectly resigned to his fate. "My friends," said he to us, "I am a native of Norfolk, Virginia, where I expect I have now a wife and three children living. The only favor that I have to request of you is that should it please God to deliver either of you from your perilous situation and should you be so fortunate as to reach once more your native country that you would acquaint my unfortunate family with my wretched fate." He now requested of us a few moments to prepare himself for death, to which we could only reply with tears in our eyes, and which he employed in fervent prayer for himself, his family and for our speedy deliverance. Having now informed us that he was ready to die, by his direction an incision was made in a vein of his left arm, while we caught and drank the blood which streamed from the wound.

We soon had the satisfaction to see our unfortunate companion expire without a struggle. The body we cut into small slices and dried as well as we could in the sun. Such alone was our food for twelve days. We must notwithstanding have perished ere this had not the frequent rains supplied us with water, which we caught by wringing our clothes, when thoroughly wet, into a bucket with which we bailed our boat. With this short allowance, which was rather tantalizing than sustaining in our comfortless condition, I and my only surviving companion now began to grow so feeble as to be unable to support ourselves long on our legs, and our clothes being continually wet, our bodies were in many places chafed into sores.

It was now nine weeks since the unfortunate night of our shipwreck. Loathsome as our only food was, we had partaken of the last of it when on the morning of the 5th March we discovered breakers about two leagues ahead. We immediately shaped our course for them and about noon discovered what we supposed to be land, which on our nearer approach proved to be a small island of about two miles in circumference, bordered with high craggy rocks, against which the sea broke with a tremendous roar. The next morning we approached the island as near as the surf would admit of, and rowed quite around it without discovering any place where we could attempt a landing with any degree of safety. This circumstance was borne by us with much impatience, for we had flattered ourselves that we should meet with fresh water at the first part of the land we might approach, and being thus disappointed, our hunger and thirst at length drove us to the extremity of even attempting a landing where there was indeed no small prospect of our being dashed to pieces.

Accordingly, at half past four o'clock we steered the boat directly in for a point of rocks, but when within about an hundred yards of them the surf upset our boat. At this critical juncture I was so fortunate as to seize an oar, with which I was enabled to buoy myself up until the swell of the sea carried me within reach of a shelving rock, which I ascended before the return of another sea. Exhausted nature almost prevented my ascending the high and craggy rocks which lined the sea-broken shores of the whole island. Having at length reached the summit, I looked around for my unfortunate companion, but alas, nothing was discernible but broken fragments of the boat, which had been dashed into a hundred pieces by the surf and which were now floating upon the foaming waves. Thus did my dreary prospects become still more terrible when I beheld the last of my unfortunate shipmates perish in our most arduous struggle to preserve our existence.

As soon as I had recovered sufficient strength to walk, I proceeded in search of something to appease my hunger and thirst and to take a more minute view of the island. But, alas, what was my surprise when I discovered that the island was barren of everything that could serve to gratify the cravings of exhausted nature—not a shrub or plant did it produce of any kind, nor was there any appearance of springs of fresh water. This island, which had no appearance of having ever before been visited by any human creature, was about half a mile in length and a quarter in breadth, and composed wholly of rocks piled one upon another in all positions, as if tumbled together by the billows. As the succeeding night approached I sought a shelter beneath a large shelving rock, where on a little rockweed that I had collected I attempted to repose my wearied limbs. In the night there was a heavy shower of rain, some of which I attempted to catch by spreading my jacket on the rocks, but in this I was disappointed, for, having been so frequently soaked with sea water, it had become quite impregnated with salt. Thus I had no other resource but to lie with my mouth open and catch the drops of rain as they fell.

As soon as the day began to dawn I renewed my search for water and found some in the holes of the rocks; but it was brackish and not fit to drink. These holes I cleared out in hopes that I might thereby be enabled to obtain some fresh water in case of another shower, which I earnestly prayed for. I was this day so fortunate as to find a few small shellfish of the size of snails, which I chewed to moisten my mouth. As night approached I again sought my lodging place, where I laid myself down, but with little expectation of ever again witnessing the rising sun. I had now been three days without food, and to add to my misery my legs began to swell and my whole body became so bloated that, notwithstanding the little flesh I had left, my fingers with the smallest pressure upon my skin sunk to the depth of an inch, and the impression remained for some moments afterwards. My eyes felt as if buried in deep cavities. It was at this moment that the recollection of the peaceful home and the fond parents whom I had left brought on such a fit of melancholy that I lost all recollection for many hours. Toward morning I enjoyed for the first time upon the island an hour's sleep. Perspiration took place and I awoke as from a dream, free from delirium but painfully alive to all the horrors that surrounded me.

As soon as I felt myself a little revived by the cheering rays of the sun I once more crawled abroad in search of something to appease hunger and thirst, nor were my researches this day so fruitless as those on the preceding one. About noon I was so fortunate as to discover in the cavity of a rock a dead seal, which, although in quite a putrid state, proved a most seasonable relief—without this discovery I must inevitably have perished.

Of my newly discovered food I had the precaution to eat sparingly, to avoid the dangerous consequences which might have resulted from my voracity in the debilitated state to which my stomach was reduced. Such parts of the carcass as remained I conveyed to my lodging place and preserved for a future meal. The sun had now disappeared and I should have enjoyed a tolerable night's rest had not my insupportable thirst prevented it. But fortunately for me the night proved a rainy one, which, although it was attended with heavy thunder and the sharpest lightning that I had ever before witnessed, yet as the rain fell in torrents it not only served to cool my parched tongue and lips but enlivened my fondest hopes that the holes in the rocks, which I had cleared out for the purpose, would furnish me with a sufficient supply for present use.

Daylight, which I awaited with great impatience, at length appeared. I hastened to the several places which I had prepared for the reception of water and found them filled. How shall I express my extreme joy when after being for three days deprived of a draught of sweet water, I was unexpectedly blessed with a sufficient quantity to last me at least ten days?

I carefully covered over my rocky cisterns with flat stones to secure their precious contents from the salt water, which would not unfrequently break with such fury upon the rocks as to dash completely over the highest part of the island. Having done this, I again returned to the rock, which was the most comfortable shelter I could find on the island. I had here collected a considerable quantity of rockweed, which made me a tolerable bed. After partaking of a few mouthfuls of the seal (which was now nearly consumed) I stretched myself upon my bed and attempted to gain that repose which nature required. But those who have not experienced the irresistible power of sleep after long watching and excessive fatigue will scarcely believe that my repose was very short. This was nevertheless the case, my lodgings being of the most uncomfortable kind.

At daybreak I left my rocky cavern for the purpose of again searching among the rocks for something that might serve for food—a dead carcass in the most putrefied state would then have been considered by me of inestimable value. But what was my surprise, what my joy, to discover the rocks bordering upon the sea covered with seals to the number as I judged of many thousands! They appeared but little affrighted at my approach but, like a small freshwater turtle, creeped moderately into the sea as I advanced toward them. I ran directly for my oar, which had once been the means of preserving my life, and which was now to be used as a principal instrument by which my food was to be obtained. Indeed there was not another stick of wood of the smallest size upon the island. As I could easily approach them within reach of the oar, they fell an easy prey. A light blow upon the head was sufficient to stun them, so that they were easily taken. For the space of an hour I had fine sport, when they all (as if by a signal from their leader) instantly disappeared.

Fortunately for me I had through my many hairbreadth escapes preserved my knife, with which I proceeded to cut the throats of the seals that they might bleed. Their blood I drank as it oozed from their wounds and thought it most delicious. Indeed I at this moment think that nothing could have been to me, in my then weak and emaciated state, more beneficial, nothing could have contributed more to my immediate relief. Had I instead of thus satisfying myself with the blood partook as heartily of the flesh, the effects might have proved fatal to me.

On numbering the seals killed I found them to exceed one hundred: a not inconsiderable quantity of provision indeed for the consumption of one man. But so valuable did I esteem the acquisition, so sensible was I of the value of provision to me at this critical moment, that had the stay of the seals and my strength admitted of it, it is probable that I should not have spared one of them. Indeed I never made use of an eighth part of the number then destroyed. Having skinned about a dozen of the largest of them I cut them in thin pieces and spread them upon the rocks to dry.

Having been thus unexpectedly provided with provision and water (for which I did not forget to return thanks to that Being through whose mercy I had been so miraculously preserved), a more comfortable shelter next demanded my attention. As I despaired of ever meeting with an opportunity that would enable me to quit this dreary island, I strove to reconcile myself to my situation as well as I could and to employ my thoughts upon things that might serve to contribute to my convenience and comfort, I accordingly now projected a scheme of forming for myself as tolerable a dwelling as my situation and the materials for building would admit of. I fixed upon a convenient spot upon the highest part of the island, being the only place inaccessible to the waves in tempestuous weather. As I had not yet fully recovered my strength and as the building was to be constructed of such detached parts of rocks as I could manage, and they to be removed by bodily strength, I made but slow progress—it was indeed four weeks before I got my house completed and rendered waterproof. It was sufficiently spacious, containing three apartments, one for the deposit of provision, one to lodge in, and another an occasional retreat from foul weather or the heat of the sun. It was built in form of a sugar loaf, the walls of which were three feet thick, the whole of which I covered with dry rock weed.

Having thus completed my hut, I saw the importance of keeping some kind of reckoning of time, without which I was sensible that I should soon lose all knowledge of the day of the week and not be enabled to distinguish one from another. But how was a reckoning to be kept, since I had neither pen, ink or paper? As I recollected that I possessed nothing brought with me but my jackknife and oar, it occurred to my mind that with the assistance of the former some kind of journal might be kept upon the latter. For this purpose I scraped the broad end of the oar and prepared it for the reception of such notches and characters as formed a kind of calendar, by which I was enabled at all times to determine the day of the week and month. Although I was thus doomed to spend my days in solitude,

I never failed to pay due regard to the Sabbath. As the only mode of worship that I could adopt, I carved a short hymn appropriate to my situation on the oar, which I never failed to chant on the Sabbath.

The seals whose unexpected appearance had afforded me such seasonable relief and in a great measure dissipated my fears of starvation I was happy to find were very frequently in the habit of visiting the island. Not a week passed but I destroyed more or less of them. As my clothing had become much tattered and torn, I made me a complete suit of their skins; but for the want of proper management they became so dry and hard that I could wear them only occasionally. As I lost my hat in my attempt to effect a landing, of a part of my flannel shirt I made me a convenient cap.

The frequent rains continued to supply me with a sufficiency of water, which lodged in the holes of the rocks, of which there were many. But as they were subject to be filled with salt water when there was a heavy sea I found it necessary to prepare something for its reception in my hut. But how was a vessel to be formed, since I was in possession of no instrument by which one could be wrought? I at length hit upon a plan of forming a hollow in as large a stone as I could conveniently convey to my house. By an incessant pounding and grinding with smaller stones, in less than five weeks I completely effected my object.

Thus I rendered my lonely situation as comfortable as could be expected. After the first year I became still more reconciled to my wretched situation. I continued to make such improvements in and about my dwelling as my helpless situation would admit of. The second year I barricaded my hut with a wall twenty feet square and ten feet in height. I was nearly two months in performing this work, and as it completely defended my dwelling from the high winds and the spray of the sea I did not conceive my time misspent. I erected likewise near my house a pillar of rocks and stones of about thirty feet in height. The foundation was formed of as large rocks as I could conveniently work in, and upon these less ones were laid, from which I made use of still smaller ones until I approached the top. The object of its erection was to enable me to discover from its peak any vessel that might perchance pass the island. And that they might discover me I made a flag of my waistcoat, which, affixed to an end of the oar, I occasionally erected from the summit of this rocky mass.

In the month of June, of the third year of my solitary confinement to the island, I descried a sail passing to the leeward but at too great a distance to discover me. The very appearance of this sail afforded me the greatest satisfaction. It convinced me of a fact that I had before in a degree doubted: that these seas were sometimes visited by navigators and that I might sometime or other be so fortunate as to be discovered by them.

In the month of March, of the fourth year of my confinement, I experienced one of the most tremendous storms that perhaps was ever before witnessed by man. It commenced at about nine in the evening with the approach of black clouds and a high wind from the southwest, which at ten increased to a hurricane, attended with incessant peals of thunder and flashes of the sharpest lightning that I had ever before witnessed. The sea, agitated by the wind, dashed with such force against the island that I was not without my apprehensions for its safety. Over every part, except the little eminence on which my habitation was erected, it made a fair breach. It was now I saw the importance of the building which enclosed my lonely hut, without which I am confident the latter could never have withstood the force of the wind and I probably should have been crushed beneath its ruins, for had I attempted to have sought shelter elsewhere I should have been swept into the sea.

It is frequently remarked that the wind that blows no one any good is indeed an evil one—but in the present instance I was happy to find that this was not the case. In the morning, the storm having subsided, I was not a little agreeably surprised to find the rocks covered with flying fish, among which there were many of the largest size. This was indeed a treat to one who had been nearly four years confined to one particular kind of food. I picked many of them up in less than half an hour, which I split and cured in the sun after the manner of cod. In visiting the southwest part of the island a few hours after, my surprise was again excited by the appearance of an enormous dead whale which the sea had thrown high and dry upon the rocks. And what added to my astonishment: I discovered a harpoon (of the common form) buried in its bowels, with a few fathoms of new line attached thereto. Thus was my hopes again revived that I should finally meet with an opportunity to quit the desolate island. The situation of the whale rendered it probable that these seas were frequented by whalemen, although this whale might have been struck many hundred leagues to windward.

As I had now made sure of at least a year's provision, I employed my time in sketching upon my oar minutes of the most remarkable incidents that had attended me since I quit the peaceful shores of America. This I rendered as intelligible as possible, the letters being of the smallest kind. A dozen letters were a day's work for me. And lest it should be my hard fortune never to meet with the long-wished-for opportunity to return to my friends, the last year of my residence upon the island I engraved or notched upon the broad end of the oar an account of my ill fate, thinking that it might in some future day fall into the hands of someone who might possibly visit the island and who would give the information requested. The following is a copy of the engraving:

This is to acquaint the person into whose hands this oar may fall that Daniel Foss, a native of Elkton, in Maryland, one of the United States of America, and who sailed from the port of Philadelphia in 1809 on board the brig Negociator, bound to the Friendly Islands, was cast upon this desolate island the February following, where he erected a hut and lived a number of years, subsisting on seals—he being the last who survived of the crew of said brig, which ran foul of an island of ice and foundered on the 26th November, 1809.

Said Foss earnestly requests that information of his fate and that of his shipmates may be made known to their friends in America.

The oar which had proved so serviceable to me in my destitute situation, and which now contained a record of my own fate and that of my shipmates, I spared no pains to preserve. As it was the only substitute for a flagstaff that I could procure, to secure it from the weather I made a covering of sealskins for it. When it could be spared I never failed to keep it erected upon the summit of my rocky observatory, with the flag attached to it, that notice might be given to any vessel that might pass within view of the island of its being inhabited. Nor was this wise plan finally without its desired effect.

Having been considerably indisposed for two or three days previous to that of my happy deliverance, I did not arise until late in the morning, when, ascending my observatory as I was accustomed to do, it is impossible for me to describe my feelings on discovering a ship with topsails aback, nearly within hail of the island! That I might be discovered I swung my cap in the air and jumped from rock to rock and soon had the satisfaction of seeing them looking at me with their spyglasses. I now made every motion I possibly could indicative of my distressed situation, which they answered by pointing to an extreme point of the island. Thither I hastened and discovered their boat (which I had not before noticed) with three men attempting a landing. After making several unsuccessful attempts, by their motions they signified to me that they must return to the ship without being enabled to effect their object! But at the greatest risk of my life I was determined not to let this opportunity to quit the desolate island pass unimproved. I seized my oar and with it plunged headlong through the foaming surf and was unaccountably successful in reaching the boat, which conveyed me immediately on board the ship.

The ship proved to be the Neptune, Captain Call, of New York, to which port she was bound from Batavia. The captain declared that he should have passed the island unnoticed, had he not observed my flag, which he conceived erected as a signal of distress. By contrary winds the Neptune had been driven far out of her course, otherwise she would not have fell in with the island, which Captain Call could not find laid down in any map or chart whatever. My being finally relieved by a vessel bound to my own country was indeed a fortunate circumstance. But from my very odd appearance the captain and crew at first could hardly credit my being one of their countrymen. My clothing was in a very tattered condition and my beard more than a foot in length. My much regarded oar, on which I had wrought so much, was viewed by all on board as a very great curiosity, which I have since my return presented to the keeper of the Philadelphia Museum, where it is lodged for the inspection of the curious. We had a quick and pleasant passage to New York, from whence I returned to my friends in Maryland, from whom I had been more than six years absent.

1826   The Sufferings of Miss Ann Saunders,

who, being shipwrecked in the Atlantic Ocean, was
so far reduced by hunger and thirst as to be driven
to drink the blood of her fiancé, for the preservation
of her own life.

FOR THE information of such of my readers as
may be unacquainted with the fact, it may not be unimportant that
I commence the narrative of my recent unparalleled sufferings with
stating that I am a native of Liverpool, where I was born in June,
1802, of reputable parents; who, although as regarding worldly riches
were ranked with the poorer class, yet succeeded in bestowing on me
what I now and ever shall conceive a legacy of more inestemable
worth, to wit: an education sufficient to enable me to peruse the
sacred Scriptures, whereby I was early taught the importance of attending to the concerns of my soul. At an early age I had the misfortune to lose my father—but, young as I was, the irreparable loss made
a deep and lasting impression upon my mind. By this melancholy
and unexpected event my poor mother was left a widow with five
helpless children and without the means of contributing but a scanty
pittance to their support. The three oldest were in consequence put
out into respectable families in the neighborhood, where I have reason to believe we were treated with as much tenderness as young
children generally are who are bound out under similar circumstances.
When I had arrived to the age of eighteen I was persuaded to take
up my abode with a widowed aunt, with whom I remained until
sometime in October, 1825. It was while with my aunt that I became
first acquainted with that peculiarly unfortunate youth, James Frier,

of whose wretched and untimely fate I shall hereafter have a sad occasion to speak.

While with my aunt I also became intimately acquainted with a Mrs. Kendall, the wife of Captain John Kendall, a lady of pious and amiable disposition and who, I believe, was very deservedly respected by all who had the pleasure of her acquaintance. It was by the very strong solicitations of this lady (and those of the unfortunate youth above mentioned) that I consented to accompany her with her husband on their passage from Liverpool to St. John, New Brunswick, in the fall of 1825.

It was early in the morning of the 10th November that I took an affectionate leave of my mother and sisters and embarked with Mrs. Kendall, whose companion I was to be, and bid adieu for the first time to the shores of my native land. The wind was favorable, but it being the first time in my life that I had ever adventured more than half a mile on the ocean, I was confined to my berth the first three days after we left port. But, becoming more accustomed to the motion of the vessel, I soon regained my health and spirits and from this moment enjoyed a pleasant passage, without any very remarkable occurrence attending us until we reached St. John, the port of our destination.

On the 18th January, 1826, Captain Kendall having obtained a cargo of timber and made every necessary preparation for our departure, we set sail for Liverpool with a favorable wind and with the prospect and joyful expectations of an expeditious passage. On board of the ship were twenty-one souls, including Mrs. Kendall and myself. Many of the seamen were married men and had left in Europe numerous families dependent on them for support. Alas! poor mortals, little did they probably think, when they bid their loving companions and their tender little ones the last adieu, that it was to be a final one and that they were to behold their faces no more in this frail world! But we must not charge an infinitely wise and good God foolishly, who cannot err, but orders every event for the best.

We enjoyed favorable weather until about the 1st February, when a severe gale was experienced, which blew away some of the yards and spars of our vessel and washed away one of the boats off the deck and severely wounded some of the seamen. Early in the morning ensuing, the gale having somewhat abated, Mrs. Kendall and myself employed ourselves in dressing the wounds of the poor fellows that were most injured while those who had escaped injury were employed in clearing the deck of the broken spars, splicing and disentangling the rigging. So that in a few hours they were enabled again to make sail, and with the pleasing hope that they should encounter no more boisterous and contrary winds to impede their passage. But in this they were soon sadly disappointed, for on the 5th they were visited with a still more severe gale from ESE, which indeed caused the sea to run mountains high. The captain gave orders to his men to do everything in their power to do, for the safety of our lives. All sails were clewed up and the ship hove to, but the gale still increasing, about noon our vessel was struck by a tremendous sea, which swept from her decks almost every moveable article and washed one of the seamen overboard, who was providentially saved. A few moments after, the whole of the ship's stern was stove in. This was only the beginning of a scene of horrid calamities, doubly horrible to me, who had never before witnessed anything so awful.

While the captain and officers of the ship were holding a consultation on deck what was best to be done for the preservation of our lives, Mrs. Kendall and myself were on our knees on the quarterdeck, engaged in earnest prayer.

The ensuing morning presented to our view an aspect the most dreary. The gale seemed to be increasing with redoubled vigor. Little else was now thought of but the preservation of our lives. Exertions were made by the crew to save as much of the ship's provisions as was possible, and by breaking out the bow port they succeeded in saving fifty or sixty pounds of bread and a few pounds of cheese, which were stowed in the main top; to which place Mrs. Kendall and myself were conveyed, it being impossible for us to remain below, the cabin being nearly filled with water and almost every sea breaking over us. The night approached with all its dismal horrors. The horizon was obscured by black and angry-looking clouds, and about midnight the rain commenced falling in torrents, attended with frightful peals of thunder and unremitting streams of lightning.

Daylight returned, but only to present to our view an additional scene of horror. One of the poor seamen, overcome by fatigue, was discovered hanging lifeless by some part of the rigging. His mortal remains were committed to the deep. As this was the first instance of entombing a human body in the ocean that I had ever witnessed, the melancholy scene made a deep impression on my mind, as I expected such eventually would be my own life.

At 6 A.M. our depressed spirits were a little revived by the appearance of a sail standing toward us; which proved to be an American, who remained in company with us until the next morning; when, in consequence of the roughness of the sea, being unable to afford us any assistance, they left us.

It would be impossible for me to attempt to describe the feelings of all on board at this moment, on seeing so unexpectedly vanish the pleasing hope of being rescued by this vessel from our perilous situation. As the only human means to prolong our miserable existence a tent of spare canvas was erected by the ship's crew on the forecastle, and all on board put on the short allowance of a quarter of a biscuit a day. On the 8th February, the gale still continuing, a brig was seen to leeward but at a great distance, and in the afternoon the same brig (as was supposed) was seen to the windward. Captain Kendall ordered a signal of distress to be made and we soon had the satisfaction to see the brig approach us within hail and inquire very distinctly how long we had been in that situation and what we intended to do. But night approaching and the gale still prevailing to that degree that no boat could have floated in the water, we saw no more of the brig.

All on board were now reduced to the most deplorable state imaginable. Our miserable bodies were gradually perishing and the disconsolate spirits of the poor sailors were overpowered by the horrible prospects of starving without any appearance of relief.

February the 11th another vessel was discovered at the northward and the signal of distress again made, but without any effect, as she did not alter her course and was soon out of sight. We had now arrived at an awful crisis. Our provisions were all consumed and hunger and thirst began to select their victims. On the 12th James Clarke, a seaman, died of no other complaint (as was judged) than the weakness caused by famine; whose body, after reading prayers, was committed to the deep. And on the 22nd John Wilson, another seaman, fell a victim of starvation.

As the calls of hunger had now become too importunate to be resisted, it is a fact, although shocking to relate, that we were reduced to the awful extremity to attempt to support our feeble bodies a while longer by subsisting on the dead body of the deceased. It was cut into slices, then washed in salt water and, after being exposed to and dried in the sun, was apportioned to each of the miserable survivors, who partook of it as a sweet morsel. From this revolting food I abstained for twenty-four hours, when I too was compelled by hunger to follow their example. We eyed each other with mournful and melancholy looks, as may be supposed of people perishing with hunger and thirst; by all of whom it was now perceived that we had nothing to hope from human aid but only from the mercy of the Almighty, whose ways are unsearchable.

On the 23rd J. Moore, another seaman, died, whose body was committed to the deep after taking therefrom the liver and heart, which was reserved for our subsistence. And in the course of twelve days after (during which our miseries continued without any alleviation) the following persons fell victims to fatigue and hunger, to wit: Henry Davis and John Jones, cabin boys; James Frier, cook; Alexander Kelly, Daniel Jones, John Hutchinson and John James, seamen. The heart-piercing lamentations of these poor creatures dying for the want of sustenance was distressing beyond conception. Some of them expired raving mad, crying out lamentably for water. Hutchinson, who, it appeared, had left a numerous family in Europe, talked to his wife and children as if they were present, repeating the names of the latter, and begged of them to be kind to their poor mother who, he represented, was about to be separated from him forever. Jones became delirious two or three days before his death and in his ravings reproached his wife and children as well as his dying companions present with being the authors of his extreme sufferings by depriving him of food and in refusing him even a single drop of water with which to moisten his parched lips. And, indeed, such now was the thirst of those who were but in a little better condition that they were driven to the melancholy distressful horrid act (to procure their blood) of cutting the throats of their deceased companions a moment after the breath of life had left their bodies!

In the untimely exit of no one of the unhappy sufferers was I so sensibly affected as in that of the unfortunate youth, James Frier—for in the welfare of none on board did I feel myself so immediately interested, as the reader may judge from the circumstances that I shall mention. I have already stated that with this ill-fated young man I became intimately acquainted in Liverpool. To me he had early made protestations of love and more than once intimated an inclination to select me as the partner of his bosom; and never had I any reason to doubt his sincerity. It was partly by his solicitations that I had been induced to comply with the wishes of Mrs. Kendall to accompany her in this unfortunate voyage, in the course of which, by frequent interviews, my attachment for this unfortunate youth was rather increased than diminished. And before this dreadful calamity befell us he had obtained my consent and we had mutually agreed and avowed to each other our determination to unite in marriage as soon as we should reach our destined port. Judge then, my female readers (for it is you that can best judge) what must have been my feelings, to see a youth for whom I had formed an indissoluble attachment—him with whom I expected so soon to be joined in wedlock and to spend the remainder of my days—expiring before my eyes for the want of that sustenance which nature requires for the support of life and which it was not in my power to afford him. And myself at the same moment so far reduced by hunger and thirst as to be driven to the horrid alternative to preserve my own life to plead my claim to the greater portion of his precious blood as it oozed half congealed from the wound inflicted upon his lifeless body! Oh, this was a bitter cup indeed! But it was God's will that it should not pass me—and God's will must be done. O, it was a chastening rod that has been the means, I trust, of weaning me forever from all the vain enjoyments of this frail world.

While almost every other person on board were rendered so weak by their extreme sufferings and deprivations as to be unable to stand upon their feet or even to detach from the lifeless bodies of their unfortunate companions that food which was now nature's only support, the Almighty, in mercy to me, endowed me with not only strength and ability to exhort the poor wretches to unite in prayer and to prepare their precious souls for eternity but to perform this office for them, for which purpose I constantly carried about with me a knife, with which I daily detached and presented each with a proportionable quantity of this their only food. My poor unfortunate female companion (Mrs. Kendall, who never failed to unite with me in prayer) seemed too to enjoy with me a share of God's great mercy. But the reader may judge to what extremity of want we all must have been driven when she, two days before we were relieved, was compelled by hunger to eat the brains of one of the seamen, declaring in the meantime that it was the most delicious thing she ever tasted. And, what is still more melancholy to relate, the unfortunate person whose brains she was thus compelled to subsist on had been three times wrecked before but providentially picked up by a vessel after being once twenty-two days on the wreck—but in the present instance he perished after surviving similar sufferings for the space of twenty-nine days and then became food for his surviving shipmates!

About the 26th February an English brig hove in sight, on which the usual signals of distress were made and, although the winds had become less boisterous and the sea more smooth, to our inexpressible grief she did not approach to afford us any assistance. Our longing eyes followed her until she was out of sight, leaving us in a situation doubly calamitous from our disappointment in not receiving the relief which appeared so near. Our hopes vanished with the brig and from the highest summit of expectation they now sunk into a state of the most dismal despair. Nature indeed seemed now to have abandoned her functions. Never could human beings be reduced to a more wretched situation. More than two thirds of the crew had already perished and the surviving few—weak, distracted, and destitute of almost everything—envied the fate of those whose lifeless corpses no longer wanted sustenance. The sense of hunger was almost lost, but a parching thirst consumed our vitals. Our mouths had become so dry for want of moisture for three or four days that we were obliged to wash them every few hours with salt water to prevent our lips glueing together.

Early in the morning of the 7th March a sail was discovered to windward. The ship's crew (with my assistance) made all the signals of distress that the little remaining strength of their bodies would enable them to do. They were indeed the last efforts of expiring nature. But, praised be God, the hour of our deliverance had now arrived. The ship was soon within hail, which proved to be His Majesty's Ship Blonde, Lord Byron, when her boat was manned and sent to our relief.

It would be in vain for me to attempt to describe our feelings at this moment or those manifested by our deliverers when they discovered who we were and what our miserable situation; and that they had arrived in season to rescue six of their fellow creatures from a most awful but certain death. My companions in misery, who for three or four of the preceding days had been only able to crawl about the deck upon their hands and knees, now became so animated at the prospect of relief as to raise themselves erect and with uplifted hands returned thanks to their Almighty preserver.

When relieved, but a small part of the body of the last person deceased remained, and this I had cut as usual into slices and spread on the quarterdeck; which being noticed by the lieutenant of the Blonde (who with others had been dispatched from the ship to our relief) and before we had time to state to him to what extremities we had been driven, he observed, "You have yet, I perceive, fresh meat." But his horror can be better conceived than described when he was informed that what he saw was the remains of the dead body of one of our unfortunate companions and that on this, our only remaining food, it was our intention to have put ourselves on an allowance the ensuing evening had not unerring Providence directed him to our relief.

When we reached the Blonde the narrative of our sufferings as well as a view of our weak and emaciated bodies caused tears to bedew those faces which probably are not used to turn pale at the approach of death. By Lord Byron and his officers and crew we were treated with all possible kindness and humanity; insomuch that we soon gained our strength to that degree as to be able in ten days after to go on board of a vessel bound to Europe. And it was on the 20th March following that I was landed in safety at Portsmouth, where for twelve days I was treated with that hospitality, by both sexes, as ought not, and I trust will not, pass without its merited reward. And on the 5th April following I was conveyed and restored to the arms of my dear mother, after an absence of nearly five months; in which time I think I can truly say I had witnessed and endured more of the heavy judgments and afflictions of this world than any other of its female inhabitants.

1841 Murder Without Malice,

a most amazing true account, compiled and written
by Joseph Fulling Fishman and Vee Perlman.

On the morning of March 13, 1841, the
American square-rigged sailing vessel, William Brown, cast loose her
lines from a Liverpool dock and worked her way slowly and cautiously
through the mist down the Mersey River toward the open sea en
route to Philadelphia—a destination she was fated never to reach.
The tragedy was not unusual for those days. But what was unusual
was the aftermath of her sinking, which was to result in what was
perhaps the most extraordinary criminal case ever heard in any court
in the United States.

The Brown carried, in addition to her cargo, sixty-five Irish and
Scottish immigrants traveling steerage. She shipped a crew of fourteen. Ill luck tormented the ship from the start of the voyage. Her
captain, George L. Harris, her first mate, Francis Rhodes, and her
second mate, Walter Parker, agreed that never before had they encountered such an unending succession of storms and impenetrable
fog. On three different occasions the wind tore every yard of her
canvas to bits. During an entire month, with the exception of a day
or two, she was forced to slough ahead under shortened sail at a
maddeningly slow pace.

About five weeks out of Liverpool, on the night of April 19, a
strangely thick fog swathed the vessel. That peculiar chill in the air,
familiar to every sailor who travels the northern route, gave warning
of the presence of icebergs. Two lookouts instead of the usual one
were posted. But in spite of all precautions, just before midnight a

towering mass of ice suddenly broke through the fog and struck the wooden vessel with a thunderous crash.

Captain Harris shouted for all hands on deck further to shorten sail and man the pumps. A sailor ran up from below to report a hole at least six feet high and three feet wide had been gashed in the vessel's bow. Investigation convinced Harris the damage could not be repaired and that the ship was doomed.

Back on deck he found a terrified crowd of men, women and children. Practically all the passengers had been asleep when the vessel struck. The men, with one or two exceptions, wore but a pair of trousers; the women were shivering in nightgowns over which they had thrown coats or shawls. The screams and shrieks of the steerage passengers, the shouted orders of the crew, added to the confusion. And as a background to all this, there was the raucous creak and whine of the tackle, the sucking noise of the pumps and the flapping of the sails as the unmanageable vessel yawed and came up in the wind. The mates and one or two of the more self-possessed seamen were trying to man the only two boats the ship carried. Rhodes, the first mate, in the temporary absence of the captain, had ordered these released from the davits and swung over the side.

Soon Captain Harris took charge. With the help of his officers, he managed to launch the longboat. But neither he nor his crew could stem the wild rush of hysterical passengers as they crowded headlong into the boat as it was lowered.

Under the captain's instructions, Rhodes went into the longboat. Parker, the second officer, took charge of the lowering of the smaller jollyboat which swung from the stern. Captain Harris then ordered Parker to attach a rope from the jollyboat to the longboat, so both could be maneuvered out of the way of the schooner and would not be sucked down in the undertow when she sank.

Only six or seven people boarded the jollyboat which had been overlooked by many in the frenzied scramble to reach the longboat. But thirty-one passengers were unable to get into either boat. They were forced to remain on the Brown. They crowded around Harris, pawing and clawing at him, beseeching him to save them.

Down on the water Parker, in the jollyboat, was shouting at the captain for God's sake to come on, that the vessel would be going down any minute, and he could not possibly do any good for himself or anyone else by remaining longer on the doomed ship.

Harris hesitated. Parker persisted in his plea. Suddenly Harris pushed the crowd away, ran aft, swung himself over the stern and slid down the davit ropes into the waiting jollyboat. Parker cast the craft loose, and the two boats, tied together, slowly drifted away from the rapidly settling schooner.

The members of the crew pulled on their oars, trying to put as much distance as possible between them and the Brown. By the time they were a few feet away, all they could see was the vague outline of the schooner, already down by the head; and looming through the fog, the faint glimmer of a lantern still alight in the rigging. The frantic screams of those left behind, their curses and prayers, their heartbreaking pleas for those in the boats not to desert them, rolled across the water. These cries followed the small boats for a dreadful half-hour. Then there was a sudden silence as the Brown heaved, wallowed drunkenly and went down, carrying with her the thirty-one passengers left aboard.

The thirty-five or forty who had crowded into the longboat were huddled close together, shivering and half-naked. In the darkness and fog, it was difficult to tell one from another.

For six hours, until five in the morning, the two boats drifted aimlessly about. At sunrise as the fog began to lift, Captain Harris shouted to Rhodes that he was going to cut loose and try to take the jollyboat to Newfoundland. He advised Rhodes, in charge of the longboat, to do the same. The mate did not reply to the suggestion. Instead he said, "Captain, we're terribly overloaded. Can't you take some of our people?"

"No," Harris answered. "We'd be swamped."

The mate persisted. "We have no sails; we're leaking badly and the boat's so low in the water she's unmanageable. I'm afraid we'll have to do something about it. Do you understand?"

"Yes," replied the captain.

"Well?"

There followed a long silence. Then Harris called slowly, "Only—as—a—last resort, Rhodes."

"Yes, sir," came the response.

The captain shouted to his men in the longboat: "Men, I'm leaving Mr. Rhodes in command. I want you to obey him. Give me your word for it."

As the crew in the longboat agreed, the jollyboat with Captain Harris in charge cut loose. The two ships parted, each a tiny shell bobbing about on the Atlantic, 250 miles from the nearest land.

Surrounded by icefloes, drenched by a freezing rain which had begun to fall, the discomfort of those in the longboat was acute. The danger of being capsized by the large floating chunks of ice was ever present. Part of the group sat on the thwarts, their feet in the icy water which the boat was constantly shipping. The rest lay huddled between the seats. The water poured in from a dozen leaks, and continuous bailing was necessary.

Daylight brought little relief. The fog still hung like a curtain of impenetrable wool. Soon the wind began to mount and the sea to rise. The depth of the water in the boat crept up, bringing new terrors to the hearts of the miserable occupants. Rhodes called Alexander William Holmes, one of the crew, and whispered to him.

Holmes, strong, young and handsome, was an exceptionally able and intelligent seaman. He had a dominating personality and the ability to handle himself well in any emergency. Unobtrusively, but nevertheless definitely, as the hours passed he had been assuming command of the little boat—giving orders about the bailing, the division of the scanty food supply and the other details essential to comfort and safety, apparently with Rhodes's tacit acquiescence. Indeed, the latter seemed stunned by the weight of responsibility thrust upon him.

The passengers watched the conference between the two men apprehensively. They had already guessed the unvoiced decision made by Captain Harris and Rhodes earlier. They knew it meant that some of the human cargo might be jettisoned. Holmes nodded assent to Rhodes's words. He called to James Murray, a colored seaman, also a man of unusual strength, and in turn whispered to him. Then the passengers heard Holmes say: "Come on, it's got to be done."

The two seamen moved toward Owen Riley, one of the passengers, who was lying near the bow. Holmes directed him to stand up. Riley understood. He shrank back and grabbed at a thwart. "Help me, Isabelle," he called to Mrs. Edgar, another passenger, "for the love of God, tell them to spare me!" The woman did not answer. The frantic man appealed to others. No one replied.

Holmes and Murray grabbed Riley, wrenched his hand away from the thwart and pulled him upright. The struggle of the three men, thrashing about in the overcrowded boat almost upset it. But Riley was no match for the two sailors. Finally Holmes picked him up, pinioned his arms and hurled him over the side. There was a scream and a splash, while shrieks rose from the other occupants of the boat. Riley was gone.

George Duffee's turn came next. The two sailors grabbed him. "I've got a wife and three children," he pleaded. "For their sakes, spare me."

But Holmes was adamant, and said quietly: "It's no use, Duffee— you've got to go, too." Again the struggle, a despairing shriek and the cries and sobs of the women in the boat. Then silence.

The next victim, James McAvoy, made no attempt to beg for his life. He said calmly, "Just give me five minutes to pray." When he raised his head and said, "I'm ready," Holmes picked him up and tossed him over the side.

During this time Rhodes, nominally in charge, had been sitting in the stern of the boat staring straight ahead. Holmes now glanced inquiringly toward him, as if awaiting further instructions. When he received none, he took hold of James Black, another passenger. For the first time the mate called out, "Let him alone; you must not part man and wife."

Holmes released his hold on Black and grabbed the arm of Frank Askins who, with his two sisters, Mary and Ellen, was huddled in the center of the boat. The girls, begging and pleading, fought to save their brother's life, alternately clinging to him and striking out at Holmes. Both swore if he were thrown overboard, they would go too. Holmes tore Askins loose and threw him into the water. A moment later the two sisters leaped after him.

That day John Welch, Robert Hunter, Thomas Nugent, James Todd, John Wilson, James Smith, Martin McAvoy and Charles Conlin were deliberately drowned; and on the next, Hugh Keegan and two more passengers followed, until sixteen persons had disappeared into the sea in order to lighten the longboat, now in complete control of Holmes. Wholesale murder had achieved its purpose. The boat rode much easier and did not ship so much water, although continuous bailing was still necessary.

Only passengers—and not one crew member—had been thrown overboard. Those who remained were so weakened by hunger, fear, cold and exposure that they lay, listless, in the bottom of the boat.

Holmes busied himself fashioning a mast out of one of the oars, attempting to rig up some kind of sail out of a shawl or coat. He knew, however, there was not one chance in a hundred that they would ever reach Cape Race, the nearest point of land, and that the odds against their being picked up by another vessel were at least a thousand to one.

But on the third day after the wreck, when the despairing occupants of the boat had given up all hope, Holmes's keen eyes discerned a vessel in the distance. He whipped a shawl from the shoulders of one of the women and waved it wildly back and forth. At the same time he ordered the members of the crew, on threat of being thrown overboard, to row toward the ship.

The half-frozen crewmen made a pitifully weak effort to turn the boat around. They had just succeeded in getting her headed toward the schooner when a small iceberg drifted between the two boats. Long minutes slipped away as the iceberg floated slowly on its course. Again the rescuers were sighted. Holmes, in the bow, swung the shawl back and forth. Suddenly he shouted: "She's coming about! She's coming about! She sees us!"

He was right. Gradually the ship came within hailing distance. It was the schooner Crescent bound from New York to Havre, France. The wretched occupants of the longboat were taken aboard and eventually landed at Havre. Practically all the survivors of the long-boat's party, including Rhodes, returned to the United States soon after. There they discovered that those in the jollyboat under Captain Harris had been picked up by another schooner, La Mère de Famille, after six days afloat.

The officers of the Crescent had been the first to learn of the mass murders which had taken place under Rhodes's direction. Soon the story spread over the United States. A horrified public opinion was aroused. Newspapers devoted entire pages to the tragedy, and editorials were written calling for action against the ship's officers as well as Holmes and Murray for their "callous inhumanity" in countenancing and carrying into effect what one paper characterized as "wholesale murder of innocent people whom it was the duty of the ship's officers and crew to protect."

Spurred to action, the Attorney General's office referred the case to William M. Meredith, U. S. Attorney at Philadelphia, the ship's home port.

Strangely enough, Captain Harris and Rhodes by this time had been offered berths on the Harry F. Thompson, a schooner engaged in the South American trade. Instead of arresting them for issuing the fatal orders, or even holding them as witnesses, Meredith permitted them to leave the country after taking their depositions. Parker, the second mate, and an important witness to the conversation between the captain and Rhodes, had disappeared. Curiously enough, the Federal authorities apparently made no effort to find him. James Murray, the Negro sailor who had assisted Holmes in throwing the sixteen passengers overboard, also disappeared. Holmes's case, however, was presented to the grand jury and he was indicted under the Act of April 30, 1790, which provided for the punishment of any sailor who commits homicide on the high seas.

Up to this time no one seemed to have bothered with Holmes's motives for what had taken place, namely, that he had disposed of sixteen persons in order to save the lives of the remaining twenty-five. But now that he alone—and not even Murray who had been his partner in the actual drowning—was to stand trial, public sentiment swung in his favor. For the first time numerous editorials now contended that under a "state of nature" such as existed in the longboat, Holmes's action had been necessary for the salvation of the remaining passengers; that of all the crew he was the only one who showed courage and resourcefulness.

On the other side there were those who asserted that if such a tragic course were necessary, rather than an arbitrary choice of victims, lots should have been drawn. Holmes's supporters answered that with the crowded condition of the boat and the immediacy of the danger, drawing of lots was out of the question. The fact that only passengers and not members of the crew had been thrown overboard called forth a great deal of comment.

On April 13, 1842, after seven months in jail, Holmes was brought to trial before Justice Henry Baldwin of the United States Circuit Court at Philadelphia. When the case finally went to the jury, the members were found to be as divided in their opinions as the general public. After sixteen hours of deliberation, the foreman reported they could not agree. Sent back for further deliberation, they spent another ten hours in constant debate before returning to the courtroom. This time they brought in a verdict: guilty—with a recommendation that the defendant receive the mercy of the court.

Holmes was sentenced to six months' imprisonment in solitary confinement at hard labor. The fact that he was also fined twenty dollars added a further strange footnote to this extraordinary case.

To this day there has been no adequate explanation why the Government made no attempt to prosecute any of the other members of the Brown's crew who were involved.

At the conclusion of the trial thousands of letters poured in to President Tyler, asking that Holmes be granted a pardon. Most of the writers of these letters believed the seaman, who, after all, acted under orders, had been made a scapegoat. The President, however, refused to commute the sentence and Holmes served out his time. Upon his release, a sympathizer offered him a berth on a schooner which he accepted. Thus ended the case which had become the most violently partisan *cause célèbre* of the decade.

1873   The Wreck of the Ville du Havre

On Board S. S. Trimountain
November 28th, 1873

Dearest Mother:

I wonder that my pen does not refuse to write the horrible narrative which I must tell you, and my own physical strength amazes me but I know how intense your anxiety will be to hear, so I will try to employ a few hours of this unreal life on shipboard by opening my heart and sorrows to you. I must ask you to send my letter to Josey and Dinkey. We hope to land next Monday or Tuesday and if we are capable of writing now the gentlemen say that our letters will be mailed at once on reaching shore. Perhaps it is better so, for I fear that after the fearful tension of excitement is over our mental and physical faculties may give way and render us incapable of action. So I will try and speak to you while I can.

We sailed, as you know, on November 15th. The day was bright. Crowds of friends were on the steamer to say good-bye. Lallie and Helen were overwhelmed with offerings of flowers and fruit, and as we looked around all exclaimed what a nice set of passengers were on the boat. But our very start was ominous, for we had scarcely been in motion four hours when we stopped an hour and a half to arrange the machinery. Sunday was pleasant. Monday morning found us all on deck, enjoying a delicious atmosphere and sunny sky. In the afternoon a fog arose. On Tuesday we had rough weather and fog and broke a blade of the screw. Almost all of the storerooms leaked owing to the condition of the roof, so that we were very uncomfortable. The fog continued Wednesday and Thursday, with head winds.

On Thursday night several of the passengers acknowledged to each other that we had been apprehensive from the very first, as there seemed to be no organized discipline on board; but on Friday the fog dispelled, the young people were on deck again, and after a pleasant evening in the saloon we all retired to our rest, more quiet in mind than we had been before on the steamer. The night was clear and starry, the sea smooth—what had we now to fear? Just as we went to bed Lallie came to me and repeated, "The Lord is my Shepherd," and kissed me two or three times.

We were aroused at two o'clock (darkness around us) by an appalling crash, shriek of the whistle and human cries. I rushed to the hall, met the steward, and also the surgeon of the ship. Both said, "Nothing is the matter." However, I hurried back and told the children to dress as quickly as possible, then went again to the door and met a Mr. Belknap, who told me to hurry up on deck. Then a sailor came by and said there had been a collision. My idea was that we must get ready for the lifeboats, so I told Helen and Lallie to put on their warmest clothes and take their satchels and valuables. We ran into the hall. I saw a crowd collected around the main staircase. I did not know then that this was the spot where the collision had taken place, but instinctively felt we must not get in the crowd, so hurried back and went on deck by the steerage staircase.

As we reached the deck all was darkness and confusion. French sailors were working at the sailboats, yelling and screaming, great flames bursting out of the ventilator. Not an officer was to be seen, not an order given; and very few passengers to be seen. We walked towards the stern of the huge vessel and stood in front of the little saloon cabin on deck. On the right was a lifeboat, black with sailors. Here, I thought, there is no hope, for these men will swamp the boat. Still I hoped that under all this outward confusion there must be some organized system going on for our rescue.

Just before us, in the starlight, a ship loomed up against the sky. Surely here must be help. Not for one moment did I suppose we were sinking. At that instant other passengers joined us, calm and collected. We all looked into each others' faces but no one could tell us where the danger was. A Mr. Wait came by with his sister, and said, "Stay here, Mrs. Bulkley, and some of us will try to lower a lifeboat." Not an ax or knife could they find. Yet in three minutes these brave gentlemen, with their delicate penknives and their desperate strength, might have cut the boat (stiffened with recent paint) loose from the steamer. But the next instant the mast fell with a crushing noise on the deck.

"Good God, we are shipwrecked!" cried a lady near us, and she burst into an eloquent prayer.

We heard Mr. Wait's voice calling out, "Rush to the upper side of the ship." We started in haste for the other side of the ship, water all about us. Some tremendous force parted us as we went down together. The sufferings of strangulation were on me. I thought that I was falling to the very bottom of the sea. With almost a start of horror I found myself rising to the surface. As I arose my hand struck a hard, cold substance. I grasped it and found it to be an iron chain suspended from a boat which was upside down in the water. A number of French sailors were clinging to the upraised keel. I spoke not a word as these men shrieked for help, for I felt it was better they should not know a woman was clinging to the bottom of the boat.

In a few moments the boat broke to pieces. For a second the shattered fragments held together like a raft, then, scattered by the surging waters, all disappeared. I saw not a human being around me. A beam struck me in the chest, I remembered that persons could be supported in the water by resting lightly on a plank; so as the chain was drawn from me this beam supported me. I was surrounded by barrels and broken timbers and my faculties were keen enough to distinguish the smell of liquor on the surface of the water. Thus I lay on the water, not struggling for life but passively waiting God's will. A woman once floated quite near me and I heard her say *Sauvez moi.*

I could no longer see the ship. I felt that I was drifting away into the ocean and never dreamed of being saved. Still, physical instinct kept me on the plank. I was alone with my God and prayed that He might take my soul. I was cold and benumbed and knew I could not live many minutes. Suddenly I felt something under me and, stretching my feet downwards, felt them sustained by a triangular piece of timber. With this support under my feet and the plank at my breast I raised my head higher above the water. But soon a faintness seemed to come over me. I felt the waters going over my head and, raising my eyes for the last time as I supposed, I saw a great white boat above me. Here I screamed for the first time: "Help a woman!"

The next instant strong arms were about me and when I asked, "Who are you?" a voice replied, "An English sailor come to save you."

I was placed tenderly in the bottom of the boat. The rowers stopped and Miss Edgar of New York was picked up. We were the last saved. We had drifted a mile from the ship and had been three quarters of an hour in the water. As we came up to the ship an English voice called out, "How many have you?"

"Six."

"Good God! Is that all? Any women?"

"Two. We could find no more."

"Hurry up with them on deck."

We were utterly helpless. The men put strong ropes under our arms and we were hauled up the sides of the ship. As I recognized faces of the passengers about me I felt as if it were a resurrection of the dead....

We lay almost unconscious in the cabin of the English ship when the news was brought in that a second ship was in sight. This proved to be the Trimountain of New York, bound for Bristol, England. Captain Robinson of the English ship was very unwilling to have us leave, but the gentlemen thought that since his ship was so much damaged it would be best to go on a sound ship, the bow of the vessel being terribly broken by the collision. We lay so exhausted that it did not seem possible for us to be moved again but the gentlemen persisted and talked with Captain Surmont, survivor of the Ville du Havre, who gave the necessary orders. We were taken up, lowered down the sides of the ship and placed in the bottom of boats.

A few moments' rapid rowing and we were alongside of the Trimountain.

The captain had a chair lowered for the ladies. We were strapped to it and drawn up.

The last hope was destroyed before we left the English ship of ever finding any more beloved faces. The boats cruised for five hours without finding any others after Miss Edgar and I were saved. Captain Urquhart of the Trimountain also tacked and cruised over the spot before pursuing his course. So we have the mournful satisfaction of knowing that everything was done to look for the lost ones.

We have been on board this ship a week tomorrow and hope to reach land next Monday. We are destitute of money and clothes. Fortunately the captain is a noble-hearted man and does all he can to make us comfortable. We are grateful that his sound ship shelters us. But we are leading such an unreal life, and all feel that we must keep up and not be burdens upon others. The very necessity of action acts like a stimulant and we hardly realize who we are and what the terrible situation is.

Imagine eleven ladies and about twelve gentlemen being in two small cabins, not a tooth brush among us and only such clothing as we had upon us when saved, which has been dried for us, and the flannel underclothing of the sailors. Only two ladies have shoes, the rest are in the woolen stockings which the English sailors gave us. I have a pair of gentleman's slippers and fortunately had my flannel wrapper on when I went overboard. All must use the captain's comb. But one of the young girls, a wonderful child of seventeen, Miss Mixter of Boston, combs our hair every morning. We have no hairpins, so we must wear it down our shoulders. This poor girl has lost her father, mother and grandfather. She and her little sister of twelve were both miraculously saved, as I was.

I dare not think of my own future and only long for my return to you. It is mysterous to think why have I been saved, when with Lallie my life's work is done. I dare not say anything more about her lest I be overcome and not able to finish my letter. All the passengers go together to Paris and as soon as we are able to travel I mean to return.

I will try to write you again before we start, and wish you or Johnny could meet me in New York. I don't dare to think beyond that. Perhaps I had better go back to the old Sand Hills for the rest of the winter, but do try to be in New York when I arrive, or if you are not strong enough to endure the climate, do ask Josey to be there. I don't like to ask Johnny to leave his business to meet me, for I may be obliged to stay in New York a little while.

The wind is very favorable now and the captain hopes to reach Cardiff on Monday. We will be obliged to get something there to cover our heads and be decently clad. If you receive this you will know that God has brought us safely to shore again. We fear that the English ship may, even in her disabled condition, get into port before we do and send the telegraphic tidings over the world before you receive the particulars from us. I have also written a letter to New York and a dispatch for Mr. Joseph Bulkley requesting him to send you, Josey and Dinkey, the news that "I alone am saved."

God bless you all.

Your loving daughter,

Mary

1912   The Last March:

being the tragic conclusion of a journal kept by the
English Antarctic explorer, Robert Falcon Scott.

SUNDAY, *February* 18.—R. 32. Temp. – 5.5°.
At Shambles Camp. We gave ourselves 5 hours' sleep at the lower
glacier depot after the horrible night, and came on at about 3 to-day
to this camp, coming fairly easily over the divide. Here with plenty
of horsemeat we have had a fine supper, to be followed by others
such, and so continue a more plentiful era if we can keep good
marches up. New life seems to come with greater food almost immediately, but I am anxious about the Barrier surfaces.

Monday, February 19.—Lunch T. – 16°. It was late (past noon)
before we got away to-day, as I gave nearly 8 hours sleep, and much
camp work was done shifting sledges and fitting up new one with
mast, &c., packing horsemeat and personal effects. The surface was
every bit as bad as I expected, the sun shining brightly on it and its
covering of soft loose sandy snow. We have come out about 2' on
the old tracks. Perhaps lucky to have a fine day for this and our camp
work, but we shall want wind or change of sliding conditions to do
anything on such a surface as we have got. I fear there will not be
much change for the next 3 or 4 days.

R. 33. Temp. – 17°. We have struggled out 4.6 miles in a short
day over a really terrible surface—it has been like pulling over desert
sand, not the least glide in the world. If this goes on we shall have a
bad time, but I sincerely trust it is only the result of this windless
area close to the coast and that, as we are making steadily outwards,

219

we shall shortly escape it. It is perhaps premature to be anxious about covering distance. In all other respects things are improving. We have our sleeping-bags spread on the sledge and they are drying, but, above all, we have our full measure of food again. To-night we had a sort of stew fry of pemmican and horseflesh, and voted it the best hoosh we had ever had on a sledge journey. The absence of poor Evans is a help to the commissariat, but if he had been here in a fit state we might have got along faster. I wonder what is in store for us, with some little alarm at the lateness of the season.

Monday, February 20.—R. 34. Lunch Temp. – 13°; Supper Temp. – 15°. Same terrible surface; four hours' hard plodding in morning brought us to our Desolation Camp, where we had the four-day blizzard. We looked for more pony meat, but found none. After lunch we took to ski with some improvement of comfort. Total mileage for day 7—the ski tracks pretty plain and easily followed this afternoon. We have left another cairn behind. Terribly slow progress, but we hope for better things as we clear the land. There is a tendency to cloud over in the SE to-night, which may turn to our advantage. At present our sledge and ski leave deeply ploughed tracks which can be seen winding for miles behind. It is distressing, but as usual trials are forgotten when we camp, and good food is our lot. Pray God we get better travelling as we are not so fit as we were, and the season is advancing apace.

Tuesday, February 21.—R. 35. Lunch Temp.—9½°; Supper Temp. – 11°. Gloomy and overcast when we started; a good deal warmer. The marching almost as bad as yesterday. Heavy toiling all day, inspiring gloomiest thoughts at times. Rays of comfort when we picked up tracks and cairns. At lunch we seemed to have missed the way, but an hour or two after we passed the last pony walls, and since, we struck a tent ring, ending the march actually on our old pony-tracks. There is a critical spot here with a long stretch between cairns. If we can tide that over we get on the regular cairn route, and with luck should stick to it; but everything depends on the weather. We never won a march of 8½ miles with greater difficulty, but we can't go on like this. We are drawing away from the land and perhaps may get better things in a day or two. I devoutly hope so.

Wednesday, February 22.—R. 36. Supper Temp. −2°. There is little doubt we are in for a rotten critical time going home, and the lateness of the season may make it really serious. Shortly after starting to-day the wind grew very fresh from the SE with strong surface drift. We lost the faint track immediately, though covering ground fairly rapidly. Lunch came without sight of the cairn we had hoped to pass. In the afternoon, Bowers being sure we were too far to the west, steered out. Result, we have passed another pony camp without seeing it. Looking at the map to-night there is no doubt we are too far to the east. With clear weather we ought to be able to correct the mistake, but will the weather get clear? It's a gloomy position, more especially as one sees the same difficulty returning even when we have corrected this error. The wind is dying down to-night and the sky clearing in the south, which is hopeful. Meanwhile it is satisfactory to note that such untoward events fail to damp the spirit of the party. To-night we had a pony hoosh so excellent and filling that one feels really strong and vigorous again.

Thursday, February 23.—R. 37. Lunch Temp. −9.8°; Supper Temp. −12°. Started in sunshine, wind almost dropped. Luckily Bowers took a round of angles and with help of the chart we fogged out that we must be inside rather than outside tracks. The data were so meager that it seemed a great responsibility to march out and we were none of us happy about it. But just as we decided to lunch, Bowers' wonderful sharp eyes detected an old double lunch cairn, the theodolite telescope confirmed it, and our spirits rose accordingly. This afternoon we marched on and picked up another cairn; then on and camped only 2½ miles from the depot. We cannot see it, but, given fine weather, we cannot miss it. We are, therefore, extraordinarily relieved. Covered 8.2 miles in 7 hours, showing we can do 10 to 12 on this surface. Things are again looking up, as we are on the regular line of cairns, with no gaps right home, I hope.

Friday, February 24.—Lunch. Beautiful day—too beautiful—an hour after starting loose ice crystals spoiling surface. Saw depot and reached it middle forenoon. Found store in order except shortage oil —shall have to be very saving with fuel—otherwise have ten full days' provision from to-night and shall have less than 70 miles to go. Note from Meares who passed through December 15, saying surface bad; from Atkinson, after fine marching (2¼ days from pony depot), reporting Keohane better after sickness. Short note from Evans, not very cheerful, saying surface bad, temperature high. Think he must have been a little anxious. It is an immense relief to have picked up this depot and, for the time, anxieties are thrust aside. There is no doubt we have been rising steadily since leaving the Shambles Camp. The coastal Barrier descends except where glaciers press out. Undulation still, but flattening out. Surface soft on top, curiously hard below. Great difference now between night and day temperatures. Quite warm as I write in tent. We are on tracks with half-march cairn ahead; have covered 4½ miles. Poor Wilson has a fearful attack snowblindness consequent on yesterday's efforts. Wish we had more fuel.

Night camp R. 38. Temp. −17°. A little despondent again. We had a really terrible surface this afternoon and only covered 4 miles. We are on the track just beyond a lunch cairn. It really will be a bad business if we are to have this pulling all through. I don't know what to think, but the rapid closing of the season is ominous. It is great luck having the horsemeat to add to our ration. To-night we have had a real fine hoosh. It is a race between the season and hard conditions and our fitness and good food.

Saturday, February 25.—Lunch Temp. −12°. Managed just 6 miles this morning. Started somewhat despondent; not relieved when pulling seemed to show no improvement. Bit by bit surface grew better, less sastrugi, more glide, slight following wind for a time. Then we began to travel a little faster. But the pulling is still very hard; undulations disappearing but inequalities remain.

Twenty-six Camp walls about 2 miles ahead, all tracks in sight— Evans' track very conspicuous. This is something in favor, but the pulling is tiring us, though we are getting into better ski drawing again. Bowers hasn't quite the trick and is a little hurt at my criticisms, but I never doubted his heart. Very much easier—write diary at lunch—excellent meal—now one pannikin very strong tea—four biscuits and butter.

Hope for better things this afternoon, but no improvement apparent. Oh! for a little wind—E. Evans evidently had plenty.

R. 39. Temp. −20°. Better march in afternoon. Day yields 11.4 miles—the first double figure of steady dragging for a long time, but it meant and will mean hard work if we can't get a wind to help us. Evans evidently had a strong wind here, SE I should think. The temperature goes very low at night now when the sky is clear as at present. As a matter of fact this is wonderfully fair weather—the only drawback the spoiling of the surface and absence of wind. We see all tracks very plain, but the pony-walls have evidently been badly drifted up. Some kind people had substituted a cairn at last camp 27. The old cairns do not seem to have suffered much.

Sunday, February 26.—Lunch Temp. −17°. Sky overcast at start, but able see tracks and cairn distinct at long distance. Did a little better, 6½ miles to date. Bowers and Wilson now in front. Find great relief pulling behind with no necessity to keep attention on track. Very cold nights now and cold feet starting march, as day footgear doesn't dry at all. We are doing well on our food, but we ought to have yet more. I hope the next depot, now only 50 miles, will find us with enough surplus to open out. The fuel shortage still an anxiety.

R. 40. Temp. −21°. Nine hours' solid marching has given us 11½ miles. Only 43 miles from the next depot. Wonderfully fine weather but cold, very cold. Nothing dries and we get our feet cold too often. We want more food yet and especially more fat. Fuel is woefully short. We can scarcely hope to get a better surface at this season, but I wish we could have some help from the wind, though it might shake us up badly if the temp. didn't rise.

Monday, February 27.—Desperately cold last night: −33° when we got up, with −37° minimum. Some suffering from cold feet, but all got good rest. We must open out on food soon. But we have done 7 miles this morning and hope for some 5 this afternoon. Overcast sky and good surface till now, when sun shows again. It is good to be marching the cairns up, but there is still much to be anxious about.

We talk of little but food, except after meals. Land disappearing in satisfactory manner. Pray God we have no further setbacks. We are naturally always discussing possibility of meeting dogs, where and when, &c. It is a critical position. We may find ourselves in safety at next depot, but there is a horrid element of doubt.

Camp R. 41. Temp. −32°. Still fine clear weather but very cold—absolutely calm to-night. We have got off an excellent march for these days (12.2) and are much earlier than usual in our bags. 31 miles to depot, 3 days' fuel at a pinch, and 6 days' food. Things begin to look a little better; we can open out a little on food from to-morrow night, I think.

Very curious surface—soft recent sastrugi which sink underfoot, and between, a sort of flaky crust with large crystals beneath.

Tuesday, February 28.—Lunch. Thermometer went below −40° last night; it was desperately cold for us, but we had a fair night. I decided to slightly increase food; the effect is undoubtedly good. Started marching in −32° with a slight northwesterly breeze—blighting. Many cold feet this morning; long time over foot gear, but we are earlier. Shall camp earlier and get the chance of a good night, if not the reality. Things must be critical till we reach the depot, and the more I think of matters, the more I anticipate their remaining so after that event. Only 24½ miles from the depot. The sun shines brightly, but there is little warmth in it. There is no doubt the middle of the Barrier is a pretty awful locality.

Camp 42. Splendid pony hoosh sent us to bed and sleep happily after a horrid day, wind continuing; did 11½ miles. Temp. not quite so low, but expect we are in for cold night (Temp. −27°).

Wednesday, February 29.—Lunch. Cold night. Minimum Temp. −37.5°; −30° with northwest wind, force 4, when we got up. Frightfully cold starting; luckily Bowers and Oates in their last new finnesko; keeping my old ones for present. Expected awful march and for first hour got it. Then things improved and we camped after 5½ hours marching close to lunch camp—22½. Next camp is our depot and it is exactly 13 miles. It ought not to take more than 1½ days; we pray for another fine one. The oil will just about spin out in that event, and we arrive 3 clear days' food in hand. The increase of ration has had an enormously beneficial result. Mountains now looking small. Wind still very light from west—cannot understand this wind.

Thursday, March 1.—Lunch. Very cold last night—minimum −41.5°. Cold start to march, too, as usual now. Got away at 8 and have marched within sight of depot; flag something under 3 miles away. We did 11½ yesterday and marched 6 this morning. Heavy dragging yesterday and very heavy this morning. Apart from sledging considerations the weather is wonderful. Cloudless days and nights and the wind trifling. Worse luck, the light airs come from the north and keep us horribly cold. For this lunch hour the exception has come. There is a bright and comparatively warm sun. All our gear is out drying.

Friday, March 2.—Lunch. Misfortunes rarely come singly. We marched to the depot fairly easily yesterday afternoon, and since that have suffered three distinct blows which have placed us in a bad position. First we found a shortage of oil; with most rigid economy it can scarce carry us to the next depot on this surface. Second, Titus Oates disclosed his feet, the toes showing very bad indeed, evidently bitten by the late temperatures. The third blow came in the night, when the wind, which we had hailed with some joy, brought dark overcast weather. It fell below −40° in the night, and this morning it took 1½ hours to get our foot gear on, but we got away before night. We lost cairn and tracks together and made as steady as we could N by W, but have seen nothing. Worse was to come—the surface is simply awful. In spite of strong wind and full sail we have only done 5½ miles. We are in a very queer street since there is no doubt we cannot do the extra marches and feel the cold horribly.

Saturday, March 3.—Lunch. We picked up the track again yesterday, finding ourselves to the eastward. Did close on 10 miles and things looked a trifle better; but this morning the outlook is blacker than ever. Started well and with good breeze; for an hour made good headway; then the surface grew awful beyond words. The wind drew forward; every circumstance was against us. After 4½ hours things so bad that we camped, having covered 4½ miles. One cannot consider this a fault of our own—certainly we were pulling hard this morning —it was more than three parts surface which held us back—the wind at strongest, powerless to move the sledge. When the light is good it is easy to see the reason. The surface, lately a very good hard one, is coated with a thin layer of woolly crystals, formed by radiation no doubt. These are too firmly fixed to be removed by the wind and cause impossible friction on the runners. God help us, we can't keep up this pulling, that is certain. Amongst ourselves we are unendingly cheerful, but what each man feels in his heart I can only guess. Pulling on foot gear in the morning is getting slower and slower, therefore every day more dangerous.

Sunday, March 4.—Lunch. Things looking very black indeed. As usual we forgot our trouble last night, got into our bags, slept splendidly on good hoosh, woke and had another, and started marching. Sun shining brightly, tracks clear, but surface covered with sandy frost-rime. All the morning we had to pull with all our strength, and in 4½ hours we covered 3½ miles. Last night it was overcast and thick, surface bad; this morning sun shining and surface as bad as ever. One has little to hope for except perhaps strong dry wind—an unlike contingency at this time of year. Under the immediate surface crystals is a hard sastrugi surface, which must have been excellent for pulling a week or two ago. We are about 42 miles from the next depot and have a week's food, but only about 3 to 4 days' fuel—we are as economical of the latter as one can possibly be, and we cannot afford to save food and pull as we are pulling. We are in a very tight place indeed, but none of us despondent yet, or at least we preserve every semblance of good cheer, but one's heart sinks as the sledge stops dead at some sastrugi behind which the surface sand lies thickly heaped. For the moment the temperature is on the · — 20°—an improvement which makes us much more comfortable, but a colder snap is bound to come again soon. I fear that Oates at least will weather such an event very poorly. Providence to our aid! We can expect little from man now except the possibility of extra food at the next depot. It will be real bad if we get there and find the same shortage of oil. Shall we get there? Such a short distance it would have appeared to us on the summit! I don't know what I should do if Wilson and Bowers weren't so determinedly cheerful over things.

Monday, March 5.—Lunch. Regret to say going from bad to worse. We got a slant of wind yesterday afternoon, and going on 5 hours we converted our wretched morning run of 3½ miles into something over 9. We went to bed on a cup of cocoa and pemmican solid with the chill off. (R. 47.) The result is telling on all, but mainly on Oates, whose feet are in a wretched condition. One swelled up tremendously last night and he is very lame this morning. We started march on tea and pemmican as last night—we pretend to prefer the pemmican this way. Marched for 5 hours this morning over a slightly better surface covered with high moundy sastrugi. Sledge capsized twice; we pulled on foot, covering about 5½ miles. We are two pony marches and 4 miles about from our depot. Our fuel dreadfully low and the poor Soldier nearly done. It is pathetic enough because we can do nothing for him; more hot food might do a little, but only a little, I fear. We none of us expected these terribly low temperatures, and of the rest of us Wilson is feeling them most; mainly, I fear, from his self-sacrificing devotion in doctoring Oates' feet. We cannot help each other, each has enough to do to take care of himself. We get cold on the march when the trudging is heavy, and the wind pierces our warm garments. The others, all of them, are unendingly cheerful when in the tent. We mean to see the game through with a proper spirit, but it's tough work to be pulling harder than we ever pulled in our lives for long hours, and to feel that the progress is so slow. One can only say 'God help us!' and plod on our weary way, cold and very miserable, though outwardly cheerful. We talk of all sorts of subjects in the tent, not much of food now, since we decided to take the risk of running a full ration. We simply couldn't go hungry at this time.

Tuesday, March 6.—Lunch. We did a little better with help of wind yesterday afternoon, finishing 9½ miles for the day, and 27 miles from depot. (R. 48.) But this morning things have been awful. It was warm in the night and for the first time during the journey I overslept myself by more than an hour; then we were slow with foot gear; then, pulling with all our might (for our lives) we could scarcely advance at rate of a mile an hour; then it grew thick and three times we had to get out of harness to search for tracks. The result is something less than 3½ miles for the forenoon. The sun is shining now and the wind gone. Poor Oates is unable to pull, sits on the sledge when we are track-searching—he is wonderfully plucky, as his feet must be giving him great pain. He makes no complaint, but his spirits only come up in spurts now, and he grows more silent in the tent. We are making a spirit lamp to try and replace the primus when our oil is exhausted. It will be a very poor substitute and we've not got much spirit. If we could have kept up our 9-mile days we might have got within reasonable distance of the depot before running out, but nothing but a strong wind and good surface can help us now, and though we had quite a good breeze this morning, the sledge came as heavy as lead. If we were all fit I should have hopes of getting through, but the poor Soldier has become a terrible hindrance, though he does his utmost and suffers much I fear.

Wednesday, March 7.—A little worse I fear. One of Oates' feet very bad this morning; he is wonderfully brave. We still talk of what we will do together at home.

We only made 6½ miles yesterday. (R. 49.) This morning in 4½ hours we did just over 4 miles. We are 16 from our depot. If we only find the correct proportion of food there and this surface continues, we may get to the next depot but not to One Ton Camp. We hope against hope that the dogs have been to Mt. Hooper; then we might pull through. If there is a shortage of oil again we can have little hope. One feels that for poor Oates the crisis is near, but none of us are improving, though we are wonderfully fit considering the really excessive work we are doing. We are only kept going by good food. No wind this morning till a chill northerly air came ahead. Sun bright and cairns showing up well. I should like to keep the track to the end.

Thursday, March 8.—Lunch. Worse and worse in morning; poor Oates' left foot can never last out, and time over foot gear something awful. Have to wait in night foot gear for nearly an hour before I start changing, and then am generally first to be ready. Wilson's feet giving trouble now, but this mainly because he gives so much help to others. We did 4½ miles this morning and are now 8½ miles from the depot—a ridiculously small distance to feel in difficulties, yet on this surface we know we cannot equal half our old marches, and that for that effort we expend nearly double the energy. The great question is, What shall we find at the depot? If the dogs have visited it we may get along a good distance, but if there is another short allowance of fuel, God help us indeed. We are in a very bad way, I fear, in any case.

Saturday, March 10.—Things steadily downhill. Oates' foot worse. He has rare pluck and must know that he can never get through. He asked Wilson if he had a chance this morning, and of course Bill had to say he didn't know. In point of fact he has none. Apart from him, if he went under now, I doubt whether we could get through. With great care we might have a dog's chance, but no more. The weather conditions are awful, and our gear gets steadily more icy and difficult to manage. At the same time of course poor Titus is the greatest handicap. He keeps us waiting in the morning until we have partly lost the warming effect of our good breakfast, when the only wise policy is to be up and away at once; again at lunch. Poor chap! it is too pathetic to watch him; one cannot but try to cheer him up.

Yesterday we marched up the depot, Mt. Hooper. Cold comfort. Shortage on our allowance all round. I don't know that anyone is to blame. The dogs which would have been our salvation have evidently failed. Meares had a bad trip home I suppose.

This morning it was calm when we breakfasted, but the wind came from the WNW as we broke camp. It rapidly grew in strength. After travelling for half an hour I saw that none of us could go on facing such conditions. We were forced to camp and are spending the rest of the day in a comfortless blizzard camp, wind quite foul. (R. 52.)

Sunday, March 11.—Titus Oates is very near the end, one feels. What we or he will do, God only knows. We discussed the matter after breakfast; he is a brave fine fellow and understands the situation, but he practically asked for advice. Nothing could be said but to urge him to march as long as he could. One satisfactory result to the discussion; I practically ordered Wilson to hand over the means of ending our troubles to us, so that any one of us may know how to do so. Wilson had no choice between doing so and our ransacking the medicine case. We have 30 opium tabloids apiece and he is left with a tube of morphine. So far the tragical side of our story. (R. 53.)

The sky completely overcast when we started this morning. We could see nothing, lost the tracks, and doubtless have been swaying a good deal since—3.1 miles for the forenoon—terribly heavy dragging —expected it. Know that 6 miles is about the limit of our endurance now, if we get no help from wind or surfaces. We have 7 days' food and should be about 55 miles from One Ton Camp tonight, 6 × 7 = 42, leaving us 13 miles short of our distance, even if things get no worse. Meanwhile the season rapidly advances.

Monday, March 12.—We did 6.9 miles yesterday, under our necessary average. Things are left much the same, Oates not pulling much, and now with hands as well as feet pretty well useless. We did 4 miles this morning in 4 hours 20 min.—we may hope for 3 this afternoon, 7 × 6 = 42. We shall be 47 miles from the depot. I doubt if we can possibly do it. The surface remains awful, the cold intense, and our physical condition running down. God help us! Not a breath of favorable wind for more than a week, and apparently liable to head winds at any moment.

Wednesday, March 14.—No doubt about the going downhill, but everything going wrong for us. Yesterday we woke to a strong northerly wind with temp.−37°. Couldn't face it, so remained in camp (R. 54.) till 2, then did 5¼ miles. Wanted to march later, but party feeling the cold badly as the breeze (N) never took off entirely, and as the sun sank the temp. fell. Long time getting supper in dark. (R. 55.)

This morning started with southerly breeze, set sail and passed another cairn at good speed; half-way, however, the wind shifted to W by S or WSW, blew through our wind clothes and into our mits. Poor Wilson horribly cold, could not get off ski for some time. Bowers and I practically made camp, and when we got into the tent at last we were all deadly cold. Then temp. now midday down −43° and the wind strong. We must go on, but now the making of every camp must be more difficult and dangerous. It must be near the end, but a pretty merciful end. Poor Oates got it again in the foot. I shudder to think what it will be like to-morrow. It is only with greatest pains rest of us keep off frostbites. No idea there could be temperatures like this at this time of year with such winds. Truly awful outside the tent. Must fight it out to the last biscuit, but can't reduce rations.

Friday, March 16 or Saturday 17.—Lost track of dates, but think the last correct. Tragedy all along the line. At lunch, the day before yesterday, poor Titus Oates said he couldn't go on; he proposed we should leave him in his sleeping-bag. That we could not do, and we induced him to come on, on the afternoon march. In spite of its awful nature for him he struggled on and we made a few miles. At night he was worse and we knew the end had come.

Should this be found I want these facts recorded. Oates' last thoughts were of his Mother, but immediately before he took pride in thinking that his regiment would be pleased with the bold way in which he met his death. We can testify to his bravery. He has borne intense suffering for weeks without complaint, and to the very last was able and willing to discuss outside subjects. He did not—would not—give up hope till the very end. He was a brave soul. This was the end. He slept through the night before last, hoping not to wake; but he woke in the morning—yesterday. It was blowing a blizzard. He said, 'I am just going outside and may be some time.' He went out into the blizzard and we have not seen him since.

I take this opportunity of saying that we have stuck to our sick companions to the last. In case of Edgar Evans, when absolutely out of food and he lay insensible, the safety of the remainder seemed to demand his abandonment, but Providence mercifully removed him at this critical moment. He died a natural death, and we did not leave him till two hours after his death. We knew that poor Oates was walking to his death, but though we tried to dissuade him, we knew it was the act of a brave man and an English gentleman. We all hope to meet the end with a similar spirit, and assuredly the end is not far.

I can only write at lunch and then only occasionally. The cold is intense, −40° at midday. My companions are unendingly cheerful, but we are all on the verge of serious frostbites, and though we constantly talk of fetching through I don't think any one of us believes it in his heart.

We are cold on the march now, and at all times except meals. Yesterday we had to lay up for a blizzard and to-day we move dreadfully slowly. We are at No. 14 pony camp, only two pony marches from One Ton Depot. We leave here our theodolite, a camera, and Oates' sleeping-bags. Diaries, &c., and geological specimens carried at Wilson's special request, will be found with us or on our sledge.

Sunday, March 18.—To-day, lunch, we are 21 miles from the depot. Ill fortune presses, but better may come. We have had more wind and drift from ahead yesterday; had to stop marching; wind NW, force 4, temp. −35°. No human being could face it, and we are worn out nearly.

My right foot has gone, nearly all the toes—two days ago I was proud possessor of best feet. These are the steps of my downfall. Like an ass I mixed a small spoonful of curry powder with my melted pemmican—it gave me violent indigestion. I lay awake and in pain all night; woke and felt done on the march; foot went and I didn't know it. A very small measure of neglect and have a foot which is not pleasant to contemplate. Bowers takes first place in condition, but there is not much to choose after all. The others are still confident of getting through—or pretend to be—I don't know! We have the last *half* fill of oil in our primus and a very small quantity of spirit—this alone between us and thirst. The wind is fair for the moment, and that is perhaps a fact to help. The mileage would have seemed ridiculously small on our outward journey.

Monday, March 19.—Lunch. We camped with difficulty last night, and were dreadfully cold till after our supper of cold pemmican and biscuit and a half a pannikin of cocoa cooked over the spirit. Then, contrary to expectation, we got warm and all slept well. To-day we started in the usual dragging manner. Sledge dreadfully heavy. We are 15½ miles from the depot and ought to get there in three days.

What progress! We have two days' food but barely a day's fuel. All our feet are getting bad—Wilson's best, my right foot worst, left all right. There is no chance to nurse one's feet till we can get hot food into us. Amputation is the least I can hope for now, but will the trouble spread? That is the serious question. The weather doesn't give us a chance—the wind from N to NW and −40° temp. to-day.

Wednesday, March 21.—Got within 11 miles of depot Monday night; had to lay up all yesterday in severe blizzard. To-day forlorn hope, Wilson and Bowers going to depot for fuel.

Thursday, March 22 and 23.—Blizzard bad as ever—Wilson and Bowers unable to start—to-morrow last chance—no fuel and only one or two of food left—must be near the end. Have decided it shall be natural—we shall march for the depot with or without our effects and die in our tracks.

Thursday, March 29.—Since the 21st we have had a continuous gale from WSW and SW. We had fuel to make two cups of tea apiece and bare food for two days on the 20th. Every day we have been ready to start for our depot 11 *miles* away, but outside the door of the tent it remains a scene of whirling drift. I do not think we can hope for any better things now. We shall stick it out to the end, but we are getting weaker, of course, and the end cannot be far.

It seems a pity, but I do not think I can write more.

R. Scott.

Last entry.

For God's sake look after our people.

Note: The curious repetition of Monday on page 220, apparently a lapse on Scott's part, appears in the London and New York editions of *Scott's Last Expedition*, 1913, Vol. I.

Sources

THE ADVENTURES OF PETER SERRANO. From Isaac James, *Providence Displayed.* . . . 1800, pp. 159-66. James reprinted the account from Garcilasso de la Vega, *Royal Commentaries of Peru,* translated by Sir Paul Rycaut, 1688.

THE TRUE RELATION OF PETER CARDER. From Samuel Purchas, *Hakluytus Posthumus or Purchas His Pilgrimes. Containing a History of the World, in Sea Voyages and Lande-travels, by Englishmen and Others,* 1625, IV, pp. 1187-90.

BY RICHARD CLARKE OF WEYMOUTH. From Richard Hakluyt, *The Principall Navigations, Voiages and Discoveries of the English Nation.* . . . 1589, pp. 700-701.

MASTER THOMAS CANDISH HIS DISCOURSE. From Samuel Purchas, *Hakluytus Posthumus or Purchas His Pilgrimes. Containing a History of the World, in Sea Voyages and Lande-travels, by Englishmen and Others,* 1625, IV, pp. 1192-1201.

A POOR ENGLISHMAN CAST AWAY. From Isaac James, *Providence Displayed.* . . . 1800, pp. 168-76. James reprinted the account from Samuel Clarke, *Clarke's Mirrour or Looking-Glasse, both for Saints and Sinners,* London, 1671, II, pp. 618-20.

A MOST DANGEROUS VOYAGE BY CAPTAIN JOHN MONCK. From A. and J. Churchill, *A Collection of Voyages and Travels,* 1732, I, pp. 504-508.

AN ACCOUNT OF THE SHIPWRECKED CREW OF A DUTCH VESSEL. From A. and J. Churchill, *A Collection of Voyages and Travels,* 1732, IV, pp. 575-87. The original account was by Hendrick Hamel. The present version was translated from the French, 1654.

PROVIDENCE DISPLAYED. From Woodes Rogers, *A Cruising Voyage Round the World,* 1712, pp. 124-31.

THE ENGLISHMAN. From Richard Steele, *The Englishman,* Dec. 1, 1713, No. 26.

THE PRESERVATION OF CAPTAIN JOHN DEAN. From *A Narrative of the Sufferings, Preservation and Deliverance of Capt. John Dean and Company,* 1711, pp. 1-21.

PHILIP ASHTON'S OWN ACCOUNT. From Romance of Sea-Faring Life, London, 1841, pp. 51-69.

THE JUST VENGEANCE OF HEAVEN. From The Just Vengeance of Heaven Exemplified. . . . Philadelphia, 1748.

THE REMARKABLE SHIPWRECK OF THE SLOOP BETSY. From Remarkable Shipwrecks. . . . Hartford, 1813, pp. 172-84.

THE MELANCHOLY NARRATIVE. From David Harrison, The Melancholy Narrative of the Distressful Voyage and Miraculous Deliverance of Captain David Harrison. . . . 1766, pp. 2-45.

THE LOSS OF H.M.S. PHOENIX. From The Mariner's Chronicle, New Haven, 1834, pp. 418-31.

DANIEL FOSS, OF ELKTON, MARYLAND. From Daniel Foss, A Journal of the Shipwreck and Sufferings of Daniel Foss, a Native of Elkton, Maryland, 1816.

THE SUFFERINGS OF MISS ANN SAUNDERS. From Narrative of the Shipwreck and Sufferings of Miss Ann Saunders, Providence, R. I., 1827, pp. 7-20.

MURDER WITHOUT MALICE. From Joseph F. Fishman and Vee Perlman, "Murder Without Malice," The American Mercury, LXI, pp. 478-84.

THE WRECK OF THE VILLE DU HAVRE. From Mary Adams Bulkley, The Wreck of the S.S. Ville du Havre, 1873.

THE LAST MARCH. From Scott's Last Expedition, New York, 1913, I, pp. 396-410. Reprinted by permission of Dodd, Mead and Company, Inc. Copyright, 1913, 1941, by Dodd, Mead & Company, Inc.

Selected Bibliography

c 1666   A narrative of the sufferings of the crew of the Catarinetta. In A. and J. Churchill, A Collection of Voyages and Travels, I, pp. 556-57.

c 1674   Mr. James Janeway's Legacy to His Friends. . . . 1674.

1699   Jonathan Dickenson, God's Protecting Providence. . . . 1699.

1719   Remarkable Shipwrecks. . . . 1813, pp. 13-26. The shipwreck of the Countess de Bourk and her daughter on the coast of Algiers.

1727   Cicely Fox Smith, Adventures and Perils, 1936, pp. 401 ff. Narrative of the loss of the Luxborough.

1758   James Sutherland, A Narrative of the Loss of H.M.S. Litchfield. . . . 1768, pp. 1-21.

c 1770   Olaudah Equiano, The Interesting Life of . . . 1791, II, pp. 27-42.

1780   S. W. Prenties, Narrative of a Shipwreck on the Island of Cape Breton. . . . 1780.

1782   Alexander Dalrymple, An Account of the Loss of the Grosvenor, East Indiaman, 1783.

1782   Captain Inglefield's Narrative Concerning the Loss of H. M. S. Centaur. . . . 1783.

1786   Richard Pierce, A Circumstantial Narrative of the Loss of the Halsewell. . . . 1786.

1788   William Mackay, Narrative of the Shipwreck of the Juno on the Coast of Arracan, 1798.

1801   Henderick Portenger, Narrative of the Suffering and Adventures of. . . . 1801.

1825   William S. Cary, Wrecked on the Feejees, 1825.

1825   Sir Duncan MacGregor, A Narrative of the Loss of the Kent, 1825.

1835   Michael Seymour, Diary of the Wreck of H.M.S. Challenger on the Western Coast of South America, 1836.

1840 "Conflagration of the Poland on her passage from New York for Havre," in S. A. Howland, *Steamboat Disasters and Railroad Accidents in the United States*. . . . 1840, pp. 302-16.

1898 Victoire Lacasse, "The Bourgogne Disaster," *Harper's Weekly*, XLII, pp. 724-25.

1912 An account of the tragedy of HMS Titanic, in Frank H. Shaw, *Full Fathom Five*, 1930, pp. 64-97.

1927 "Drifting to Death," in David Master, *S.O.S.*, 1934.

1942 Harold F. Dixon, "Three Men on a Raft," in *Life*, XII, No. 14, April 6, 1942.

1943 Mark Murphy, "Eighty-Three Days," in *The New Yorker*, XIX, August 21, 28, and September 4, 1943.

1944 Paul Madden as told to Pete Martin, "Tragic Voyage," in *Saturday Evening Post*, CCXVI, June 10 and 17, 1944.